Konstantin Mochulsky

ANDREI BELY:
His Life and Works

Translated by
Nora Szalavitz

Ardis / Ann Arbor

PG
3543
Z 7813
1977

Table of Contents

268849

A Note on the Translation

My primary aim in working on this book has been accuracy in transmitting meaning, both in the translation of Mochulsky and in his quotations from Bely. I have attempted, secondarily, to make the book as readable as possible, a feat more easily achieved in the case of Mochulsky than in that of Bely. Mochulsky writes beautiful Russian, which makes translating his work a pleasure, although what is most effective in the original can never be as much so in translation. I only hope that some of the beauty of the Russian shines through the English. Rendering Bely readable is extremely difficult, if not impossible, as he constantly plays with sounds and abounds in puns, neither of which correspond to the English; word play often takes precedence over sense. Where possible, I have included transliterations, so that the reader can hear the sounds and arrive at some appreciation of what Bely presents to the Russian reader.

I wish to thank the following people who assisted me in preparing the translation:

Rose Raskin of Columbia University, and Oksana Chikalenko, for their help with some of the difficult Russian.

Professor John Malmstad of Columbia University, for his information on Bely.

Karen Doran, for her help with the German.

Helene Iswolsky, for her information on Mochulsky.

My father, Aaron Levenstein, for his help in finding information on many of the people mentioned in the text.

My husband, Miklos Szalavitz, for reading the work and encouraging me to continue.

My daughters, Maia, Kira and Sarah, for putting up with the endless hours of typing.

Nora Szalavitz

The period of the predominance of the Symbolist movement in Russia has been called the "Silver Age of Russian Literature," or the "Russian Renaissance," and Andrei Bely was one of its greatest poets and the greatest of its novelists and theoreticians.

In the field of poetry, Bely invented a new form of lyric — the "symphony," where the sounds of words and the repetition of motifs play as important a role as their meaning. Its origin was based on the Symbolist theory of the close connection of all the arts and the primacy of music. Much of Bely's verse is constructed on the basis of internal rhyme, word repetition, and sound associations. While most of his poetry lacks true greatness, it has performed an important function for Russian prosody: through his experiments in verse, Bely introduced into Russian versification the equivalent of Verlaine's *vers liberé* — a more flexible use of traditional prosody emphasizing tonic values at the expense of syllabic scheme — and did much to reveal new poetic possibilities for subsequent generations of Russian poets.

His novels were also noteworthy in their literary inventiveness. Bely was the originator of what later became a school of "ornamental prose," a prose which concentrates the reader's attention on small detail, independent smaller units. But where his successors allowed the independence of the small units to destroy the unity of their works, Bely maintained this unity by balancing the details against the musical composition of the whole. His novels abound in the interplay of sounds, "orchestration," and the repetition of motifs. His first novel, *The Silver Dove,* is astounding in its rendition of Gogolian prose and its transmission of the sensation of a mystical trance. His next novel, *Petersburg,* was declared by Vladimir Nabokov to be one of the four greatest prose works of the 20th century, in the company of Joyce's *Ulysses* (with which it has many affinities), Kafka's *Metamorphosis,* and Proust's *Remembrance of Things Past.* Its appearance in 1913 initiated a new era in Russian letters, and it has been noted even by Communist critics that all of Russian prose during the 1920's advanced under its banner. Its influence is evident in the works of such Soviet writers as Zamyatin, Pilnyak, Fedin, Tynyanov, Olesha and Esenin. Bely's next novel, *Kotik Letaev,* was an attempt to portray the beginnings of consciousness in a young child and has been called a "work of genius" by the noted Russian critic, D. S. Mirsky.

Bely's contributions to literary theory were no less significant. He is among the founders of statistical stylistics. His methods of analyzing Russian verse were adopted in the 1920's by the Russian formalists and structuralists (a school which has much in common with the western "New Criticism") and still retain their value and interest. Vladimir Nabokov had recourse to Bely's techniques in his commentary on Pushkin's *Eugene Onegin.*

7

In the Soviet Union, Bely suffered a period of "official" eclipse in the years after his death in 1934, but in recent years he seems to have become more acceptable. None of his novels were printed after 1935. In 1940, a small volume of his verse was published, as was another in 1966-67. Both were immediately sold out. *Petersburg* is scheduled to be published in the Soviet Union next year, and the orders for it have already greatly exceeded the announced volume of the printing. He is of great interest to the younger Soviet critics and readers.

In the United States, there has also been a growth of interest in Bely among Slavic scholars. In 1959, a translation of *Petersburg*, by John Cournos, was published by Grove Press. It has gone through six printings. In 1968, Oleg Maslennikov published a study of Russian Symbolism entitled *The Frenzied Poets. Andrei Belyi and the Russian Symbolists* (Greenwood Press, New York). In 1971, *Kotik Letaev*, translated by Gerald Janecek, was printed by Ardis Publishers. An English translation of *The Silver Dove* appeared in 1974. A new translation of *Petersburg*, using all of Bely's varying editions, is being prepared at present by Professors Robert Maguire and John Malmstad at Columbia University. Doctoral dissertations have been written on Bely's poetry (Malmstad), his usage of grammatical person in the novels (D. F. Robinson), and his literary theories. However, with the exception of Mochulsky's work, there is no other monograph devoted to Bely in Russian.

At the time he was writing (during World War II), Mochulsky had little access to information on the last years of Bely's life. It might be interesting for the reader to refer to the portrait of Bely in Nadezhda Mandelstam's *Hope Against Hope* (Athenum, New York, 1970), where the author tells of the loneliness in which Bely lived as he was forced to watch the persecution of his fellow Anthroposophists, and even the arrest, several times, of his own wife, while he himself was not touched. We learn from the introduction to the 1966 Soviet edition of Bely's poems that his wife apparently survived Stalin and has written her memoirs, but they have remained unpublished.

Andrei Bely was a remarkable person to see and know. All who came in contact with him speak of the electrical excitement he radiated; he was the immediate focus of attention everywhere he went. The impression he made was apparently unforgettable. None who were acquainted with him, regardless of their personal feelings, had any doubt but that he was a genius, and his works bear witness to this.

Like many of the prominent literary and artistic members of his generation, Bely was a seeker of religious revelation. During an important part of his literary life, he was an admirer of Rudolf Steiner and remained an Anthroposophist of sorts until his death. It was perhaps in the religious respect that Mochulsky's interest in Bely was aroused, for Mochulsky himself had undertaken a similar quest. Some background on Mochulsky may be helpful to the reader in understanding his approach to his subject.

Konstantin Vasilievich Mochulsky, the biographer of Dostoevsky,

Vladimir Soloviev, and several of the Russian Symbolist poets, was born in Odessa on January 28, 1892, and died in Cambo, France on March 21, 1948, from tuberculosis. His father was Russian, a Professor of Russian Letters at Novorosiisky University. According to some sources, his mother was Greek, and to others, a Karaite Jew.

As a child, Mochulsky suffered from poor health and because of this received his early education at home. He later attended a gymnasium at Odessa, and, upon his graduation at eighteen, entered the philological faculty at St. Petersburg University. After receiving his degree, he continued to work at the University, studying Romance literatures. In 1918, he obtained the post of lecturer at Saratov University, but, because of complications arising during the Revolution, was unable to take up his duties. He taught instead at the university in Odessa, where his father had taught before him.

The next years brought him terrible personal losses. His younger brother died in an accident in the Caucasus while Mochulsky was still in Russia. In 1919, he left Russia, and his mother, who remained behind, died there the following year. In 1923, in Switzerland, his remaining brother died in his arms of tuberculosis.

After he left Russia, Mochulsky taught first at the University of Sofia, in Greece, from 1920 to 1922, and then in Paris at the Sorbonne, with which he was associated until 1941. He was among the group of Russian scholars who were given the opportunity to teach Russian subjects there on an extra-curricular basis. These scholars were allowed the use of small auditoria and paid a nominal fee. Under these conditions, Mochulsky gave the lectures on Dostoevsky and Soloviev which formed the basis for his biographies.

Compared to many Russian emigres during this period, Mochulsky was quite well-off. He tutored in wealthy Parisian families, in both Russian and Spanish, and translated *Don Quixote* into Russian. He attended the literary circles in Montparnasse, and became associated with the Russian weekly *The Link (Zveno)*. He published essays on the theater and literature, as well as short stories, under the pseudonym "Versilov."

At the end of the 1920's or the beginning of the 30's, Mochulsky experienced a sort of religious conversion. At some time during this period, he spent his summer holidays in Biarritz. Growing restless, he traveled about the Pyrenees and stopped in Lourdes, where he paid a visit to the Grotto.

As it happened, this was a day when a large pilgrimage came to Lourdes and Mochulsky was so impressed by the spectacle of religious faith manifested by the pilgrims that he abruptly turned toward religion himself and became deeply involved in Russian Orthodoxy, which at this time in Paris was experiencing a "Renaissance."

His "conversion" was a serious matter, and sharply altered his whole way of life. He gave up tutoring (his new religious views were offensive to the wealthy families where he taught) and ceased to attend his literary meetings. He began, instead, to associate with Nikolai Berdyaev's Religious and Philo-

9

sophical Academy. He was greatly influenced by the teachings of Father Sergei Bulgakov and by the practices of a Russian nun, Mother Maria (Skobtseva); he began to devote a great deal of his time to the Society for Orthodox Action. Because he had lost most of his income by giving up his tutoring, he was now forced to live in a garret. During the summers, he worked as a gardener in Mother Maria's home for the tubercular and was, according to those who knew him during this time, perfectly content with his new way of life. At one point, he even considered becoming a monk, but was dissuaded from this by Mother Maria, on the grounds that he could be far more useful to others working outside a monastery. He became an active member of the League of Orthodox Culture, the Student Christian Movement, and the Fellowship of St. Alban and St. Sergius; he remained a member of the faculty of the St. Sergius Theological Academy until a year before his death.

When the Germans occupied Paris in 1940, Mochulsky remained in the city and endured all the hardships of that period. Mother Maria and many of his other friends were arrested by the Nazis for aiding Jews, and died in concentration camps. Mochulsky himself only avoided arrest because he was not with them when they were summoned by the Germans. His health was undoubtedly damaged by the physical and spiritual sufferings of the times. In 1946, he was found to have an advanced case of tuberculosis and was sent to a sanatorium at Fontainebleau, and from there to Cambo in the Pyrenees. In 1947, believing that he was better, he returned to Paris, but was shortly obliged to go back to Cambo, where he died the following year.

During the 1930's, Mochulsky published two books, *Gogol's Spiritual Path (Dukhovnyi put' Gogolia)* in 1934 and *Vladimir Soloviev* in 1936. During the war, in spite of the difficult conditions under which he was living, he completed his famous biography of Dostoevsky, *Dostoevsky: His Life and Work (Dostoevskii: Zhizn' i tvorchestvo)*, which was not published until 1947. According to a letter written to his friend, Helene Iswolsky, on July 26, 1945, and published in *The New Review (Novyi Zhurnal)*, vol. 95, 1969, in which he describes how he lived during the war, Mochulsky in 1944 had begun a study of the Russian Symbolists, primarily Blok and Bely, as well as Valery Bryusov. Originally planned as one book, it became three, all of which were published posthumously by YMCA Press in Paris: *Alexander Blok* in 1948, *Andrei Bely* in 1955, and *Valery Bryusov* in 1962. The biography of Bely was actually put together for publication by friends of the deceased. Mochulsky had not succeeded in completing it. The Russian edition contains three appendices of material Mochulsky had collected but was unable to incorporate, which in the English translation have been integrated into the main body of the text.

At least in part because the book remained unfinished, it does not compare in quality to Mochulsky's biography of Dostoevsky (translated into English by Michael A. Minihan and published by Princeton University Press in 1967), and long recognized as a definitive work. Nevertheless, although in-

10

complete and unfinished, Mochulsky's work on Bely is at present the only biography of Bely in Russian or English which studies all of his works — poetry, prose, literary criticism — in detail. Mochulsky's brilliant perception as a literary critic is as apparent in his treatment of Bely as it was of Dostoevsky.

Mochulsky examines Bely's poetry as completely as Bely himself might have wished. He demonstrates to the reader what Bely was attempting in his experimental verse, examining the repetition of motifs and sounds, the orchestration of the poems, and their meaning — philosophical, mythological, autobiographical. He quotes the poems at length and, where Bely was imitating earlier Russian poets, he furnishes examples of their verse.

In his treatment of Bely's novels, Mochulsky employs much the same techniques. He provides passages which give the reader the flavor of the work and, in the case of *The Silver Dove,* a reference to Gogol to reveal Bely's use of Gogolian prose. He discusses plot, structure, language, and literary antecedents. Mochulsky's critique of *Petersburg* is as polished, brilliant, and complete as those of the novels of Dostoevsky. He quotes and examines the different versions of the book, discusses the plot from the point of view of both historical and autobiographical content, examines the major characters, and analyzes the use of language.

Bely's literary criticism and studies of language are explored in detail, both in terms of their basic tenets, and in terms of their influence on later critics. Examples are presented of Bely's verse analysis, and his findings are cited on the qualities presented in the poetry of previous Russian poets, as well as that of his contemporaries. Bely's theories on Symbolism as a philosophical, religious, and literary movement are thoroughly examined.

As in his biography of Dostoevsky, Mochulsky examines the works he discusses in relation to the writer as a human being, the period in which he lived, and the people and ideas that influenced him. The reader thus obtains not only a portrait of Bely, but one of the entire Symbolist movement. Such a method is particularly appropriate in dealing with Bely, who was an intensely autobiographical writer, in addition to being an extraordinary human being.

Mochulsky devotes a good deal of attention to Bely's religious and philosophical ideas. Himself an admirer and to some extent a follower of the Russian religious philosopher Vladimir Soloviev, Mochulsky was well equipped to understand Bely's attraction to Soloviev's beliefs and to mysticism in general. Where earlier critics dismissed Bely's religious ideas and mystical experiences as exaggerated, silly, or even insane, Mochulsky examines them seriously and is thus able to arrive at an understanding of both the man and his works. (This is not to say that Mochulsky attaches any intrinsic importance to Bely's attempts at philosophy; he is well aware that they have no lasting value. But in order to arrive at any comprehension of either Bely or his works, they cannot fairly be dismissed in silence or in ridicule.) Patient and understanding in dealing with most of Bely's "eccentricities," even Mochulsky cannot treat Bely's Anthroposophy without some bias, foreign as it was to Mochulsky's Russian Orthodoxy, and destructive as it was of Bely's poetry. He has no patience with Bely's "Steinerist" reaction to Jerusalem and seems to lament his abandonment of Christianity.

Nevertheless, Mochulsky's portrait of Bely is profoundly sympathetic, even when, as Mochulsky recognizes, Bely indulged in his most vicious literary attacks, his wildest religious fantasies and visions, and his subservient lies to ingratiate himself with Soviet power. In Mochulsky's biography, the reader is given a sympathetic understanding of Andrei Bely as a human being, and of the tragedy of his life-long, hopeless quest for an exit from chaos into cosmos.

ANDREI BELY

Chapter One: Childhood and Youth

Boris Nikolaevich Bugaev (Bely was his pen name) was born in Moscow on October 14, 1880; Alexander Blok, with whom his fate was joined so intricately and mysteriously, was only a month younger than he. His father, a well-known mathematician and professor at Moscow University, was Nikolai Vasilievich Bugaev.

The son of a military doctor, N. V. Bugaev made his way through persistent labor: he left home in order to study mathematics in Moscow, went hungry, gave lessons, studied nights on end, and received high scholarly degrees. His is the original theory of "evolutionary monadology," which was highly esteemed by the French mathematician Poincaré. He was unusually ugly, clever and eccentric. His son describes him: "Large-headed, bespectacled, with his hair falling onto his forehead, he leaned toward his right side with his shoulder lowered and somehow twisted."

The independent and powerful personality of the father had a tremendous influence on the son. Bely writes:

I was already an "eccentric," following in the footsteps of my father. From him I learned humor and my future "decadent" grotesqueries; the very oddities of my father were taken at face value. An "eccentric:" that is, not to act like everyone else: that's how one should act, but for my father puns and oddities were "art for art's sake;" for me they became a goal in themselves: to destroy the ordinary way of life.

Bely's mother — Alexandra Dmitrievna — was a beautiful society woman. She posed for the artist K. Makovsky as the model of the "bride" in the "Wedding of a Boyar."

Between the father and mother there was unceasing conflict, sometimes hidden, sometimes obvious. The mother was unhappy in family life, suffered from hysteria and an "illness of sensitive nerves." The little boy very early became aware of a "boundary" between his parents; they fought over him and tore him to pieces. He recalls:

My mother's love for me was powerful, jealous, cruel; she ruled me like her "little kitten," her little beast.... The whole source of nightmares was the drama of life; any equilibrium was broken down in me, and of course my father and mother did the breaking; above all, I already instinctively sensed that they themselves were broken down.

The child's first burst of consciousness illuminated the adversity of the world; the family drama became for him the source of a tragic disposition. He was born under the sign of the destruction of the old world.

15

I was overflowing with the apocalyptical mysticism of the end to the point of Apocalypse.... The theme of the end is inherent to my development; it is overcast with the theme of another end: the end of one of the professorial apartments, typical nevertheless, for in it lay the end of the ordinary way of life, the end of a century.

Bely maintains that he knew already as a student in the fifth grade: "the life in the good apartment will vanish: and the art glorified by this apartment will vanish as well; with Machtet and Potapenko, with Klever and Konstantin Makovsky, with the academician Beklemishev and with Nadson instead of Pushkin."

Reality attacked his childish consciousness like a nightmare; the shock and fear remained with him for his entire life. Bely's literary work is an attempt to exorcise the chaos in and around himself; to save himself from destruction, to find solid ground, to find reason in the confusion of delirium. At the heart of his writing is amazement and horror at life.

In his third year, the little boy caught the measles, and then scarlet fever; to this time he ascribes the birth of his consciousness. Flashes of recollections through the delirium and fever of illness comprise the theme of his last story, *Kotik Letaev.*

At first the world of the child is limited to the close square of the nursery; then it broadens to the boundaries of the apartment, beyond which lie "unknown, perhaps terrifying voids." The faces of father, mother, nurse, a strip of wall, reflections of sunbeams flit past. The figure of the German maid, Raisa Ivanovna, floats by, reading him the verses of Uhland, Goethe, Eichendorff. Music is heard from the drawing-room. His mother is playing Beethoven and Chopin. "The world of sounds was completely adequate for me; and I for it. In this resounding space I was both God and priest...."

The religious education of the little boy was superficial; he was told that there are no devils, wizards and other evil forces, and that there could not be; that "God, so to speak, is the source of evolutionary perfection." The liberal professorial milieu of the 1880's was nourished on Darwin and Spencer. Nevertheless, the Gospel was read to the child, and he confessed that "the images of the New Testament filled his being to overflowing."

"The period from five to eight years of age," writes Bely, "was one of the most dismal: everything I noticed as wrong I intensified incredibly." His mother began to teach him reading, writing, and music: he was afraid to upset her with his lack of understanding and grew stupid from fear. She became irritated, shouted at him, cried. The lessons were transformed into torture for both of them. Finally, in 1889, a "deliverer" appeared, the governess Bella Radek. She grasped the character of the little boy and attempted to wean him away from pretense and affectation. "I don't understand you," she would say. "Why do you put on airs? Everything you are doing makes people think poorly of you. Why this pretense that you are a fool? You are not that way at

16

all!"

But the little boy could not help "putting on airs." It was his self-defense, his "diving-bell," without which he would have drowned in a sea of reality inimical to him. But then the "bell" became a habit. Psychological conflicts and contradictions became part of his nature, gave birth to duality, to "two-facedness." He began to read Cooper, Mayne Reid, Jules Verne, to play Indians, soldiers; the playing continued for a decade and became a second life. It intensified the splitting of his consciousness.

During the summer, the Bugaev family lived in Demyanovo; its owner, Vladimir Ivanovich Taneev, rented summer houses. This estate was located three versts from Klin at the highway leading to Shakhmatovo. Only seventeen versts separated the Beketov estate from Demyanovo; the future friends — Blok and Bely — spent their summers virtually side by side during their childhood. Not far away, near Kryukovo, in Dedovo, lived Sergei Mikhailovich Soloviev, Blok's second cousin and a friend of Bely's youth. Chaikovsky, who visited the brother of Taneev, the composer Sergei Ivanovich, was living seven versts from Demyanovo, in Frolovsky village.

In October, 1890, Bely was taken ill with diptheria. "I remember," he writes, "not so much the illness, as Gogol, whom my mother began to read aloud to me during my illness; Gogol was my first love among the Russian prose writers; he struck me like a clap of thunder with the brilliance of his metaphors and the intonations of his phrases."

Bely the writer comes from Gogol. In *The Silver Dove* and in *Petersburg* he complicates Gogolian grotesque and reworks his stylistic methods.

The home of Professor Bugaev was visited by the entire scholarly world of Moscow: the zoologist Sergei Alexeevich Usov — a Darwinist and authority on Shakespeare, "of gigantic height, a massive man with a great curly beard and fiery eyes;" Nikolai Ilich Storozhenko — "the average resultant force of the liberal literati; spineless, slight, but innocent and kind;" Alexei Nikolaevich Veselovsky — "eyes empty and protruding, bluish, bleary; much the same was his forehead, as well as the hair above this forehead, and the same for his beard!" Maxim Maximovich Kovalevsky — "his extremely white vest was rounded out by his heavy stomach: his jacket was blue; he glistened with satisfaction and starch, and, turning up his black little well-groomed beard, he would dissolve in such extremely good-natured laughter."

During the '90's, the philosophers Grot and Lopatin made their appearance in the Bugaev home. Bely depicts them in his album of caricatures. Nikolai Yakovlevich Grot, a professor and editor of the journal *Questions of Philosophy and Psychology,* was "handsome, animated, endearing, and a kind of mildly bombastic person! Frizzy hair, black as a crow's wing, a pleasant, soft beard, a pale face with regular features, a straight nose; he came across as a sort of Figner going in for philosophy." It was said of Lev Mikhailovich Lopatin, "Levushka," a friend of Vladimir Soloviev, that he was "an angel of kindness." And the little boy imagined him as an angel with little wings. When he

17

saw him, he was astounded: "He doesn't have wings, but a beard, long, like a goat's; fearsome red lips, just like those of a Moor; glasses with gold frames; and behind them the eyes of a sheep (at once frightened and frightening); the forehead on his small head is small, thinly covered with slicked-down thinnish hair; weak little hands powerlessly rubbing each other."

In September, 1891, Bely entered the gymnasium of Polivanov; it seemed to him that "the door into his life had opened." His childhood was at an end. Lev Ivanovich Polivanov, a pedagogue of genius, an inspired teacher, an authority on Russian philology and the author of a number of textbooks, revealed the world of Russian literature to Bely. The student remembered forever the tall, bent figure, the worn face with its mane of hair and clipped beard, the glasses with their gold frames, the blue jacket too short and too tight, the eternal cigarette in his mouth, the flying, impetuous gait. The director instinctively grasped the complex and gifted nature of the boy and often helped him in his continual "dramas." In the first grade, Bely was an excellent student, received "Fives,"[1] and was intoxicated with success. In the second grade, the decline began. He was terrorized by the Latinist Pavlikovsky: "Something of Peredonov[2] plus the 'man in a case'."[3] The little boy lost his taste for studying; he was scolded at home; his friends grew cool toward him. "An amazing degeneration," he writes, "from the first to the fourth grade: from a victor to 'the insulted and injured'." In the fourth grade, Bely began to study at home, rebelling against the introduction of irrelevant subjects. In the sixth grade, he became acquainted with Baudelaire, Verlaine, Wilde, Hauptmann, Ruskin... "Ibsen was the explosion of a bomb within me." Instead of attending the gymnasium, he went to the reading room at the Ostrovsky, where he read through Ibsen and Dostoevsky. At last the deception was revealed. Polivanov called him in. A dramatic explosion took place. The boy cried and confessed everything; the director forgave him.

"I became a Symbolist," recalls Bely, "by paying the price of murdering Abel. The Abel within me was a clean conscience."

His first love occurred when he was thirteen. At the summer house near Tsarytsin, he fell in love with a little girl, Manya Muromtsova, but, upon returning to the city, he promptly forgot her. He was captured by the theater: the plays of Ostrovsky at the Maly Theater, Yermolova, Sadovsky. He writes:

My strange games, interweaving contemplation, thoughts on Schopenhauer's esthetics, and stylistic exercises with simple childish play had already begun in the fifth grade of the gymnasium when I gave myself up utterly to the sounds of music and the rays of the moon.

In the summer of 1896, he went abroad with his mother and traveled in Germany, France and Switzerland. In Paris he became acquainted with the famous professor Paul Bouex and on the return trip met the Catholic priest Auget, who told him about the French decadents.

His literary attempts began during this period; he wrote an extremely long poem in imitation of Tasso; a fantastic story in which there is a yoga who kills with a glance; and lyrical passages "with a huge dose of homegrown, not yet book-learned, decadence." Here is one of his first verses:

> Who so wildly howls
> At the rotten cross?
> Is it wolves?
> No: it is my shade crying.

It is a feeble quatrain, but already characteristic of the author of *Ashes* and *The Urn*. He read more and more new books and underwent a dizzying shift in literary enthusiasms. The intellectual avidity of youth was insatiable. In 1922, in the book *Notes of an Eccentric,* Bely makes an attempt to explain the disorderly reading of his adolescence as the only path to "initiation." He writes in his diary:

I was a well-read youth. I would find myself in my father's study, reading books on the sly; I would pore over *Questions of Philosophy*. There was Vera Johnston's translation, *Excerpts from the Upanishads*. I began to read it. I understood something of Buckley; and I understood everything in Smiles' *Thrift*. I was even reading Carpenter. In *The Upanishads,* I lived before my birth. *The Upanishads* filled my soul, like a chalice, with warmth. Everyone would say that my philosophical tastes were influenced by Schopenhauer, but no: my aspirations in later years were influenced by the Vedas, *The Upanishads;* and – Schopenhauer was a mirror: in it the Veda was reflected.... By reading Schopenhauer, I reduced the Buckleys and the Smiles's to ashes within me. The rules of sober morality were destroyed; thus I turned to the devil....

* * *

In the evening, pretending that I was preparing my lessons, I noticed at times that I would sit for hours, doing nothing or listening to the soaring melodies audible to me from afar.... I abandoned the sciences; and at this point, the pedagogues noticed that the student B. had become a loafer; he had become a pessimist, a Buddhist, – and from then on, Fet became my favorite poet. Tortured by the life which had been taught to me, I gazed into the wilderness. Pessimism was an unconscious transition to the rich, surging life which was revealed within me shortly thereafter.... As a schoolboy, I already preached to schoolboys: asceticism is a duty; the way it is practiced (attempts at the alteration of consciousness) is a social matter. I was already a specialist in imponderable actions. And the means for attaining consciousness of the new world was art; and – I began to do an occasional bit of writing....
The world of the gymnasium had become a universal wilderness....

A muddle in my head at the fourth lesson; at the fifth — I would sleep or suffer cosmically, becoming transformed into a dull, weary, senseless body.

In 1896 an event took place in Bely's life which defined his fate as a writer: he became acquainted with the family of Mikhail Sergeevich Soloviev, the brother of the philosopher. The Solovievs lived in the same house as the Bugaevs. Their eleven-year-old son Seryozha met the sixteen-year-old Borya Bugaev. "Seryozha," Bely recalls, "was in a long black velvet little jacket with a white lace turn-down collar and long stockings: a little boy right out of the 17th century; without any arrogance, he would wrinkle his large forehead and shake his bright ashen curls." He invited Borya to his house and Bely soon adopted the Soloviev family as his own.

Mikhail Sergeevich Soloviev was perhaps no less remarkable than his famous brother. Earnest, penetrating, modest, he inspired and supported the philosopher in his research. With him, he translated Plato and, after the death of Vladimir Sergeevich, he worked on the complete edition of his brother's works. Mikhail Sergeevich had a pure classical soul and a profound esthetic sensibility. He understood the poetic world of Pushkin, Tyutchev and Fet; he loved Shakespeare. For all his noble conservatism, he was capable of daring: decadence and symbolism did not frighten him. He was one of the first to recognize Bryusov as a poet and thought highly of Merezhkovsky's *Tolstoi and Dostoevsky*. He was Bely's patron.

Externally, Mikhail Sergeevich was the complete opposite of his tall, dark-haired brother. Blond, with blue eyes, a curly beard and a pale, tired face, he was taciturn and only rarely did he become caught up in inspiration. Bely remembers him with grateful love:

There was something magnificent in the way the unpretentiously smoking Soloviev sat quietly at the tea table wearing an Italian cape with a warm yellow vest under his jacket. And the conversation, to which he only listened, acquired a special, inexpressible imprint, lapsing at times; it was not a tea table, but rather a meeting of the Florentine Academy.... In this unbeautiful figure there was tremendous beauty; one was struck by the thinness, weakness, sickliness of the small body so sensitive to cold with its disproportionately large head, which seemed even larger because of the frizzy cap of blond hair.

The wife of Mikhail Sergeevich, Olga Mikhailovna, an artist and translator, lived for art, religion and mysticism; her insatiable, restless soul was always seeking something new. She loved the English pre-Raphaelites, the French Symbolists, Wilde, Ruskin and Maeterlinck, and subscribed to *Jugend, Studio,* and later to *The World of Art.* Bely is indebted to her for his love of Vrubel and the Impressionists. He writes:

Olga Mikhailovna wore a long black house-coat which resembled the habit of a novice, and which made her seem thinner, more dried up, more in miniature. Her coiffure was astounding — a veritable little tower of black hair perpendicular to her temples and drawn up with a black ribbon tied in a bow.

With Seryozha Soloviev, the future poet, philologist and critic, who completed his spiritual path by accepting the priesthood, Bely maintained a passionate friendship. Not long before his death, he wrote: "I consider the significance of Seryozha in my intimate, as well as my social, life, irreplaceable, tremendous."

In the poem "First Meeting," Bely portrays the Soloviev family in charming verses.

> During the winter, half-frozen, he knocks at a familiar door.
> Mikhail Sergeich Soloviev
> Opened the door for me wordlessly.
> Thin and pale, he covered with a rug
> His chest which long ago had caught cold.
> With the radiant golden trace
> Of his candle, he showed me the way,
> Rocking with his measured gait,
> With his golden-haired head,
> With his golden-haired beard,
> Squinting, weak, but animated.
> This is Olga Mikhailovna Solovieva:
> O. M., his wife, my friend
> An artist — ...
> Would pray from the Cheti-Minei,
> She translated de Vigny,
> Was captivated by the Pyrenees,
> Carmen, Barbey d'Aurevilly.
> She always corresponded with Alya,
> Whose son wrote poetry,
> Who, by an act of fate,
> The wind-fallen wood of life sent to me;
> Thus the name of Alexander Blok
> Was mentioned at the table.
> This is Seryozha Soloviev:
> Seryozha Soloviev — a child,
> A lively, clever little angel.
>
> * * *
>
> Logos was revealed to him at age three
> At six — Grigory Bogoslov,

At seven – the French vocabulary.
He could explain what he held sacred
From the time he was fourteen
In harmonious Latin.
Here he is – a prophet and poet,
The holder of the key to the heavens, an inveterate mystic,
A blue-eyed schoolboy.

Their close friends would gather at the Soloviev house: Vladimir Serge-evich Soloviev came to play chess with his brother and rumbled intermittently with his strange laughter; the philosopher Sergei Nikolaevich Trubetskoi – awkward, tall, emaciated, with small restless eyes and a charming childlike smile – was striking in his nervousness and abruptness. The historian Klyu-chevsky was there, as well as the Solovievs' sister, the poetess Poliksena Ser-geevna (Allegro); later there were visits from Bryusov, Merezhkovsky, Zinaida Gippius.

In the seventh and eighth grades at the gymnasium, Bely was totally in-volved in literature and music. He wrote verses and attended concerts; his favorites were Grieg, Wagner and Rimsky-Korsakov. At the gymnasium he held his friends in terror: his "mailed fist" was Symbolism; he brandished it among his confounded classmates. In the hall of the Soloviev apartment, Ser-yozha and Borya staged plays: scenes from *Macbeth, The Bride of Messina,* and *Boris Godunov.* Mikhail Sergeevich was the director.

In 1899 he graduated from the gymnasium and, under his father's influ-ence, entered the science faculty of Moscow University.

From 1899 to 1906 Bely spent his summers at the Silver Well Estate in Tulskaya Guberniya. In the book *Notes of an Eccentric* (1922), he ascribes to this place a tremendous influence on his destiny. The old house with nine windows, surrounded by poplars, stood on a hill; a river flowed at the foot of the hill; a dark avenue of lime trees led sideways from the house. The garden ended in a ditch. Beyond it there was an incline on the opposite side of which hung wild cliffs. Fields of golden rye lay beyond.

Bely writes:

Standing in the middle of the plateau, I did not see the ravines. Like a gaze, my thoughts flowed across the plains in the leaps of history; they spread over me. All the *Symphonies* had their origin here – in this place: in the azure of the heavens, in the noisy gold of the rye (and later *Ashes* was also written from here).... When the Silver Well was sold, the style of my books changed as a result; the architechtonics of the phraseology of the heavy *Dove* (the novel *The Silver Dove*) replaced the flying arabesques of the *Symphonies....* Here I was once reading through Schopenhauer.... Indeed, all the sources of my knowledge orig-inated here; here I thought out *Symbolism;* Zarathustra came to me –

to initiate me into his secrets.

After he had passed through the Anthroposophic school in Dornach, the Bely of 1922 interpreted his past as the path to "secret knowledge;" it seemed to him that even in his youth, on the plains of the Silver Well, he was hearing the mysterious voice calling him to a lofty goal.

The experiences of the summer sunsets provoked in me the role of a church servant; I directed a liturgy in the fields, and from them in fact came the themes of the later *Symphonies*.... During those years I studied attentively all the nuances of the sunsets.... Until 1900, some gave light; later new ones burst forth:
The ascents of the dawn of the not yet risen sun
...This voice arose within me in the fields.

When liberated from its recent Anthroposophic commentaries, this vague mystical experience of early youth is astounding in its resemblance to Blok's experiences of the same years. Just like Bely, the young Blok gazed at the same sunsets on the plains of Shakhmatovo, heard the same secret call and waited for Her appearance:

And I await Thee, suffering and loving...

Duality was Bely's tragic fate. In his university years, the duality was revealed in the incompatibility of the two worlds in which he was living: the world of art and the world of science. He writes:

The first month after graduating from the gymnasium was not a month of rest, but a month of work, doubts at the magnitude of the "scissors"[4] and the feeling that the "scissors" would not be closed. On the one hand — work on dramas, "symphonies," "mystery plays," and on the other — histology, comparative anatomy, botany, chemistry. I needed to combine the incompatibles, to find a reconciliation for the contradictions, to create a theory of double unity.

Bely wanted to validate esthetics as a precise experimental science and even invented terms for himself, such as "esthetic-scientist," or "scientific esthetician." These constructs met with no sympathy in the Soloviev circle, and the professors of the science faculty noticed that the student Bugaev was becoming indifferent to laboratory work. In reality, it was difficult for him to concentrate on histology and anatomy because at this time he "was defining himself as a beginning writer in earnest," and working out a plan for the mystery play, *He Who Hath Come*. The first draft dates from the spring of 1898. It was reworked in 1903 and appeared in *Northern Flowers*. Bely describes the origin of this mystery play in *Notes of an Eccentric.*

During his years at the gymnasium, he interpreted church services as theatrical performance; the deacon and the sexton seemed like pagan priests at a sacrifice, and being in church was difficult for him. He always thought that somewhere there must be another service in which he might join. And at this point, during Holy Week, he had a vision:

> It was as if one wall of the church opened into the void. I saw the End (I don't know of what — my life or the world's), but it was as if the road of history rested upon two domes — upon a Temple; and crowds of people thronged toward it. To myself, I called the Temple I saw the "Temple of Glory," and it seemed to me that Antichrist was threatening this Temple. I ran out of the church like a madman.... In the evening, in my little room, I drafted the plan for a mystery drama, and I gave it the title "He Who Hath Come"; and soon after, I drafted the entire first section (extremely incomplete). I did not finish the drama.

After the mystery play, two very wild dramas were written and read only to Seryozha. Then a poem in prose in the form of a "symphony" was begun and destroyed. Finally — poetry.

But science also "cut sharply" into Bely's consciousness. He read a great deal, wishing to master the facts of the precise sciences. In November, 1899, he delivered a lecture "On Problems and Methods in Physics" at a physics seminar. He attended the lectures of Menzbir, Tikhomirov, Zograf, and Sabaneev. He had no luck in science; the captiousness of one professor discouraged him from studying microbiology; in the laboratory of another, they could not find room for him. The "stupid" student's composition "On Ravines" was a burden to him. Thus the double unity of science and art fell apart. Chemistry and anatomy were conquered — by the philosophy of Nietzsche. Bely writes:

> Since autumn, 1899, I have been living in Nietzsche; he is my relaxation, my intimate moments, when I push away textbooks and philosophy and give myself up completely to his phraseology, his style, his words.

The new 20th century began for Bely under the sign of Nietzsche.

Gazing back at the last years of the departing century, the poet characterized them in terms of the changing coloration of the atmosphere:

> Since 1896, I have noted a change in the coloration of ordinary existence: from a gray December coloration, it has clearly revealed to me its February dark blue.... I experienced this to the utmost toward 1897; a pre-spring feeling of anxiety, including both joy and fear of inundation, seized me.... The transition to 1899, however, was a transition

24

from February twilight to the March skirmish of spring and winter. The years 1899-1900 were the March of my spring. As of 1901, I had already entered my May...

These poetic metaphors are developed more fully in the book *Reminiscences of Blok.*

Bely maintains that on the brink of the two centuries, the psychological atmosphere changed sharply. Until 1898, the North wind blew and the sky was gray. Balmont's verses *Under Northern Skies* reflect this period. Chekhov reigned as the "poet of social stagnation"; Nina Zarechnaya (in *The Seagull*) and "Uncle Vanya" were languishing and bored. Ibsen's *Ghosts* spoke of the irreparability of fate; Maeterlinck's *The Blind* wandered in the dark night. At theatrical performances, scenes of autumnal twilight were predominant, with gray clouds over the woods and "pale maidens with water-lilies behind their ears." In *Questions of Philosophy and Psychology,* Gilyarov wrote about "thoughts of death in France"; S. A. Andreevsky in his *Literary Essays* maintained that "all forms of poetic creation were finally immobilized," that for poetry "the cycle of time is complete," poetry is finished. The void was imminent, the abyss yawned (the poetry of N. Minsky). The pessimism of Schopenhauer and the nirvana of Buddhism were ruling all souls. "My first sermon," recalls Bely, "was a sermon on Buddhism to the Arsenievsky schoolgirls, who listened to me with respect. My classmates shrugged their shoulders, angry at my success among the young ladies."

The verses of Fet were read aloud; the prophetic wisdom of India was divined in his Russian landscapes and the "wholeness of oblivion" was sought. The poisonous flowers of Baudelaire were in bloom and "the sea gulls flew with mournful cries over the anguish-covered plain" (Balmont). Thus, in refined impotence, esthetically admiring its own impotence, the 19th century was dying.

As of 1898, a new wind blew. "Boundlessness rushed toward the banks of the old life," writes Bely; "we sensed this invasion of the eternal as an earthquake of life." The atmosphere was purified; the dawn of Symbolism arose out of the shadows of Decadence preceding it. Balmont abandoned the torpidity of *Silence* and, drunk with the sun, glorified the *Burning Buildings.* Friedrich Nietzsche, the destroyer of idols, stood at the door of the new century. The younger generation seized upon his great book, *The Birth of Tragedy*; the recently melancholy Decadents were transformed into admirers of Nietzsche, anarchists, revolutionaries of the spirit. The brink of the year 1900 was a "rent in time," "a crisis of consciousness," the entry into a new, "tragic" epoch.

* * *

Toward the end of 1900, Bely finished his first literary work, *The Northern Symphony (the First Heroic).* He tells of its origin in the book *The Turn of the Century*:

I conceived a cosmic epopee, sprinkling the wildest phrases throughout the text with all my might; when I had finished this masterpiece, I noticed that it had not grown into a universal poem; and then I began to narrow the subject... to subjective improvisations and simply fairy tales; it was nourished by the melodies of Grieg and my own improvisations on the piano; Grieg's romance, "The Princess," was a great influence. The depths of the forest were evoked by a ballad of Grieg which lay at the heart of the second and third parts of the *Symphony*. The *Northern Symphony* arose from these youthful exercises toward the end of 1900.

There is no need to dwell on the imperfection of this "youthful exercise"; the feebleness of the construction, the decadent mannerism of the style, the confusion of the contents are striking. But in rereading it now, almost half a century after it was written, it is impossible not to feel its old-fashioned charm.

The scenario of the "fairy tale" is constructed from literary impressions: there are northern heroes in the spirit of the early Ibsen, and a princess in a tower extending her slender hands to the sun, exactly as in Maeterlinck, and a hodge-podge of German ballads, and medieval knights seeking faraway princesses, and old kings rising from their graves, and giants, and wizards, and black swans. In this romantic atmosphere, a romance takes place between a princess "with blue eyes and a mournful smile" and a knight "thirsting for transcendental dreams." The princess lives in a tower and against the background of the fiery sky she appears like a white lily on scarlet satin. And around the tower are woods filled with evil spirits and ghosts. There old gnomes, hunchbacks, giants, and centaurs are wandering; there goat-bearded knights are dancing the devilish "goat dance." Dvoretsky, the wizard, lures the knight into the "goat rites," and he prepares a satanic banquet in his castle. But the princess prays for her faraway friend and saves him from destruction. She says to him, "My kingdom is not of this earth. There will come a time when you will see it... I too have the royal purple: it is the purple of the morning sunrise, which soon will catch fire over the world. Days will pass and you will see me in this purple."

And at last the time comes; the princess descends from the tower. With the crucifix in her hands, she goes to dispel the darkness. The knight repents and dies. Behind the princess a white bird comes flying. Her throne is consumed by a white light, and she disappears. With this the poem concludes: the fourth part, written in a different style, serves as an epilogue. The story is written in "musical phrases" with repeating leit-motifs; the major theme is the struggle between light and darkness, bright eternity against dark time.

The motif of Eternity and light is embodied in the princess: her colors are whiteness and purple; she is the one who ascends over the darkness. The leit-motif of sunrise is emphasized by verses which suddenly flow into prose:

You are laughing, all unconcern, all like Eternity,
   golden above our ancient world.
Do not be confused by our belated banquet; flare up
   over the woods, with a bright scarlet flame.

The atmosphere of sunrise in which Bely was living on the brink of the
new century illuminated even his first literary work. His princess is as much
imbued with the azure of the sky and the purple of the sunrise as is Blok's
"Lady Beautiful." At the end of the poem, the old northern king sings a
hymn to the sunrise:

   The starlight is dying; sorrow is easing.
   Oh, dawn!
   Let the morning of the days sparkle
   Like thousands of mother-of-pearl fires.
   Oh, dawn!
   The shadows are melting!

Bely's romantic tale has the charm of light fantasy, youthful enthusiasm, morning freshness. But its "literariness" is diffuse and inexpressive.
The author begins with musical impressions (the romances and ballads of
Grieg) and selects his words almost at random, attempting primarily to transmit the sounds. He writes in "musical phrases," melodious, but of short endurance. This is not the sweeping harmony of a symphony, but the sentimen-
tal melody of a romance. The fourth part, only externally connected with the
history of the princess and the knight, is devoted to a description of the kingdom of the blessed, where the heroes of the Symphony are to be found after
their death.

With tender humor, the author describes his "holy eccentrics." The
kingdom of the blessed consists of blue lakes, sandy banks, little islands, thickets of reeds; there in huts are sitting anchorites casting their long fishing rods
into the water; Adam and Eve wade in the water to their knees along the
sandy banks. A little old man — a saint — walks along the bank striking a
heavenly mallot. Among the reeds sits the blessed simpleton Avva with his
merry wrinkled face, and he catches the watery bounty with his fishing rod.
All around are growing the snow-white flowers of oblivion, lotus and iris; red
flamingoes are flying; in a white mist, white men and women in crowns of
white roses pass by. At sunset, the Lord God Himself, surrounded entirely in
mist, marches along the thickets of blue iris.

The former princess, now a saint, sits on a little island and gazes into
the distance. A drowned man floats up to the island; the princess recognizes
her faithful knight, "who had drowned in the abyss of stagnation." She leads
him into her hut of reeds and they live in a "dream-like fairy tale." The
blessed rejoice around them.

They made merry. They were not dancing, but taking wing
in elegant, interplanetary accords.

This fantastic fusion of the Biblical paradise with pagan Lethe is crowned
— quite unexpectedly — by the coming of the Kingdom of the Spirit.

The preceptress of these places is speaking.
The day of our ascension is dawning:
And the joy of twilight dwindles before the new, third
    joy of the Spirit of the Consoler.
An old man, living at the lake, arises at dawn, ascends
    the craggy rock, and rings a silver bell.
It was a sign that the star of the Dawn has already
    flashed from the East.
Daybreak.
The silver bell has rung.

Bely's poem is the birth of Symbolism. A new feeling of life, a new
"mood." The sunrises and sunsets give off a different light; the air has another
scent.
  The Northern Symphony remained in manuscript form for three years.
It was published in *Scorpion* in the second half of 1903, a year after the appearance of the *Second Symphony*.

Chapter Two

In the spring of 1900, in the family of Mikhail Sergeevich Soloviev, Bely made the acquaintance of the philosopher Vladimir Soloviev; they held a "significant conversation" and agreed to meet after the summer. But in July, Vladimir Soloviev died. In the home of Mikhail Sergeevich there was a real cult of the deceased philosopher. "The year 1901," writes Bely, "passed for me and Seryozha under the sign of Soloviev's poetry." The singer of Eternal Femininity played a tremendous role in his life: "the mystical dawn" of the beginning of the new century was always connected for him with the name of Soloviev. "The dawn of the century," Bely continues, "was for me the flowering of hopes, the year of my coming of age, of personal successes, strengthened health, first love, new acquaintances who defined my future, the year of the writing of the *Symphony,* and of the birth of 'Andrei Bely'." On the roof of the university laboratory, during breaks between classes, the students Bugaev, Vladimirov and Pechkovsky would meet. They were all enthusiastic about the new art, poetry and mysticism. There were stormy arguments; a special language was invented with strange metaphors, aphorisms, words with special allusions. The friends would descend from the roof of the laboratory to stroll about Moscow, in the environs of Novodevichy Monastery, frightening the passers-by with the impetuous gallop of centaurs in the spirit of the *Northern Symphony.* Bryusov mentions this "theater for oneself" in his diary. He notes in 1903:

Bugaev visited me several times. We talked a lot. Of course about Christ, Christian feeling.... Then about centaurs, satyrs, about their way of life. He told me how he went to search for centaurs behind the Devichy Monastery, on the other side of the Moscow River. How a unicorn walked around his room. Then Bely sent his acquaintances little cards (visiting cards) as if from unicorns, satyrs, etc. Bely himself was embarrassed and began to assure me that it was a "joke." But formerly it had not been a joke for him, but rather a desire to create an atmosphere — to make everything seem as if unicorns existed.

In the evenings, the students would meet in Vladimirov's apartment where poetry and debates alternated with music and dramatic improvisations. This was the origin of the future circle of "Argonauts" — the hotbed of Moscow Symbolism. Vladimirov, a person much given to gaiety and fantasy, betrayed natural science for art and later devoted himself to painting; Petrovsky, "a little chemistry student with a sickly appearance," was of a revolutionary frame of mind: he preached that the old world must burn to ashes and that only then would come the dawn of a new era. Pechkovsky, with large blue eyes, embarrassed over his slight deafness, was engrossed in reading the poetry of Vladimir Soloviev. Gradually new people entered the group: Chelishchev, a mathematics student and a musician and composer; Ivanov, a learned eccenric, punster, "seizing upon nonsense and inflating it into a farcical crescendo." But the most picturesque figure in the circle was the law student Lev Lvovich Kobylinsky; Marina Tsvetaeva calls him "a man of genius" in her memoirs; Bely speaks of him as an astonishing improvisor and mime. He could have become a great actor, an outstanding orator, a talented poet – and he became nothing. Kobylinsky was chaos embodied; he burned with ideological passions. The list of his metamorphoses is very instructive: an educated economist and Marxist, he was attracted by Baudelaire and became a poet and a student of Baudelaire. He adopted the pseudonym Ellis, worshipped the "great magician" Bryusov, and worked selflessly on the *Scales*. Then the cult of Dante began; later followed anarchism in the spirit of Bakunin, pessimism, occultism, Steinerism, and, finally, conversion to Catholicism. This ideological Proteus admitted only the extremes. "There is no third way," he cried. "Either the bomb, or Vlas-like submission;[1] either anarchism or Catholicism!"

Kobylinsky had a face as white as a plaster mask, a blue-black beard, green phosphorescent eyes, and weak red lips. Storms of misunderstandings, scandals, confusion arose in the life around him. He lived in furnished rooms at the "Don" with its blue tavern sign, on the Smolensk market. "Darkness reigned in his cell;" the blinds were never raised; only before the bust of Dante were two candles constantly burning. He would eat in a restaurant for shop-keepers, under the rumble of snare-drums, and he always had problems with his stomach. He lived at night, slept during the day. He wrote mystical erotic verses and translated Baudelaire. He dreamed of a new inquisition by the "order of madmen," on the bonfire of which the universe would be consumed. Ellis has long been forgotten as a poet and critic, but in his time, he was the "spirit of the age," one of the creators of the decadent life-style.

Vladimirov's circle was a free union of buoyant youth. "Fun," commedia del'arte, prevailed; the laughter was unceasing. The romances of Glinka as executed by Vladimirov alternated with the improvisations of Chelishchev, the parodies of Ivanov, the buffoonery of Ellis. Bely's *Second Symphony*, a witty satire on the Moscow mystics, was created in this atmosphere.

In the author's memory, its first part was connected with spring, with the melting of the snow on Holy Week, with early Easter, with walks along the Arbat. At this time. Borya Bugaev and Seryozha Soloviev were experiencing their first love. One was in love with a "society lioness," the other with an Arsenievsky schoolgirl.

We described sharp zigzags in twisting alleys. The picture of spring, of the streets and passers-by, suddenly burst forth in the first part of the *Symphony* like a diary.

The sketches were read at the Soloviev tea table. Mikhail Sergeevich approved;
Bely began to think of the subject, but examinations were at hand, and the
poem was put aside. After twenty years, the poet returned in memory to the
spring of 1901, the happiest time in his life. His youth is resurrected in the
poem "Three Meetings:"

> Oh, unforgettable walks,
> Oh, unforgettable dreams,
> The twisting alleys of Moscow...
> All has swept past; where, oh youth, are you!
>
>   * * *
>
> Tall, pale and round-shouldered,
> Where are you, Seryozha, dear brother;
> Your eyes — prophetic rumblings,
> Your eyes, fixed on the sunset;
> You are leaving for Eternity; for the Arbat.
> You would wander without speaking
> And I would hear and see more clearly
> The youthful spring of the Arbat,
> Your bent back,
> Your raised shoulders,
> The first grass on the boulevards...

The romantic spring concluded with the prose of examinations. He
passed physics at last. Bely was alone in Moscow, in an empty apartment. He
carried his table to the balcony overlooking the Arbat. On the eve of Whitsunday and on Whitsunday itself, he wrote the second part of the *Symphony*. He
spoke the lines aloud and wrote them down — doing this the night through
under the unextinguished dawn. On Whitmonday, Seryozha arrived from Dedovo. Bely read the poem to him. Seryozha was struck by the description of
the Novodevichy Monastery and the friends went there to compare the image
with the original. The golden light of Whitmonday burned low there on the
crosses in the graveyard; nuns wandered among the lilac bushes; the sounds
of the harmonium were heard; the red icon-lamp shimmered on the grave of
Vladimir Soloviev — absolutely as it was in the *Symphony*! All Moscow
seemed to the friends to be illuminated by the light of the poem. Life and
poetry merged. The next day they went to Dedovo, and Bely read two parts
of the *Symphony* to the Solovievs. He writes: "Mikhail Sergeevich said to me,
'Borya, this must be published: you are contemporary literature. And it will
be printed.' " But out of respect to his father the professor, Bely decided not
to be published under his own name. They began to think up pseudonyms.
The young author proposed: "Boris Burevoi (Boris the Stormy)." Mikhail
Sergeevich began to laugh: "When the pseudonym is revealed later," he said,
"people will make puns: 'Burevoi — Bori voi (Borya's wail)'!" And he thought

31

up: Andrei Bely (Andrei the White).

"Thus the natural scientist, in his junior year," concludes the author, "became a writer against his will."

In Dedovo, four "unforgettable days" passed. One night Bely and Seryozha spent in a boat in the middle of a pond, reading the Apocalypse in the light of a floating candle. At dawn, Mikhail Sergeevich came, and the three of them went to look at the white campanula transplanted from the Pustynka Estate, where Vladimir Soloviev had lived. The mystical white flowers were angels of death for the philosopher; he wrote about them:

> Bold designs
> In a sick heart
> The white angels
> Arose all around.

From Dedovo, Bely returned to Moscow, for an examination in botany.

The third part of the *Symphony* was written in the country at the Silver Well, between the first and fifth of June; the fourth was finished in July.

* * *

In the foreword to the *Symphony,* the author explains that his work has three meanings: musical, satirical and ideologically symbolic.

> First, it is a symphony, the goal of which is the expression of a number of moods connected to each other by a basic "general mood" (harmony); hence the necessity of dividing it into parts, parts into sections, and sections into verses (musical phrases).... The second meaning is satirical; some of the extremes of mysticism are ridiculed here.... Finally, the ideological sense, which, predominating, destroys neither the musical nor the satirical meaning. The combination in one section or verse of all three aspects of Symbolism.

Thirty-two years after writing the *Symphony,* in the book *The Turn of the Century,* Bely returned to his first "Symbolist" work. He did a large part of the work in the country, during the summer, not at a desk, but on horseback; eyes and muscles took part in the work. He writes:

> I dance out and shout my rhythms in the fields, with sweeps of the hands, groping for the connections between words and leg, ear, eye, hand.... The influence of bodily movements on the architechtonics of a phrase is the America I discovered in my youth. The gallops in the fields were reigned in by the gallops of phrases and the dynamics of the images that flashed by.... I became accustomed to writing in motion; I write this way even now.... The form of the *Symphony* took shape under specific conditions — in running, in the saddle, in my tempo in the field....

Concerning the second, satirical, meaning of the *Symphony*, the author says that at the beginning of the century, he thought out a whole series of "symphonies," to portray "religious eccentrics," but that he had paints enough for only one. When the *Dramatic Symphony* was written the mystical type had only just been born. Bely was acquainted only with the followers of of Soloviev and had heard of Anna Schmidt. In his caricatures there is more imagination than observation. However, his satire proved to be prophetic: soon there appeared not imaginary, but very real "religious philosophers" — Lev Tikhomirov, Berdyaev, Ern, Florensky, Sventsitsky. The "World Soul" became famous — Anna Schmidt with her mystical treatises. Bely adds:

Anna Schmidt was an appendix to my *Symphony* free of charge. She exceeded even my caricature.... Her teaching about the Third Testament is the basis of the parodies portrayed in the *Symphony*, the sole difference being that to me the "Woman clothed with the sun" is a beauty, and not an old woman very unpleasant in appearance.

* * *

The *Second Dramatic Symphony* is an attempt at the creation of a new literary form; the author tears apart the traditional structure of the narrative, the sequential flow of events joined by a causal and temporal link. His prose is broken into pieces, smashed into fragments. The numbered "musical phrases" are the simplest units of the composition. Each of them is an independent whole. Here are a few examples:

The poet wrote a poem about love.
The two people quarreled over a cup of tea about people great and small.
It was already Whitmonday. Everyone was napping and having good dreams.
On the emptied sidewalk, illumined by streetlights, a little man minced along with a pince-nez on his extended nose.

These "motifs" are self-enclosed like monads. They are not united with each other, but are presented side by side. The method of "juxtaposition" suggests the technique of Impressionist painting; the colors are placed side by side without half-tones and transitions. This produces an impression of brilliant multi-color, sharp contrasts, unexpected dissonance.

A talented artist on a large canvas depicted a "miracle."
While in the butcher shop hung twenty skinned carcasses.

The phrase-monad must evoke in the reader a definite "melody of the soul." To produce this effect, it combines in the greatest tension all the emotional elements of style: rhythm, sound, meaning and image. The author is unusually inventive in devising "rhythmic gallops." His "phrases" run the whole gamut of "general moods," from poetic sadness and mystical trepidation through disgust, boredom, horror, to blasphemy and cynicism. Thoughts, feelings, moods circle in a whirlpool. It seems as if we are standing in the center of a circle, and along the circle with a roar and a clatter a multi-colored carousel is rushing. Faces, figures, costumes are borne past; they disappear and appear again in a different illumination. The old immobile world has been torn from its place and carried into wild motion. Bely has created a new dynamic composition and laid the basis for impressionism in art.

But in the *Second Symphony,* the problem of form is not all that is resolved; an "ideological, symbolic" meaning is included. After shattering the world into atoms and allowing it, like a top, to spin along a circle, the poet demonstrates the senselessness of the flow of time by means of form. The content corresponds to the form. In the first part, momentary photographs of Moscow on a hot spring day are presented. By recording "events" and "incidents" occurring simultaneously on the streets and in the homes of the city without selection, Bely in reality reveals the mystical horror of the temporal process. Time without end, "Eternal Time," is eternal boredom and eternal banality. The leit-motif of boredom is maintained, growing stronger, throughout the entire poem. Here is the introduction:

Everyone was pale and above everyone hung the dome of heaven, blue, gray-blue, sometimes gray, sometimes black, filled with musical boredom, eternal boredom, with the sun-eye in the middle.

Next is an inventory of events: pedestrians are walking; street-cleaners pass on their water-tanks; martial music is played on Prechistensky Boulevard; a pale hunchback strolls with his lame son; in a store, the salesman flies along the storeys on the elevator; a coachman resembling Nietzsche sits in his box; a student in front of a bookstore looks at a German translation of Gorky... And the leit-motif:

From the dome of heaven rush the despondent and grim songs of Eternity... And these songs are like scales. Scales from the invisible world. Eternally the same and the same. Hardly have they concluded than they have already begun again.

At the end of the first part, the theme of time shifts into an elegaic key:

The sounds ran together with the minutes. A group of minutes comprised Time. Time flowed without pause. In the flow of Time hazy Eternity was reflected... It was like a huge bird. Its name was the bird of sorrow. It was sorrow itself.

The world is suffocating from the boredom of the cosmic scales, the endlessness of the closed circle, eternal return, the senselessness of time. This is the thesis. It was suggested to the young author by the philosophy of Shopenhauer, Hartmann, Nietzsche, theosophy and Buddhism. In the second part, the antithesis appears. The meaning of time lies in the fact that it must end, that a moment will come when "there will be no more time." The theme of "eternal return" is opposed to the theme of the Apocalypse.

At the end of the 19th century, Vladimir Soloviev was seized by a presentiment of the approaching end. He said that world history was complete, that the last battle between Christ and Antichrist was drawing near ("Three Conversations"). In one private letter, he confessed that "The approaching end of the world is wafted toward me like a certain clear but indefinable breath, — as a traveler, approaching the ocean, senses the ocean air before he sees the ocean."

The group of Moscow mystics, followers of Soloviev, to which Bely belonged, experienced eschatological moods acutely. Hope for a new revelation, worship of Eternal Femininity, the expectation of the end was their credo. But they could not escape seeing how this credo was distorted as it grew into a way of life, becoming transformed into "mystical jargon." Bely ridiculed the distortion of "Apocalypticism," sparing neither himself nor his friends.

Bely depicts the "ideological landscape" of the beginning of the century with great skill. He is a master at grotesque, parody, caricature, and already in this early work his talent as a satirist appears. At first he presents the general spiritual atmosphere of the age. In a literary circle, Drozhzhikovsky (Merezhkovsky) makes a speech; he preaches the synthesis of theology with mysticism and the church and points to the three transformations of the Spirit. The cynical mystic Shipovnikov (Rozanov) is shouting from St. Petersburg to all of Russia while Merezhkovich (Merezhkovsky again) writes an article on the unification of paganism with Christianity. The Marxists are addicted to philosophy and the philosophers to theology. The mystics multiply and their web covers all Moscow. One studies a mystical haze (Blok?); another attempts to posit the question of the resurrection of the dead on practical soil (Fedorov?); a third interviews elders; a fourth makes inquiries about the possibility of the appearance of the Beast (of the Apocalypse). Max Nordau gives a public lecture and inveighs against degeneration. At a meeting of theosophists and orgiasts, a person coming from India exclaims: "For how long, how long, will they not understand thee, oh Karma!" In the midst of these ideological storms stands the figure of the hero of the *Symphony* — the mystic Sergei Musatov. "He was tall and blond with dark eyes; he had the face of an ascetic." For Musatov, the symbolic images of the Apocalypse are immediate reality; he knows that the Kingdom of the Spirit is already approaching, that the "Woman clothed with the sun" is giving birth to the white horseman who will rule the peoples with an "iron rod." He believes in the messianic calling of Russia.

35

The Babylonian whore is Europe; from her will come the Beast which will persecute the Woman; but she will flee from him and hide in Russia, in the Solovetsky Cloister. Musatov feels that he is a hierophant and pagan priest. "Is not my stick an iron rod!" he exclaims. "Is not the straw of my hat gold!" Bely makes the mystical mania of his hero into buffoonery.

Friends inform Musatov that the family of the approaching Beast has been found, that the Beast is not yet out of the cradle. For the present, he is a good little boy, blue-eyed, living in the north of France. Fortunately, the mystic's anxiety for the fate of the world is soon dispelled. He discovers from his agents that "the Beast was a victim of a stomach disorder, that he has given his soul up to God, not yet even five years old, having taken fright at his dreadful significance." Musatov meets a woman, the blue-eyed "Fairy Tale," and the image of the "Woman clothed with the sun" is embodied for him in this blonde beauty. He approaches her. "Fairy Tale listened carelessly, wishing to send him away as quickly as possible. Suddenly a handsome little boy with blue eyes ran out." Musatov is shaken: the Beast from the abyss! But the boy turns out to be a girl — the daughter of the hostess — and he calms down.

Thus all the "insights" of Musatov collapse. "Eternity whispered to her pampered favorite: 'I was joking. And you joke too.... We are all joking.' "

But the counterpoint of Bely's *Symphony* is complex. The caricature of the unsuccessful mystic is submerged in a mystical twilight; irony and enthusiasm are indivisible. There is pure poetry in the description of the Novodevichy Monastery on Whitsunday and that of Moscow on the mysterious night of Whitmonday, when the deceased Vladimir Soloviev, in a pelerin cape, strides along the roofs and blows a horn, while the author himself gazes at the illuminated city from his balcony.

> Onto the balcony of the three-storey house came a man
>   neither young nor old.
> He held a candle in his hand. The candle burned like
>   Whitmonday.
> The sound of a horn carried clearly over Moscow, and
>   from above were heard luminous storms, luminous
>   floods like Whitmonday.

The self-proclaimed prophet Sergei Musatov distorted the truth and was punished. But the truth shines as formerly "like Whitmonday." The deceased Vladimir Soloviev rides in a carriage, sits on the parvis of the Church of the Burning Bush, and whispers: "The end is near; what has been long desired will shortly come to pass." Then he goes around the city and makes the sign of the cross over his friends.

And in these words of pathos, sorrow and tenderness, all the dissonances of the *Symphony* are resolved.

Again spring approaches; again in the Novodevichy Monastery under the apple trees the nuns are sitting and between the graves wanders the fabled beauty (Fairy Tale), and it seems to her that "something precious, impossible, sadly pensive is drawing near." "Before her the future was revealed and she burned with joy. She knew. Little lights gleamed forth somewhere on the graves."

The *Second Symphony* is the literary birth of "Andrei Bely," the birth of a genuine poet.

Mikhail Soloviev gave the poem to Bryusov; he praised it, but informed them that the Scorpion publishing house had no funds; however, it would give the beginning poet its seal. The *Symphony* was published with the seal of Scorpion at the expense of Mikhail Soloviev in April, 1902.

At the beginning of April, the *Second Symphony* appeared. The newspapers and journals greeted it with frenzied abuse. A friend of the author, Ellis, authoritatively announced: "The book was written by a lost soul; no one but a madman could have written it!"

The Scorpion publishing house announced the new writer — Andrei Bely — to all Moscow. He became a "rising star." He was castigated; strange rumors circulated about him. He was "a certain unusual person, a poet, mystic and 'Decadent.' " In his whole appearance, there was something "special" — could it be the portent of a new religion? Zaitsev recalls:[2]

They saw in him something like Prince Myshkin in *The Idiot*. The rumor went that in the University there was a similar incident involving him: at a student meeting, in the heat of an argument, someone slapped him across the face. He turned the other cheek.

During the summer, in the Ekaterinoslavsky newspaper, the *Dnepr Region*, there appeared a sympathetic review of Bely's symphony by Emily Medtner, in which he demonstrated that the meaning of the *Symphony* lay not in the mystics and not in the lunatics, but in the symbol of joy, in the heroine who bore the name "Fairy Tale." Medtner later told Bely:

One breathes the *Symphony* like fresh air after a storm. I love the air and the dawns in it. You have plucked a piece of fresh air from the ashes. Moscow is illuminated in a new way. The *Symphony* is the music of dawn.

But the music of the *Symphony* really reached only one kindred soul. Blok wrote about it not a review, but a poem in prose.[3] In it he captured the new, still vague melody of the poem. He wrote:

Better than anything I ever dreamed. I dreamed in the uncertain, blazing boundary which divides the brief sleep of rest from the eternal sleep

37

of life.... And, like a candle caused to flicker by the wind at a window, I looked ahead into the calmness of the night, and back, into the daily abode of labor... "The morning cometh, and also the night" (Isaiah). Its music is vague. The twinkling stars ring, the dawn appears, pearls rain down, the incarnation draws near. She has arisen and whispers in my ear: my dear one, my tender one, is it you? But "he that hath the bride is the bridegroom" (John). He will recognize the voice of his companion before the others. He who yearns for the mountains will hear the voice beyond the pass. But you will not sleep in the "golden-purple night!" In the morning you will say gently at the same window: Greetings, rosy Friend, Fairy Tale that is dawn!

* * *

Having finished the *Second Symphony*, Bely immediately began a third. He worked on it in November and December in the "histological tea room" of Moscow University. Toward spring, the symphony was finished; but the author was not satisfied with it. Its publication was postponed until 1905.

Return: The Third Symphony develops the theme of "universal boredom," which had already resounded in the *Second*. But in the few months separating the two works, Bely's poetic world had drastically changed. The mystical dawn was extinguished, and the universe was submerged in unmitigated darkness. As an epigraph to the poem, one might take a verse from the 1902 poem, "Sunset."

> There is nothing... And there will be nothing.
> And you will die.
> The world will disappear and God will forget it.
> What, then, are you expecting?

In the "histological tea room," the sobered dreamer was absorbed in physics, embryology, chemistry. After flights into "sapphire ether," revelations and ecstasies, came austere positive science. The "scientific world-view," the last word of wisdom at which European civilization had arrived, was revealed to the student. And it proclaimed: "Emptiness; emptiness ahead and emptiness behind. Nonbeing. The world is an idea, a dream, a phantasm."

The *Symphony* is the result of the scientist's studies of precise sciences. It is colored by the powerful influence of Schopenhauer and Nietzsche, but basically it honestly transmits the despair of a disappointed mystic, the tragedy of a prophet who deceived himself. The *Symphony* tells the "boring history" of the chemistry teacher Khandrikov. He has an unattractive, tiresome wife, Sofya Chizikova, and an unpleasant, sickly child. Khandrikov's enemy, the chemistry docent Tsenk, weaves a complicated intrigue around him; the psychiatrist Orlov defends him. Khandrikov writes a dissertation, becomes entangled in his constructs, and goes mad. He is put in a sanatorium for the mentally ill; there he kills himself. This everyday story in the spirit of Chekhov is placed in the framework of a romantic fairy tale. The wretched figure of Khandrikov and his dismal life is only one of its embodiments. His soul had been blissfully at peace in the lap of the cosmos, was sent into the world to suffer, and, after conquering the absurd dream of life through madness and death, again is returned to the embrace of "silver Eternity." The prologue to Khandrikov's life takes place on the banks of a cosmic ocean; the happy child is digging in the velvet sand with a mother-of-pearl shell. "The ashy-gray sea was shot with tender silver as if purified from filth." Eternity in the image of a magnificent elder cares for the child.

The silver-white chasubles, the blinding rod of the old man trembled in orange sparks. On his breast swung a mysterious diamond necklace. It seemed as if lights were all catching fire on his breast. And from the necklace was suspended the sign of immutable Eternity.

But in the kingdom of the blessed there is also a serpent, "with the head of a calf crowned with little golden horns." On him rests the bearer of universal evil, unceasing and senseless motion — "Tsar Wind, who is mentally ill." He "bites at his wolf's beard, he glares with his green eyes, he twists his felt cap in his hand, not daring to put it on in the presence of the snake-like monster."

Old Man Eternity sends the child's soul to embodiment in the world. He says:

I crown you with suffering. You will depart. We will not see you. The wilderness of suffering will expand above, below, and on all sides. In vain you will run through space — the boundless wilderness will keep you in its cold embraces. Your voice will be in vain. But the hour will come. The solution will arrive; and then I will send an eagle to you.

In the second part, the unhappy soul passes through the wilderness in the form of the chemistry teacher Khandrikov. Tsar Wind is embodied in the figure of the evil docent Tsenk; Old Man Eternity takes the image of the psychiatrist Orlov.

In the sanatorium, the mad Khandrikov dimly distinguishes behind the mask of the doctor the familiar ancient features. The doctor says to him: "What do your madness and my health mean before the universal phantasm? The universe has surrounded us with its embraces. It caresses and kisses us. Let us die. Silence is good."

And Orlov sends him the promised eagle. Khandrikov throws himself into the water.

The epilogue returns us to the cosmic homeland. Again the ashy gray sea is shot with tender silver. Old Man Eternity, resembling Dr. Orlov, speaks to the returning soul:

Many times you departed and came, borne by the eagle. You came and again departed. Many times you have been crowned with suffering, with its burning fires. And now for the first time I place on you these stars of silver. Now you have come and, sun-like, you will not set. I greet you, oh my unsetting child.

Khandrikov has overcome the law of eternal return through his madness and suicide. He has earned contentment in the embraces of the cosmos. The risings and settings of his "planet" are finished. Henceforth, he is the "unsetting child" crowned with silver stars.

The central place in the *Symphony* is occupied by Khandrikov's brilliant improvisation at the celebration after the defense of his dissertation. This "serious" resumé of the contemporary scientific theories on the nature of the universe and "progress" resounds like a funeral knell over the "positive world-view" of the departing 19th century. The exposition of the chemistry teacher, confined to strictly "scientific" tones, is more comical than the most unbridled buffoonery.

Khandrikov says:

Perhaps, the universe is only a flask in which we are precipitated like crystals, life with its motion being only the falling of the crystals to the bottom of the vessel and death the cessation of this falling. And we do not know what will be: will we be decomposed, chased into other universes, treated with sulphuric acid to turn us sulphuric; do they want to dissolve or reduce us to fragments in a mortar.... Perhaps all is returned. Or all is changed. Or all returns changed. Or only similar. Perhaps the change, of something which was, has returned more perfect than this thing which was. Or less perfect. Perhaps neither more nor less perfect, but of equal value. Perhaps progress moves in a straight line. Or in a circle. Or in a straight line and in a circle — in a spiral. Or a parabola replaces progress. Perhaps the spiral of our progress is not the spiral of the progress of atoms. Perhaps the spiral of the progress of atoms is wrapped around the spiral of our progress. And the spiral of our progress, to the degree to which we can foresee it, is wrapped around a single link of the spiral of the higher order... And thus without end... Everything flows. Rushes. Whirls along on obscure circles. The huge water spout of the world carries every life in its stormy embraces. Before it is emptiness. And behind it the same.

Docent Tsenk announces that "Khandrikov is rebelling." And it is in reality a rebellion. In the person of his hero, Bely had flung a challenge to the "old world." Let it crumble with its atomic evolution and spirals of progress into its own emptiness! The world of nonbeing — let it return to nonbeing!

Bely screams of the crisis of contemporary mankind, of the approaching ruin of European culture. And in his rebellion, he is a prophet of the imminent world-wide catastrophes.

The *Third Symphony*, artistically less perfect than the *Second*, exceeds it in its prophetic enthusiasm.

* * *

Bely in 1902

Zaitsev recalls Bely as a student:

On the Moscow Arbat I see him as a student in a double-breasted jacket and a cap with a blue band. His eyes were especially memorable — not simply blue, but enamel azure, the color of the heavens, with very thick, magnificent eyelashes shading his eyes like huge fans. Thin, slight, with a large forehead and a chin jutting foreward, always tilting his head back a little, it seemed as if he was not walking, but "flying" along the Arbat. The authentic "Kotik Letaev," in a halo of tender, bright curls. A well-groomed Kotik, of aristocratic birth.

At the beginning of 1902, Bely wrote essays in response to Merezhkovsky's book on Tolstoi and Dostoevsky, and signed them "A Science Student."[4] In them, he summarized his apocalyptical credo: at present, religious anguish is becoming unendurable; in it the approach of Antichrist is sensed. "Eternal Femininity," "the Woman clothed with the sun," already spreads through the air; but the great whore also does not sleep. Christianity, from its rose color, must become white, of the nature of John. And the final thesis: "One must be prepared for the unexpected so that "it" will not take him unaware, because the storm is imminent, and the waves are raging; something threatening is emerging from the waters."

One might think that it was not Bely who wrote the letter, but the hero of the *Second Symphony,* Musatov.

The "Science Student's" confession of faith made a great impression on Merezhkovsky. Zinaida Gippius wrote to Olga Solovieva that they had guessed who the author was; that Dmitry Sergeevich was very excited, while Rozanov called the letter "a work of genius." In February, Merezhkovsky came to Moscow and gave a lecture on Gogol. On the following day, at a reception at Bryusov's house, he entranced the young mystic with his tenderness and humility. Bely wittily parodied Merezhkovsky's manner of speaking:

Perhaps you are right, and we are wrong, but you — in contemplation, and we — wretched, weak, sickly — in action; you are strong, we are weak. But in our weakness our power is created; we are united, and you are alone; we know nothing, and you know everything; we are ready to reject even our thoughts, but you are adamant... Then go, teach us.

41

And Bely adds: "Merezhkovsky could turn people's heads." Zinaida Nikolaevna also praised him: she called him "remarkable and new," invited him to Petersburg to work with them on the *New Path,* and promised to introduce him to Rozanov, Filosofov and Kartashev.

Solovieva, already ill, had a mystical fear of Merezhkovsky. For her, Zinaida Nikolaevna was the devil and Dmitry Sergeevich the serpent from the lair of Rozanov, who had so cruelly attacked the deceased Vladimir Soloviev. But Borya Bugaev would be Siegfried and overcome the Dragon.

For the present, Siegfried and the Dragon parted on the friendliest terms. When he was leaving Moscow, Merezhkovsky said to Bely: "You are a close friend: we leave you here as if in an enemy camp. Believe in us; do not forget; do not listen to gossip." A "mystical" correspondence was begun with Zinaida Gippius; for greater conspiracy, she wrote to him at the address of the university laboratory. With great excitement, he awaited her long, dark blue envelopes, addressed in a fine Gothic hand.

At the *World of Art* exhibit in Moscow, Bely made the acquaintance of Diaghilev and Benois. They proposed that he collaborate in the journal, and his article "Forms of Art" was accepted. In the chronicle *The Turn of the Century,* there is an excellent caricature of Diaghilev:

> The most magnificent figure of Diaghilev was distinguished from the point of view of color and graphics. I recognized him from his portrait, by the coquettishly fluffed up quiff of hair with a silver lock on the black growth, and by the rosy, brazenly moustacheless face, as rich as a fresh-baked bun ready either to be captivatingly buttered or to freeze in the icily insulting pose of a viscount. I marveled at the delicacy. According to Somov, the lips were heart-shaped. Suddenly he twitched, twitched again, frozen. The devil take it — some sort of "Caracalla," if not a rouged Isabel cutting off the heads of the Roman senators.... What a vest! What a knot and pinhole in his necktie! What blinding cuffs, like alabaster, barely visible!

In the spring of 1902, the student Bugaev was freer from university obligations than he had been in the preceding year; during the transition from the third to the fourth course, final examinations were replaced by periodic tests. In May, he lived alone in an empty city apartment. Amidst furniture in slipcovers smelling of napthaline, he read Nietzsche, Merezhkovsky and Rozanov. The little "revolutionary student," A. S. Petrovsky, would drop by. Every evening, they went to the Vladimirov circle where they argued about questions of form. Bely was overflowing with plans for the construction of a theory of the new Symbolist art.

During the autumn, the author of the review of the *Second Symphony,* Emily Medtner, came to Moscow, and a "stormy friendship" developed between him and Bely. The brother of the well-known composer N. K. Medtner,

Emily Karlovich — a Russified German — was a man of great culture, a philosopher, critic and musical theoretician. His grandfather, an artist, had been acquainted with Goethe and the cult of the author of *Faust* reigned in the Medtner family. Emili Karlovich was a member of the "Goethe Gesellschaft," and his study was crammed with the works of this scholarly society. His other idol was Wagner, and Medtner perceived reality through the symbolism of the *Ring of the Nibelungenlied*. The principle of good was embodied for him in the image of Siegfried, evil in the person of the perfidious dwarf. The Medtners' apartment was a conservatory of sorts: Konius, Gedike and Goldenweiser studied there; Koussevitzky, Scriabin and the critics Kruglikov and Engel attended lectures there. Bely is indebted to Medtner for his musical education: Medtner led him into the music of Beethoven, Handel and Bach. Under his influence, the poet attended concerts in the conservatory and became familiar with Schubert, Schumann and Mozart. He experienced Chaikovsky and Wagner with a passion, and heard the first works of Scriabin. Medtner said to him again and again: "Culture is music," and, under this inspiration, Bely wrote his first theoretical articles.

The spirit of German culture, embodied by Medtner and his cult of Goethe, Nietzsche and Wagner, stood in opposition to the spirit of Romance culture, the bearer of which was the French Piotr Ivanovich d'Alheim, the founder of the "House of Song." An elegant stylist, poet, publicist and an admirer of Mallarmé and Villiers de l'Isle Adam, gray-haired, round-shouldered, clean-shaven, he was an attractive, witty causeur, fantasist and dreamer. He planned the creation of musical centers like the "House of Song" in all countries of the world and believed that art would perfect the revolution of life. His wife, the well-known singer Maria Alekseevna Olenina d'Alheim, educated the musical taste of Moscow with her evenings of song. Very thin, intense and austere, with amazing blue eyes, she created a new artistic style of "song." Bely devoted an ecstatic article to her, entitled "The Singer."[5]

The German and Romance cultures were at war with each other. Medtner hated d'Alheim for his Catholicism, "sick mysticism," and love of Liszt. He called him Klingsor and warned Bely: "He will destroy you, I tell you; Goethe would not have approved." And the new Parsival was torn between the two warring camps.

Under Medtner's influence, Bely wrote his first theoretical article, "Forms of Art."[6] The development of all the arts, he maintains, is connected with music, which "ever more powerfully places its imprint on all the forms of the manifestation of the good." In music, the essence of motion is perceived, and hints of future perfection are heard. "The mood of any image must be understood as the 'general mood' of this image, as its musical harmony." And after references to Schopenhauer, Wagner and Ibsen, the author concludes: "Will not all forms of art increasingly aspire to occupy the place of overtones in relation to the basic tone, i.e., to music?"

Thus, in reducing all the arts to music, Bely attempts to place a theoretical foundation under his *Symphonies.*

* * *

Bely in 1903

Bely had known of the existence of "Sasha" Blok for a long time. As early as 1897, the Solovievs had told him about their relative — a schoolboy who also wrote poems and was interested in the theater. In 1901, Bely and Seryozha Soloviev read Blok's first verses with enthusiasm. In 1902, after reading Bely's *Symphony*, Blok wrote to Mikhail Soloviev: "The heart of Andrei Bely is in absolutely terrifying, almost shuddering bloom. It is strange that I have never met and never spoken one word with this person so close and dear to me."

In the first days of January, 1903, a correspondence began between the poets. Bely wrote Blok a flowery letter with quotations from philosophers. It crossed a letter coming from Blok. Thus, symbolically, both their letters and the paths of their lives crossed. Soon their correspondence was discontinued by a sad event. In January, Mikhail Soloviev died, and on the night of his death, his wife, Olga Mikhailovna, shot herself. The "Soloviev circle" fell apart. It was a dreadful blow for Bely. In August, Blok married Lyubov Dmitrievna Mendeleeva and invited Bely to the wedding as his best man; the sudden death of his father did not permit Bely to accept the invitation.

Andrei Bely spent the year 1903 in creative tension, inspiration, in university work, and in the turmoil of literary circles. At Easter, in Scorpion's third anthology, *Northern Flowers,* his verses (later included in the collection *Gold in Azure*) and a passage from the mystery play *He Who Hath Come* were published. The intention of the author was to transmit the fiery atmosphere of the expectation of the Second Coming and the appearance of Antichrist, taking the image of Christ. The action takes place at the seashore near the Temple of Glory. The people are excited, in anguish; the students believe and doubt, wait and despair. The First Teacher Elijah appeals, "My God, my God, why hast Thou forsaken us?" An excited student runs up and says in agitation that he has seen a man sitting on a stone, "with a face wild and strange. Above his head was a rosy cloud, and a voice was heard: 'Here is the Calf.' " The students divide into two parties. The preceptor Nikita warns those of little faith: "Have fear... the fiery world will run with blood. The titan of evil and pride is taking over the world." But Elijah calls upon the people to meet him. And now he comes. His beautiful, pearly-amber face and clear blue eyes are sadly fixed upon the distance. His forehead is too high. He speaks in a quiet, sad voice: "Is there no other way?" A dull thunder answers him: "It is late."

He Who Hath Come (wringing his hands above his head):
Have mercy on me!

44

The voice: There is no mercy.
He who hath come apathetically rises to his feet with a face
turned to stone, frozen, like a mask. Lowering his head and hands,
he ascends a mountain path. The higher he rises, the gentler and
more beautiful the expression on his face becomes... At the top
of the cliff, he stands with his hands lowered, proudly raising his
beautiful head. His enraptured, sunlit profile is brilliantly etched
against the background of the sunrise... Mute silence. He stands
in a shining crown and in a gray mantle bestrewn with the roses
of Eternity.

Bely's apocalyptical figure is portrayed without the influence of Vladimir Soloviev's *Tale of Antichrist*. His sadly beautiful hero is not Antichrist,
but a false Christ, a prophet who, in madness and conceit, thought himself to
be the Messiah. There is more decadent refinement than true symbolism in
the poem.

The author was weakened by the burden of a problem beyond his
strength, and the mystery play remained incomplete. But in the music of
words, images, moods, there lives something "impossible, sad, precious"
(Bely's words from the *Second Symphony*).

In the spring, Bely passed his state examinations: the professors did not
have much pity on the "little Decadent." At the examination in comparative
anatomy, one of the docents attempted to trap him with a question about the
embryology of the nostril of the frog. Another well-known professor, who
had known him as a child, refused to shake hands with the author of the
Symphony. Nevertheless, he completed the course with a diploma of the first
degree. His father was in ecstasy: "Well, Borenka," he said, "you have surprised even me. I did not expect such a thing from you. In a word, you played
the fool for a year: that's all over now. A diploma of the first degree all the
same. Of course! Yes sir!" His father was especially warm with him; he made
his peace with the "Decadence" of his son; he even liked Bryusov and Ellis.
He was ready to accept the fauns, centaurs and other fauna of the *Symphony*.
Father and son were preparing to go to the Black Sea beach – and suddenly,
in the beginning of June, Nikolai Vasilievich Bugaev died from angina pectoris.
Crushed by this unexpected sorrow, overtired from examinations, Bely went
to rest in the country.

The student Leonid Semenov, an anarchist and passionate admirer of
Blok, came to him from Petersburg on the very day of his father's burial. He
visited Bely every day until his departure and accompanied him on walks in
Novodevichy Monastery. There he visited the graves of his father, Vladimir
Soloviev, Mikhail and Olga Soloviev; he wandered among the lilacs and icon
lamps, in the rosy air of the sunset, and remembered Blok's verses:

At the forgotten graves grass has sprung up.

We have forgotten yesterday and forgotten the words.
And silence has fallen all around...

Leonid Semenev had an unusual destiny; he published a collection of poetry in the style of Blok; then he became a terrorist, and finally a follower of Dobrolyubov; he went on foot to Tolstoi and perished tragically during the Civil War.

Bely spent the three summer months in the village of the Silver Well; he grew a beard, wandered about the fields without his cap, became sunburned and strong; he recited his verses aloud. When he was writing the *Symphony*, he had been carried away by a musical flow: rhythm and sound. Now the image began to separate itself from the melody; the poet was attracted by sharp metaphors, refined rhythms, expressive words. "Never again," he writes, "did the lyrical wave so completely engulf me."[7] The poems written at the Silver Well form the basis of the book *Gold in Azure*. "Gold" is the ripened cornfields, "azure" — the air. Roaming the fields, he gazed into the sky, the clouds, smelled the breeze, noted all the shadows of illumination. Hence the special lightning of the poems in *Gold in Azure*: like a barometer, they take note of all the oscillations of air currents.

And in the evenings, all alone, he immersed himself in Kant's *Critiques*, planning to lay a firm gnoseological foundation under the shakey edifice of Symbolism.

In October, Bely returned to Moscow, entered the philological faculty and enthusiastically gave himself up to the stormy life of literary circles. In 1903, the atmosphere of Moscow had changed: the new art celebrated its first victories; new poets appeared — Max Voloshin, Krechetov (Sokolov). The names of Blok and Bely acquired even more fame, and Bryusov reigned, ackknowledged as the "maitre" by everyone. Sologub and Gippius published their best collections. "The Decadent broke into song everywhere like a mosquito," Bely recalls. As if from under the earth, there arose swarms of modernistic girls: thin, pale, hoarse, mysterious, languishing, like the heroines of Maeterlinck; they overflowed the hall of the Literary Artistic Circle and the Symbolist salons. Young poets and critics united around the Scorpion publishing house. Under the leadership of Bryusov, they worked out problems of artistic form. Here there were no mystical flights, philosophical quests; persistent work on the "craft of a poet" went on. Voloshin, Baltrushaitis, Victor Hoffman, Roslavlev, Kursinsky, and the three Koiransky brothers took part in the circle.

A second circle was grouped around the Griffin publishing house, at the head of which stood the lawyer Sergei Sokolov, who published verses under the pseudonym of Krechetov. Bely depicts him:

A handsome man, resembling an eagle, of very dark complexion. He curled his jet-black moustache. His hair was the color of a crow's wing.

His eyes were black, his frock-coat glossy black... He would throw down his pince-nez devilishly from his straight upturned nose.

Sokolov-Krechetov loved literature passionately, organized publishing houses and journals (the Griffin publishing house, the journals *Art* [1905], the *Golden Fleece* [1906], the *Divide* [1906]). There were also literary meetings in Moscow "salons," a theosophical circle, a literary artistic circle and regular meeting days for the poets. But his major energy Bely devoted to the group he created, the Argonauts. It met at his apartment on Sundays, having neither rules nor regulations. Its soul was the wild Ellis, who brought with him the "argonaut" stamp and stamped everything which pleased him: verses, book-covers, manuscripts.[8] This collaboration was the extreme wing of Symbolism and developed a program of action. It was called into life by Blok's essay, "Symbolism as a World-View." Debates and arguments continued throughout the winter. Members of the new "commune" wanted to construct not only art, but life as well. Like the ancient argonauts, they sailed on unknown seas for the golden fleece, wanted to blow up the old world and to be the first to settle on the banks of the country of the Blessed. The name "Argonaut" was taken by Ellis from Bely's poem, "The Golden Fleece:"

> Our Argo, our Argo,
> Preparing to fly,
> Beat his golden wings.

"At the table, up to twenty-five people would be gathered," Bely recalls. "We made music, sang, read poetry. On the initiative of the always possessed Ellis, the tables were often moved back and dances, parodies, improvisations began." Bely, Ellis, Sergei Soloviev, Ertel, Rachinsky, Petrovsky, Astrov, Nilender and others took part in the circle. There were visits from many guest poets (Blok, Balmont, Bryusov), artists (Borisov-Musatov, Feofilatov), musicians (S. I. Taneev, Medtner), philosophers (Schpett, Gershenzon, Berdyaev, Bulgakov, Ern), the academician Pavlov, and professor Kablukov. The "Argonauts" were in existence until 1910; then they joined the Musaget publishing house. Bely maintains that the "Argonauts were the only Moscow Symbolists among the Decadents, that the journals, the *Scales,* the *Divide* and the *Golden Fleece,* and the publishing houses Musaget and Orpheus were animated by their spirit.[9] The evaluation undoubtedly is an exaggerated one, but so natural from the mouth of the "ideologue of Russian Symbolism."

All that autumn, Bely led a "most distracted way of life:" Sundays they met at his house, Mondays at Vladimirov's, Tuesdays at Balmont's, Wednesdays at Bryusov's, Thursdays at Scorpion. There were also evenings at Griffin (at Sergei Sokolov's) and a reception at Professor Storozhenko's house. He wrote articles and reviews in the *World of Art* (on Balmont, the staging of Julius Caesar, and "Several Words of a Decadent Addressed to Liberals and

Conservatives"). His poems and passages from the *Fourth Symphony* appeared in a Griffin anthology. In the *New Path,* no. 9, there was an inspired article "On Theurgy." In it, the author revealed the "god-like," theurgical nature of the word. The words of Christ, the apostles, the prophets possessed miracle-working force, capable of resurrecting the dead, of stopping the sun. This force is contained in every prayer. But with the development of European culture, the theurgical element of the word was driven out. The god-like action degenerated into artifice — and it often consoled people with emptiness. Now mankind is living through a crisis: with the pressure of its despair, it bores into art and broadens the boundaries of spiritual life. The height of art is music: the spirit of Apollo is always subordinate to the spirit of Dionysius, and now, at the present time, the summits of thought and feeling have caught fire with the aspiration to express music by both word and deed. Yet the musical element is double-edged; it can become not only theurgy, but demonic magic as well. To control the forces of the world by calling the soul not to the glory of God is sin and horror. Theurgy is only separated from magic when it is imbued with passionate love and the greatest hope for the mercy of God.

After pointing out the theurgical element in the poetry of Lermontov and the music of Medtner, the author summoned the "aspirants" to courageously take the tragic path. He writes:

So that this theurgism may at last resound with an ineffably enchanting, unexpectedly holy, new inflection, the best of us had to undergo a great break-up of personality.... Our path is through despair, through the gaping horrors of tragism.

One must pass through chaos; to stop before it would mean never to know anything, not to see the light.

To remain in chaos would mean to lose one's mind. Only one thing remains: to pass quickly through... Lermontov remained in chaos, but the summons of Soloviev calls boldly:
Still unseen, already the coming spring resounds
And wafts the breath of Eternity.

But in order to complete this feat of the transformation of the world, man must regenerate himself, spiritually, psychologically, physiologically and physically.

The article concludes with a lyrical description of the "new people:"

But they, these children, do not even know what is written on their faces, and only the blue eyes, questioning, amazed, in the depths of which gleam secrets unknown to us, are peacefully and mournfully fixed on the scrolls of life unrolled before them.

Bely was living in the sphere of Vladimir Soloviev's esthetic ideas; his work was a bold conclusion to his teacher's articles: "Beauty in Nature" and "The General Meaning of Art." During the 1880's, Soloviev had proposed to write an "Esthetics" in the form of a "free theurgy." Bely in part fulfilled his intention. But the philosopher assumed that the transformation of the world by human creation and the beauty created by art could occur only "at the end of the entire universal process." Bely acts more decisively: he believes in the coming of a new universal age, the appearance of a new, regenerated man. His article is the manifesto of the Symbolist movement. Merezhkovsky, Bryusov, Blok and especially Vyacheslav Ivanov are united by the idea of theurgical art.

* * *

1903 was marked for Bely by the tragic crossing of his life and literary path with the path of his friend and enemy, Valery Bryusov. Recalling this event twenty years later, in the book *The Turn of the Century,* the poet could not hide his enmity for the man who cut into his life "with a sharp dagger."

In the article "On Theurgy," Bely called for the embodiment of art in deed, for the transformation of life into mysteria. And compliant reality hastened to create the conditions for experiment and "god-like action." He met Nina Ivanovna Petrovskaya,[10] and found in her unusually receptive material for his mystical experiments. Nina Petrovskaya, the daughter of a civil servant, married the publisher of Griffin, Sokolov-Krechetev, and quickly left him. Bely describes her:

A little thin, short, she gave an impression of angularity; with narrow shoulders, she seemed a little dumpy. She fluffed up her sinister black hair in two bunches; but her tremendous, black, sorrowful, amazing eyes penetrated the soul.... She powdered her pale, yellowish face with huge circles under the eyes; huge sensuous lips; she would smile, and something kind, childlike, obliged one to forget those lips.

Nina was a hopeless child tormented by an unfortunate life, a kind, tender and hysterical woman, submitting like a medium to foreign influences. The inimitable coloration of the age marks her destiny. Revealing herself little in literature (she wrote some not-bad stories), she realized her Symbolism in the creation of her life. About the people of that time, Khodasevich writes:

They lived in ferocious tension, intensity, in a fever. They lived on several planes at once. Ultimately, they were very intricately entangled in a common web of loves and hates, personal and literary. Only unceasing enthusiasm, motion was demanded from anyone entering the order

49

(and Symbolism in a certain sense was an order). It was decided that one could be possessed by whatever he liked; complete possession was all that was demanded...

Such was Nina: from Symbolism she grasped only its decadence and was a true victim of that decadence.

The boundaries between art and life almost completely disappeared. Poems were perceived as life; life created poems. Not only verses about love, but the very loves of the poets became common property; they were discussed, approved, rejected. And everyone was always in love and experienced their feelings "in public," as actors perform a play. Being in love served as a source for lyrics, while lyrics submerged reality. "It was sufficient to be in love," says Khodasevich, "and the person was guaranteed all the objects of the first lyrical necessity: passion, despair, rejoicing, insanity, vice, sin, hate, etc."

Nina Petrovskaya was responsive to the "trends" of the age. She demanded plenitude, tension, tragism, poetry from life and, in reality, lived a fiery life and perished tragically.

The first to fall in love with her was Balmont; he proposed to her that they make a poem from love, that they catch fire and be consumed. Bely says that Balmont came to Nina "pale, exalted, golden-eyed," and demanded that the two of them "cover themselves with rose petals." She assured herself that she was also in love, but this "consuming passion" left in her a bitter aftertaste. She decided to "purify herself," put on a black dress, shut herself up in her room, and repented. At this point on her path, there appeared the golden-curled, blue-eyed Andrei Bely. He took pity on her. He began to save her. She was unhappy and inwardly divided; he wrote "Stages in the Development of Normal Spiritual life" especially for her guidance. She exaltedly acknowledged in him a "teacher of life," fiercely believed in his lofty calling, began to wear a big black cross on a black string of wooden rosary beads. Bely also wore such a cross.

Nina's spiritual condition improved with each day that passed; the obsessive ideas of tuberculosis, morphine and suicide receded. Bely felt like Orpheus leading Eurydice out of hell. And suddenly the catastrophe occurred: heavenly love exploded in the fire of earthly love. Orpheus experienced this as a fall, as the soiling of his pure chasubles, as deceit to his calling. Relations with Nina entered a tragic phase — there was both passion and repentance, and common sin and mutual torture.

At this point in her life, the "great magician" Bryusov appeared; he became her secret confidant; she told him about Bely as a "burning soul," and through her delerium, Bryusov vaguely distinguished the outlines of their real relations. One thing was clear to him — the golden-haired prophet seemed to Nina to be an angel bearing the blessed news of a new revelation.

At this time, the author of *Urbi et Orbi* was occupied with occultism, black magic, spiritism, and was reading Agrippa of Nettesheim and planning a novel on alchemists and wizards. As a representative of demonism, he was to "languish and gnash his teeth" (Blok's words) before the prophet of "Eternal Femininity." He suggested a secret union to Nina. But to her disturbed imagination, the friendship with Bryusov represented a pact with the devil. It seemed to her that he was hypnotizing her, shadowing her, that his influence intruded into her thoughts, that his dark shadow was looming in the corner.

The affair with Bely ended in a dramatic break; he fled "from seduction," from the temptation of earthly love. And his admirers came to Nina and reproached her: "Young lady, you have almost sullied our prophet for us! You are inspired by the beast from the abyss." Bryusov was transformed from confidant into lover; he took revenge upon his recent rival. But he hid this from Nina and worked with her on magic experiments, supposedly to return Bely's love to her. Nina's hysterical confessions, in which truth was mixed with delerium and lover's insult with mystical fantasies, served Bryusov as material for the creation of the image of the possessed Renata in the novel *The Fiery Angel.* He portrays in the plot the complicated history of their triangular relationship, presenting Bely in the image of the mystical Count Heinrich and himself in the crude covering of the warrior Ruprecht.

In the meantime, Nina-Renata began to love her Ruprecht-Bryusov. It appears that he also loved her for a while: he dedicated verses to her. Half of the poems in the anthology *The Crown* are addressed to her. But, after completing *The Fiery Angel,* the poet began to cool toward his heroine. Nina's double romance ended in a dramatic denouement.

In the spring of 1905, after a lecture delivered by Bely in the hall of the Politechnic Museum, she approached Bely and fired a Browning; the revolver misfired, and it was seized from her hands. In *The Turn of the Century,* Bely gives another version of this incident: Nina wanted to shoot him, but had second thoughts and aimed at Bryusov; he seized the revolver from her. We lack the evidence on which to determine which variant is more reliable.

Nina's subsequent fate was dreadful. Abandoned by Bryusov, she became a morphine addict and went abroad in 1911. She lived in Rome in complete poverty, went hungry, drank. In Paris in 1928, she killed herself by letting gas into her hotel room.

* * *

After his unsuccessful attempt at the "transformation of life" with Nina Petrovskaya, Bely experienced sharp disillusionment: inert reality opposes the ascendancy of the spirit. In circles, meetings and salons, the litterateurs were excited and seething with activity, but new religious forms of intercourse, a new spiritual brotherhood, were not obtained. The theme of dawn deteriorated, became banal, as a result of entering the literary collective. Oceans of words, streams of poems, inspired articles, prophetic essays – but where was the religious deed? Bely had dreamed of other forms of life:

We are all sitting around the table; we are in garlands. Amidst the fruits is a chalice, a cross. We are silent, we harken to the silence. And now a voice: "It is soon."

Now he understood that this "harmony" was unrealizable. "After all," he adds, "you won't get Ellis to wear a toga. Gnashing my teeth, I attempted to impart a quiet rhythm to the argonauts; the argonauts made noise."[11] The theurgy of words was a total failure in literature; the lack of self-control in words devastated the soul. Bely's consciousness, like a sensitive barometer, pointed to the change in atmosphere. "The dawn was murdered," he writes. "It was an accomplished fact: there was absolutely no dawn. It expired there on the inclines of 1902; 1908 was only a year of reminiscences." His prediction came true: with the mental and spiritual unreadiness of the "aspirants," theurgy was transformed into evil magic, and the dawn was drowned in chaos. But the poet could not, did not want to acknowledge that the sky was no longer radiant, that it was covered with mist. He was lying to himself and deceiving the argonauts; they believed him.

Bely's poems of 1902 and 1903 reflect the gradation of his spiritual states from bright and joyous expectation to mournful disillusionment. He collected these poems in the anthology *Gold in Azure*, which was published by Scorpion in 1904.[12] The early poems, written during the period of the *Second Symphony*, are connected with it by the theme of "dawn." Radiance spreads over the gold of the warm cornfields, through the azure of the vault of the heavens, through the transparent air of a summer day. The author is correct in calling himself a "pleinair'ist": his eye seizes upon all shades of light, all the tints of coloration; he generously lavishes color epithets. The forms of objects are hardly noticed − all attention is focused on quality, on the combination of tonalities, on the "general mood." Bely dissects the sun's rays, and they turn about like the fan of a rainbow. The impression of an ocean of light is obtained by piling up epithets − luxurious, refined, gleaming like precious stones.

> The golden ocean roars around us
> In a drunken radiance.
>
> (1902)

The day is "A Golden Banquet."

> In pale, wine-golden sorrow,
> Hidden by a cloud,
> And fringed with her fiery
> Silver-burning arc,
> The sun sets, red-golden.
> And there flies anew

Along the yellow cornfields a holy excitement
Sounding in the oats.
(1902)

"The scarlet strip of the sunset," the gliding patches of clouds," "the red-amber sunset," "a stream of melted rays," "purple air," "the gold wine of the sky," "in the golden distance, clouds like rubies," "the blueing velvet of ether," "the gold-colored amber ray," "the peaceful light purples," "pale-azure satin," "the sun in amber sunset sorrow," "the amber-red gold of the sunset," "the purple cloud bank" — these are the basic colors on Bely's palette. He loves to unite them in compound epithets ("red-amber" or "amber-red") and put them in a multi-colored pattern on a background of gold. And in this triumph of azure, purple and fire, the world awaits revelation from the sky. Like a bride, she is prepared to meet the bridegroom.

And the world, catching fire, rejoices,
And the world glorifies the father;
And the wind caresses, kisses,
Kisses me endlessly.
(1902)

And at the feast of nature, "the ecstasy of loneliness," "exaltedly drunken sadness" grows in the poet's heart. The "gold wine" of the sun is too heady, the azure of the sky too piercing.

Why is this air radiant,
Why is it light and bright to the point of pain!
(1902)

But this pain is from excess. "The children of holy spring" know that they will grow wings, that they will soon drown in the "blue ocean" of the sky.

Someone lifted his hand:
The blueing velvet of the ether is
Drowned in the rejoicing of the world
And extended toward us.

And the feeling of being predestined is ever more powerful, the faith in a lofty calling firmer; and the mysterious voice already is heard:

To pure tears, to spiritual joy,
To being,
My fallen son, son of my blood,
I summon you.

53

The religious ecstasy, solidifying, forms into the crystals of myth. A period of myth-creating arrives for the poet. One of the most successful poems in the collection embodies the theme of "dawn" in the legend of the "argonauts." The ecstasy of flight is contained in its impetuous rhythm. The whole sky is embraced by fire, and the argonaut blows a golden horn:

> Blowing
> Into the world becoming gold.
> All the sky is enrubied.
> The ball of the sun has disappeared.
> All the sky is enrubied
> Above us.
> On the mountain heights
> Our Argo,
> Our Argo,
> Preparing to fly,
> Beat his golden wings.

This poem became the hymn of the early Moscow Symbolists; Blok responded to it in the poem "Our Argo," dedicated to Andrei Bely. In the last verse is the same call to flight:

> We will hear sounds at the bright moment
> Of departing storms,
> We will silently join our hands in song,
> And we will fly off into the azure.

From the dream of flight into the blue ether toward the golden sun was born the myth of the "magic king," who, in a "faraway place" flies with his daughter on the "golden back of a dolphin." This little poem is a mosaic of precious stones: there are "blue herds of sapphires," and "red rubies of the sun," and "turquoise smoke," and "pearly gray silver," and "the red ruby of the air," and "the fiery garb of the stars." And amidst the gleaming magnificence of the fiery world, the old king says, laughing into his beard:

> Beloved to us are
> The heights of great aspirations:
> The flights
> Of universal disturbances!

The poet's imagination peoples the sky with threatening giants, belted with the fire of storms, with crowds of fabled giants, shooting red-purple arrows. Here on the horizon stands a giant remote and angry; he causes the wind to blow, he explodes with anger, gives out a deafening, thunderous roar,

54

and tears apart the clouds in the "dark turquoise sky." Here in the azure, a crowd of giants passes on to battle:

> The earth trembled in fear from the heavy blows.
> Shreds of shining snow-white beards shook in the azure...
> And they are no more: pierced by the substance of the pure
>   gold fire,
> The many-towered city floats, mistily distant.

Now the bellicose Thor does battle with a Viking who seizes his fiery beard. Thor strikes him with a thunderbolt.

Thus, from fire, from the rumble of storms and sun shafts, Bely creates his myths of nature. They are saturated with dynamism and stormy motion. In comparison with them, the "pictures of nature" of his teacher Fet seem like motionless panoramas.

Bely's gift for creating myths is heightened to prophetic inspiration when he touches upon his cherished theme of "the end." In the poem "The Friend of Old," dedicated to E. K. Medtner, he is borne in spirit through a long line of millenia, and "from the darkness of centuries" sees the light of a general resurrection. Through the dark gaps the stream of centuries rushes; iron coffins are silent; caves gape like jaws; the poet lies in a grave, in a white shroud. And now the coffin opens: above him bends, smiling, his friend of old.

> Crossing ourselves, we both set off for
> The celebration of the universal resurrection.
> And — the dead arose from their coffins,
> And — victorious singing was heard.

The last verse is excellent:

> In the country of coffins, harbingers of spring,
> Twittering swallows — fly!
> Twittering swallows — fly
> From the air to the shoulder of the Savior.

And now, at this summit of religious ecstasy, the prophet's head whirls. He, the creator of cosmic symbols, the harbinger of the future kingdom, pre-destined, beloved — who is he? And how is he, the bearer of the new revela-tion, possessing the secret of the transformation to come, how is he to live with people "in low places?" The poem "Return" already burns with a dif-ferent light: not azure radiance, but lilac, Luciferian purple. The poet is an omnipotent magician living over the abyss in "a mountain cave." He is alone in his pride. At his summons, a "fettered race of people" rises into the mountains to the summit. He has prepared for the guests a sun banquet, he, "clothed in red sunsets, as in the skin of striped leopards." The tables blaze with gold pieces; aromas of incense and spikenard fill the air; a drink of sun flows onto the lips.

My faithful gnome carries above his head
On a round dish: the amber ball of the sun.

But soon the pathetic, greedy people inspire his disgust. He drives them away; the faithful gnome hurls rocks after them...

I am again alone in my mountain cave,
Above my head, the rapid flight of centuries.

Thus the self-deification of the prophet is completed; thus Lucifer overshadows the angel.

In the poem "The Legend," the memory of the affair with Nina Petrovskaya is transformed into an esoteric mystery play. Its Symbolist pretensions are irritating. He was a prophet, she — Sibyl in a temple; their love "burned with roses in sunset incense." He floats away in a golden canoe on the waves of the Styx. As he abandons Sibyl, he puts on her curls a wreath of lily of the valley and says:

Conquering death with love
And conquering passion with death,
I will float away, and again on solid ground
I will alight, like God, revealing my visage.

Sibyl cries quietly.

The process of self-deification is complete. He is God and must reveal his visage to the world. But the poet does not stand for long on the sharp summit of the Luciferian cliff. And his fall will be dreadful. In the same year in which "The Legend" was written (1903), sobering and disillusionment begin. In the poem "The Subdued One," thematically connected with the mystery play *He Who Hath Come*, we have before us the image of a sad prophet with a waxen face and bedimmed eyes. He stands before the "steep sheer slope," "subdued" and powerless:

In a silvery wreath and in a pale blue mantle,
Extending his benumbed hands above the world.

The Luciferian fire is extinguished; the bold hopes were deceptive. Now he knows: he is a false Messiah; the voice summoning him to save the world was the voice of the temptor.

56

The universe is extinguished. The waxen face is lowered.
The universe is extinguished; with the sunrise embracing his knees,
In his failing gaze is emotion insanely mute.
In what has fallen asleep, in what is past is the imprint of
    universal inspiration.

The magnificent, beautiful demon has been torn from the mountain peaks, and a pitiful, deformed, bloodied man fell down. The last poems of 1903 are full of unsparing mockery at himself, self-contempt, self-castigation.

And there is so much true despair in these words, so much human suffering, that it is impossible not to believe in the complete justice of the poet's avowals. In the poem "Evening Sacrifice," the madness of the prophet-Messiah is shown without the covering of symbols:

> I stood like a fool
> In my fiery crown,
> In a gold tunic
> Fastened with amethyst.
> I stood alone, like a post,
> In remote deserts
> And awaited crowds of people
> On their knees.

But the crowds did not come, and the prophet exclaims:

> Be damned, Beelzebub,
> Sly seducer,
> Was it not thou who whispered to me
> That I am the new savior?

Another poem is entitled "The False Prophet." It begins as follows:

> Preaching the imminent end,
> I stood as if I were the new Christ,
> Having put on a crown of thorns
> Adorned with the flame of roses.

On the street, passers-by heard him in surprise; cabs rumbled:

> They laughed at me,
> At the insanely funny false Christ.

And the end:

They dragged me into a lunatic asylum,
Driving me on with kicks.

Finally, in the poem "The Fool," a mad prophet is portrayed sitting before a barred window. A female voice is heard from afar, speaking of a meeting soon to come; he waves to her with his cap.

Filled with joyful sufferings
The fool falls quiet.
Quietly there falls from his hands to the floor
The madman's cap.

In this self-accusation, an act of religious repentance is completed. But the image of the false Messiah, objectified by the poet, inspires in him not only contempt and wrath, but pity as well. In "The Subdued One," insulted, laughed at, there is a sort of pale luminescence. Impotence, exhaustion, defeat, loss — this is the new lyrical theme. In the poem "Not He," the false prophet, in mist, under the coral moon, weaves a wreath from white violets. Above him, tonelessly cawing, jackdaws are flying past. He is frightened and pitiful. And the poet addresses him:

You appeal for help, mourning,
Like a bird of the swamp...
Oh child,
All your scarlet is in rags.

* * *

Your insane blue eyes
On your face of snow
Are misted with the sleep
Of the floating night.

* * *

Gold in Azure is a lyrical reflection of the blinding light which momentarily flamed in Bely's soul. He experienced "religious lunacy," dreadful temptation, but also a great illumination.

In January, 1904, Bely and Blok finally met in person. The newly-wed Bloks came to Moscow and visited Bely to get acquainted. At first contact, the friends sensed how close they were to each other and how far apart. Blok was restrained, silent, reticent; Bely — expansive, fidgety, restless and talkative. For both the first impression was a disappointment. But mutual attraction conquered the force of repulsion; from their first meeting they began to love each other, and for both this love became their destiny. Their paths crossed and again diverged; they caused each other much suffering, but that same friendship-enmity itself basically defined their lives — both personal and literary. Bely concludes the description of his first meeting with Blok with the words: "Blok is the crucial hour of my life, a variation on the theme of destiny; he is both unexpected joy and sorrow; all this was heard during our first visit; it arose in our midst."

The Bloks spent two weeks in Moscow; central to their literary and social life was daily contact with "Borya" Bugaev and "Seryozha" Soloviev. Seryozha, the nephew and fiery admirer of the philosopher Vladimir Soloviev, united the friends in a kind of "mystical brotherhood," an inspired cult of Sophia the Divine Wisdom. An exalted mystic, he suggested to the "brothers" that Lyubov Dmitrievna Blok was destined to embody the heavenly Sophia in earthly form.

At a meeting of a university circle, Bely delivered a lecture, "Symbolism as a World-View." The curve of the development of European thought goes from Kant through Schopenhauer to Nietzsche. Schopenhauer awakened mankind from the dream of life; now we hear the music of symbols. It speaks to us of other worlds, pours out upon us "enchanting streams of Eternity." Symbolist art is knowledge of genius; its goal is to make us understand the depths of spirit. The forerunner of Symbolism is Nietzsche; he is no longer a philosopher in the former sense of the word, but a sage, and his aphorisms are symbols. But art is not our ultimate goal. It must be surmounted by theurgy, and in theury lies the end of Symbolism. We aspire to the embodiment of Eternity by means of the transfiguration of the resurrected personality. This is a difficult and dangerous path. The theurgist must go where Nietzsche halted. And go by air. In illustrating his thoughts, the lecturer cited the poems of Lermontov and Blok.

After the stormy winter, Bely felt devastated. He saved himself by flight from the turmoil of literary circles and from the tangle of relations with Bryusov and Nina Petrovskaya; he went to Nizhny Novgorod to his friend Medtner. Ten days of quiet, concentrated life calmed him. With Medtner and his wife, Anna Mikhailovna, he strolled aglong the Volga, talked about Nietzsche and Wagner, read the poems of Goethe and Novalis. Medtner loved Blok's lyrics, but sensed in them the dangerous spirit of Khlystovstvo.[1] He did not approve of theurgy in poetry; he said that it was impossible to destroy the laws of art without penalty: he warned against the derangements threatening Symbolism.

At the beginning of July, Bely and Sergei Soloviev met at Blok's estate, Shakhmatovo. The days Bely spent in the company of Alexander Alexandrovich and Lyubov Dmitrievna remained in his memory as "days of a real mysterion." Echoes of them are preserved in the lyrical essay "The Green Meadow," in which Russia is portrayed as a great green meadow with green flowers illuminated by rosy dawns. Sergei Soloviev developed his idea of the "mystical brotherhood," and the "Blokists" surrounded Lyubov Dmitrievna with a semi-mystical, semi-amorous cult. This "playing at mysterion" was irksome to Blok, and he withdrew into gloomy silence.

Upon his return from Shakhmatovo to Moscow, Bely went to the Silver Well estate and there became absorbed in Kant's *Critiques,* Wundt's *Metaphysics* and James' *Psychology.* He experienced great spiritual enthusiasm: it seemed to him that in Shakhmatovo a new era had begun, the order of the morning star had been formed, a mystical triangle had been constructed — Blok, Bely, Sergei Soloviev. The cult of Eternal Femininity was recognized by them now as worship of the Madonna. He tried to give his faith a philosophical basis and wrote the essay "On Expediency."[2] In it he spoke of the unity and wholeness of experience which creates the values of life; these values are symbols. The highest symbol-prototype is Mankind as a living unity. Even positivist philosophy in the person of Kant arrived at the acknowledgment of "Le Grand Etre." Soloviev identified this cult with the medieval cult of the Madonna. Now we unwittingly move from the concept of the symbol to His image.... "The spirit of the Woman clothed with the sun is spreading." Thus scientific knowledge is united with religious revelation. Those with knowledge are transformed into knights for the "Lady Beautiful." And the author concludes: "A new knightly order is forming, not only believing in the morning of its star, but knowing Her as well."

In this quite incoherent essay the impressions of the summer at Shakhmatovo — three knights at the feet of the Lady Beautiful, Lyubov Dmitrievna — are reworked with the help of Wundt, Höffding and James. The uninitiated reader can hardly penetrate its esoteric meaning.

During the autumn, Bely spent time in the Sarov and Serafimo-Diveevskaya cloister. The Sarov pine trees and the spring of Saint Serafim mystically merged in his memory with the fields and woods of Shakhmatovo.

Upon returning to Moscow, he entered the philosophy faculty; his classmates were Sergei Soloviev, Vladislav Khodasevich, the poet B. A. Sadovsky, V. O. Nilender and B. A. Griftsov. He seldom attended lectures; soon he stopped entirely; his time was devoured by literary work on the *Scales,* various societies and circles. But in the university he learned a great deal from Prince S. N. Trubetskoi, who gave a course on Greek philosophy and conducted a seminar on Plato. His work was less satisfactory in L. M. Lopatin's seminar where Leibnitz's *Monadologies* were read and discussed. Both professors were close friends and in a sense students of Vladimir Soloviev and, in working with them, Bely did not go beyond the circle of Solovievian ideas already familiar to him. But parallel to Soloviev's metaphysics, he studied Kantian literature as well and became absorbed in the gnoseology of the neo-Kantians Vaihinger, Natorp and Cohen. Professor Boris Alexandrovich Fokht, surrounded by a circle of Kantian students, had a great influence on him. Bely characterized him as the "Figner of philosphical Moscow, 1904." "Abrupt, pale, beetle-browed, with a chestnut beard and curls like goats' horns," "a most magnificient man of sense and a great pedagogue," he initiated Bely into the secrets of neo-Kantianism. Looking back after many years on this, his "philosophical period," Bely came to the sad conclusion that he was confused once and for all in his own philosophical tactics; a great amount of time was lost in studying Kant (with the commentaries of Karl Stange), Riehl and Rickert. The attempt to construct a system of Symbolism on the basis of gnoseology ended in failure: the theory of this tendency was thus not ever written. Bely figuratively writes: "The youthful 'air-raid' into all the spheres of culture ended with a heavy 'Okh' and the groan of the injured aviator who only toward 1909 began to slowly mend from the ideological mutilations which he himself had inflicted in 1904."

Bely's literary Sundays were resumed during the autumn, but the major activity of the "Argonauts" was transferred to the "Wednesdays" of Pavel Ivanovich Astrov, who opened his large apartment to the circle. A public-spirited lawyer and esthetician, Astrov, abrupt, angular, nervous, was an admirer of the priest Grigory Petrov and a patron of the young Symbolists. At his Wednesdays were Professor I. Ozerov, P. D. Boborykin, assistant professor Pokrovsky, Ellis, Sergei Soloviev, Rachinsky, Berdyaev, Ern, Florensky and Ertel. In this circle, Bely gave the lectures "Psychology and the Theory of Knowledge," "On Scientific Dogmatism," and "The Apocalypse in Russian Poetry."[3]

The author postulates the crisis of philosophy. The fateful moment has arrived for it: all the objects of investigation which at one time belonged to it have gone over to science. But science cannot be a world-view: scientific explanation of the phenomena of life inevitably leads to the disappearance of life itself.... "The soul, desiccated by knowledge," says Bely, "mourns deeply for the paradise lost — for childlike levity, for thought in flight."

In the article "The Apocalypse in Russian Poetry," the author attempts to contrast the integral Symbolist outlook with the sterility of philosophy and the fractionalization of science. The Symbolist outlook grows from the mystical experience in Shakhmatovo and is inspired by the personality and poetry of Blok. The goal of poetry is to discover the face of the muse expressing the unity of universal truth. The goal of religion is to embody this unity. On the religious plane, the image of the muse is transformed into the visage of the Woman clothed with the sun. Soloviev predicted Her coming; Lermontov

61

saw Her under a "mysterious demi-mask;" in the poetry of Blok She is already approaching us. With joy and excitement Bely exclaims: "She is already in our midst, with us, embodied, vital, near — this finally recognized Muse of Russian Poetry has proven to be the Sun." The article concludes with a passionate, prayerful appeal:

> We believe that Thou wilt reveal Thyself to us, that ahead there will be no October fogs and February yellow thaws.... Let them think that Thou art still sleeping in an icy coffin.... No, Thou hast arisen.... Thou Thyself hast promised to appear in rose, and the soul prayerfully bows down before Thee and in the sunrises — crimson icon lamps — is overheard Thy prayerful breath of life.
>
> Appear!
>
> It is time; the world has ripened like a golden fruit pouring forth sweetness. The world is yearning for Thee. Appear!

Bely's voice had never before resounded with such fiery faith. Cloaking himself with the appearance of literary criticism, analyzing the poetry of Pushkin, Tyutchev, Bryusov and Vyacheslav Ivanov, he was glorifying his love. Bely's article is illuminated by reflected light — its source is in Shakhmatovo. By it, one may judge what a sun Blok was for him at this time, for whom "She" had become "embodied, vital, near" — a bride, a wife... So personal and intimate is Bely's address to "Her," that it seems as if he sees Her in reality, golden-curled, in a rosy dress among the ripe sheaves of wheat...

* * *

The articles Bely wrote in 1904 are full of prophetic inspiration and joyful faith in the coming of a new era. But his life was not joyful; the preacher of universal brotherhood felt lonely; he was oppressed by the confusion of ideas, circles, people, the whirlpool of hours and days. The dregs came to the surface; vital forces were exhausted in arguments and manifestoes. "From a distance," he writes in *The Turn of the Century,* "the year 1904 seems very gloomy to me. It stands before me as the antithesis of 1901; not without reason did I characterize 1901 and 1902 as years of 'dawn.' I felt solid ground beneath me. From 1904 until the very end of 1908 I felt that the ground was slipping from under me." Therefore, in Bely's mystical "credo" of this time, one must see not an expression of his spiritual condition, but the attempt to exorcise chaos. When he pathetically exclaims at the "wisdom" of the Symbolists and calls them the "central station from which new paths begin," he is functioning as a theurgist transforming reality by means of religious will. "We are Decadents," he maintains, "because we have separated ourselves from moribund civilization. No matter what, we are moving toward our joy, toward our happiness, toward our love, firmly believing that love 'thinks no evil' and 'is worth everything,' "[4]

The phrase "no matter what" is very indicative.

But to Bely's "incantations" Bryusov responded ironically: he wounded the "prophet" in the most exposed and painful place: in his theurgical calling. He said to Bely: you are calling for the transformation of the world and the embodiment of a new revelation in life — but are you capable of this? You know, this is an act of heroism — can you become a hero? In order to sanctify life one first must become a saint himself. Of what does your saintliness consist? Such is the sense of the "attack" which may be found in Bryusov's remarkable letter to Bely, the only one extant from their correspondence of 1904. Bryusov writes:

> And nevertheless you want an answer. Or rather, not an answer, but a sad confession, which seems to me to belong to both of us. Here it is. We lack sufficient will-power for an act of heroism. That for which we all are thirsting is an act of heroism, and no one of us dares to perform it. Everything follows from this. Our ideal is the selfless act of heroism, but we timidly retreat before it and ourselves are conscious of our betrayal, and this consciousness takes vengeance upon us in a thousand different ways. Betrayal... to the behest: "He that loveth mother or father more than Me." Balmont and I put as an epigraph to our works the words of the Elder Zossima: "Seek rapture and ecstasy," but are we seeking them? That is, are we always seeking, boldly, confessing our faith openly, not fearing martyrdom? We think up all sorts of justifications for our iniquities. I make reference to the fact that I must preserve the *Scales* and Scorpion. You ask for four years of time in order to think it over well. Merezhkovsky hypocritically created for himself a whole theory for the necessity to remain "at one's duties." And everyone is the same.... Having come for an act of heroism, we obediently remain under the four conditions of "society life:" we obediently don our frock-coats, and we obediently repeat words which have lost both their primary and even their secondary meanings. We habitually lie to ourselves and others.... Two paths lay before us — to crucifixion or beneath little whips; we preferred the latter. Yes, I know — a different life is coming for people. A life when everything will be "rapture and ecstasy." We cannot accomodate at present all this plenitude, but we can foresee it, can take it into ourselves as much as we are able — and we do not want to. We cannot. It would be just were we to endure torture as well.

In the mouth of the "skeptic" Bryusov, these words, addressed to the mystic, Bely, acquire a terrifying significance. On the eve of the leap off the summit, destiny was sending him, Bely, a warning. The kingdom of the Spirit "requires strength;" there is only one path to it — crucifixion. The prophet must be a performer of heroic deeds — he must bear his cross. All other paths are self-flagellation and literariness: the Symbolist movement in Russia, of course, is not only literature and not only art. All its leaders — Minsky, Merezhkovsky, Bely, Vyacheslav Ivanov, Blok, Gippius — affirmed its religious nature. To put it more precisely: Symbolism is the religious tragedy of the Russian spirit on the brink of our catastrophic century. In Bryusov's letter, the major tragic theme resounds for the first time: the failure to take up the cross and the theme of torture or retribution flowing from it.

* * *

Bely — 1905

Bely arrived in Petersburg on the historic day of January 9, 1905, the day of the firing at the workers on Dvortsovy Square. He went to the Merezhkovskys, in the house of Muruzi, on the corner of Panteleimonovskaya and Litennaya. Zinaida Gippius welcomed him with the words: "Well, some day you picked for your arrival." Many times in his memoirs Bely returns to a description of her appearance — all the portraits are very similar, but the most important, the unique, is not captured in them. Here, curled up in a ball, in her loose white shift, she lies on a couch; her luxurious golden-red hair is illuminated by the red fire in the fireplace: tremendous azure-green eyes, orchid-red lips, a wasp-like waist, a slender hand holding a lorgnette, rosary beads with a black cross on her breast; and beside her on a little table a red lacquered box with perfumed cigarettes. All this created about Gippius a special, refined, "hothouse" atmosphere. She went to bed at dawn and arose at about three in the afternoon; even in the most extreme cold she slept at an open window and sometimes went to sleep with snow in her hair; she said that she had a tendency to tuberculosis and could live no other way. When she got up, she would take a hot bath and, after breakfast, she would curl up her legs on the couch before the fire where she would spend days without going out.

In *The Turn of the Century*, Bely emphasizes the double aspect of Gippius: she was both a fashionable poetess and a "timid schoolgirl." Here she is in the first aspect:

A glitter came from the rocking chair: Zinaida Gippius was like a wasp of human size: a ball of distended red hair (which seemed as if it would reach her heels) lay over her very small and somehow crooked face; powder and the shine from the lorgnette in which she placed her greenish eye; she fingered faceted beads while staring at me; from her little forehead, like a shining eye, hung a stone on a black pendant; from her flat chest rattled a black cross; and the clasp from her boots flashed sparks, leg over leg; she tossed back the train of her close-fitting white dress.

And alongside this parody of the "decadent lioness" is her other aspect:

64

In a black skirt and a simple blouse (black and white checked), with a cross, modestly hidden in a black necklace... she sat simply; and the rosy color of her face came out on her cheeks; she smiled alertly, trying to please.... Later, gazing at Zinaida Nikolaevna, I constantly collided with this other aspect of hers — the aspect of a timid schoolgirl.... Her style of reading was intimate; she read quietly, in a very slight sing-song, lowering her eyelashes, and not serving us with metaphors, like Bryusov; on the contrary, she withdrew them into the depths of her heart, as if forcing us to follow them into her quiet cell, where it is pensively austere.

On Sundays, friends would come to tea at the Merezhkovskys. Here Bely made the acquaintance of the contributor to the *World of Art* and friend of Diaghilev, V. F. Nuvel; the philosopher-poet N. Minsky, the student contributor to the *New Path*,[5] A. A. Smirnov. Dmitry Merezhkovsky was small, thin, with a dull, pale face, sunken cheeks, a large nose, and bulging, dim eyes — he would come out of his study for a minute, shout out his aphorisms in his unexpectedly loud voice, and disappear. Bely saw at once that he did not hear a thing that was said to him. When the sayings of Dmitry Sergeevich seemed too inappropriate, Zinaida Nikolaevna would say to him capriciously, "Dmitry, you are out of order!"

On the evening of the day of his arrival, Bely accompanied the Merezhkovskys to a meeting of representatives of the intelligentsia at the Free Economic Society. There was an excited crowd, discussion of the events, arguments, resolutions, calls to battle. Zinaida Nikolaevna, in a black satin dress, took a seat and, smiling, gazed at the participants through her lorgnette. Bely noticed Gorky and, next to him, a certain clean-shaven, pale man calling for arms. Later, he found out that this was the famous provocateur Gapon.

The poet settled in at the Merezhkovskys: a genuine friendship arose between him and Zinaida Nikolaevna. Until late at night, standing before the hot fireplace, they spoke about the church, the trinity, the flesh. Dmitry Sergeevich would knock on the wall and shout: "Zina, this is horrible! Let Borya go! It's four o'clock! You're not letting me sleep!"

Bely also became friends with the sister of Gippius — the artist Tatyana Nikolaevna ("Tata"), who kept an album-diary: in it she depicted her dreams, fantasies, images, and wrote down her thoughts. The second sister, also living in the Merezhkovsky apartment, Natalya Nikolaevna ("Nata"), blue-eyed, pale and silent, sculpted statuettes; she kept to herself and seemed like a nun.

Every day, toward tea-time, the closest friend of the Merezhkovskys, the critic Dmitry Vladimirovich Filosofov, would appear.

Elegant, freshly shaved, with an irreproachably accurate part in his smooth light-blond hair, in a blue necktie, with a rounded, haughty, always neatly trimmed beard and with a small moustache, holding a cigarette, he walked across the soft rungs on very small legs which did not correspond to his tall, very tall build.

His kindness, integrity and selflessness corresponded to the stern appearance of the "examiner." Bely wittily called Filosofov "a kind aunt, an old maid, the housekeeper of Merezhkovsky's ideological inventory." Filosofov brought Dmitry Sergeevich into the "light" of the general public, defended his ideas in print, letting them past his own censorship.

Often Anton Vladimirovich Kartashev, a professor at the Spiritual Academy, slight, emaciated, with a sharp nose and abrupt movements, would dash headlong into the Merezhkovskys' salon. Covering his eyes and nervously shaking his head, he would produce his brilliant improvisations. Bely writes:

> Anton Vladimirovich always seemed a remarkable person to me, sparkling, talented (to the point of genius), eternally bursting with ideas: he was necessary to Merezhkovsky because he gave dynamism to his thoughts.... At that time the combination of the *intelligent* in a revolutionary frame of mind with the splendid ancient tradition was natural in him. The Golden-tongued was interwoven in him with Pisarev.

Once Bely read an essay in his presence; Kartashev put his two index fingers to his temples like horns and chanted in his little South-Russian tenor: "Yes, yes, yes, yes! Here we are shown with tails and horns! But we do not agree to them." Passionate and impetuous, he destroyed the harmony of the commune; there was constant competition between him and Zinaida Nikolaevna. After a typical quarrel, Anton Vladimirovich would fly out of the apartment, slamming the door. Merezhkovsky and Filosofov would act as conciliators.

During the time he was at the Merezhkovskys, Bely met many remarkable people. In the house of Muruzi, in the red-bricked living room steeped in the scent of the tuberose "Lubain" with which Gippius perfumed herself, were all the representatives of the Petersburg intelligentsia: V. V. Rozanov, S. N. Bulgakov, A. S. Volzhsky, N. A. Berdyaev, F. K. Sologub, R. A. Ternavtsev, P. P. Pertsov, G. I. Chulkov, N. Minsky, S. Andrievsky.

The "religious community" into which Bely plunged enthusiastically in Petersburg led him away from Blok. But ultimately, the "ideological rites" in the salon of Gippius, the literary Sundays at Sologub's and Rozanov's, the meetings at Minsky's and attendance at editorial meetings of *Questions of Life* wearied him. He went to Blok to rest.

This is how Bely lived in Petersburg — a double life. From the Bloks he fled to the Merezhkovskys, from the Merezhkovskys to the Bloks; the former had an abstract community, the latter personal intercourse. Zinaida Nikolaevna was jealous, reproached him with betrayal, and called his conversations with Blok a "howl in the wilderness." "Why are you silent all the time there?"

she asked Bely. "I know... somewhere, and something, and someone.... Akh, this is all old, it is simply mystical rites, decadence."

Finally Bely prepared to leave; Alexander Alexandrovich and Lyubov Dmitrievna saw him to the station. They agreed to meet in Shakhmatovo during the summer.

In 1905, Merezhkovsky's journal, the *New Path*, folded. Its place was taken by the monthly *Questions of Life*. Georgy Chulkov tells of this literary event in his memoirs.[6]

The crisis at the *New Path* had already begun in 1904. Georgy Ivanovich Chulkov, a poet and critic, exiled to Siberia for "organizing political demonstrations in the city of Moscow in February, 1902," returned to Petersburg after the amnesty and published his first anthology of poems, *Silaceous Path* (1904). Zinaida Gippius gave it her attention and instructed Poliksena Solovieva to write a review of it for the *New Path*. Chulkov went to the Merezhkovskys to make their acquaintance; he told Zinaida Nikolaevna about life in Siberia. She called Dmitry Sergeevich: "Come quickly. I have with me a re-vo-lu-tionary. He is telling very interesting tales." They began to talk about the *New Path*. Chulkov criticized it sharply. And suddenly Merezhkovsky announced: "I invite you to take upon yourself the duties of a secretary of our journal. You will be our closest collaborator. Yes, I propose it.... The problem is that the political tendencies which are sometimes expressed in our journal have grown odious to us too. The journal must be cleansed of this semi-Slavophile, semi-reactionary inheritance.... We present you with the right of veto."

The Merezhkovskys went abroad, leaving the journal in Chulkov's hands. The official editor, Filosofov, demonstrated no energy. The double censorship — church and civil — was oppressive. The newspapers continued to attack it, and subscriptions decreased. When the Merezhkovskys returned to Petersburg, a plan was made to attract the group of "idealist-philosophers" to the journal. Chulkov went to Koreiz for discussions with Bulgakov. Agreement was reached — the "idealists," Bulgakov, Berdyaev, Lossky, Frank, Novgorodtsev, joined the *New Path*. The last three issues for 1904 were published under the broadened editorship. But it was difficult for the "philosophers" to get along with the "New Path-ists" who were suspected of decadence, estheticism and amorality. This transitional period ended in Chulkov's break with the Merezhkovskys: he refused to print a certain article by Gippius; the Merezhkovskys gave him an ultimatum: either they went or Chulkov. Bulgakov was summoned to Petersburg by telegram. At the editorial meeting the majority announced that it was impossible to continue the journal without Chulkov. And the *New Path*, after a two-year existence, was discontinued. But Lossky had authorization for a journal named *Questions of Life*. D. E. Zhukovsky obtained the money. The first edition of the new monthly appeared in January, 1905 under the editorship of Berdyaev and Bulgakov. After January 9, bitter reaction set in. Chulkov's *Chronicles of Internal Life*, devoted to the workers' movement, was not published due to circumstances independent of the editors.

Bely was present at the editorial meetings of *Questions of Life* during the stormy revolutionary days; there were always crowds; the rumble of voices was heard; protest petitions were signed, appeals and declarations were composed. Chulkov, pale, emaciated, disheveled, growing a beard, was arguing with someone, trying to convince someone; Bulgakov brought about reconciliation with quiet gestures. Bely describes him:

> Bulgakov, with sloping shoulders, of medium height, with a tendency to stoop, brilliant, fresh, vigorous, his pale face flushed; a straight nose; thin crimson lips, eyes like cherries; a thick beard slightly curly. There was something in him of bilberries and cherries.... His mildness was very pleasant; he bore a whiff of the woods, spruce-cones, an odor of resins among which is built the hut of a hermit, a warrior, a native of Orlov or Kursk.... The stoical, black-browed philosopher appeared to me in a carpenter's spruce-grove. He impressed me with his vitality and health.

The reddish little Lossky, bald, bespectacled, would run up to him with an expression of perplexity. Bulgakov would lend Lossky his ear, reply with suppressed ardor, moving his hand in a cutting gesture; and there was a sense of wilfulness, stubbornness... He would speak sharply..., recovering himself, would become confused, fall silent, sit down, stroke his beard...

S. Volzhsky would appear, "shaggy, bespectacled, transparent, nervous and tubercular, in gold eye-glasses; he would shake his beard above his sunken chest and the forest of hair on his hunched shoulders."

It is curious to compare Blok's humorous story of his first visit to the editors of *Questions of Life* with Bely's ironic sketches. Blok wrote to his mother on August 29, 1905:

> After dinner, I went to the editors at 7 Rozhdestvenskaya (I must say that Dostoevsky has risen again in the city). I found it and climbed the staircase and heard a shout from behind one door: "Mystical theomachist!" I almost guessed by this alone that *Questions of Life* were shouting. Their apartment proved to be dark and small; while waiting for electricity, with candles in bottes, Bulgakov, Chulkov and Zhukovsky were sitting in the office, and Bulgakov was ridiculing Zhukovsky, shouting, "Mystical theomachist!" Then Bulgakov took Chulkov's tie from him and, laughing, led Zhukovsky off to Vyacheslav Ivanov. I began to drink tea with Chulkov and his sister near the same candles in bottles. At this point, as Dostoevsky would say, I discovered to my confusion that *Qu. L.* might be completely discontinued, that Zhukovsky had no money, and that the idealists are very much opposed to me.... Chulkov, as formerly, makes much of me and is making plans (with

Berdyaev) for a new journal, etc. Not a word was said about my receiving the money "due me" but a lot was said about new reviews. So we conversed, and when I made up my mind to ask about the money (I was already in my coat in the hall), Bulgakov returned and treated me with his customary softening good-nature (as if he is always wanting to speak with me and somehow never gets around to it... and won't I drop in, etc.). Thus it became clear to me that I will not write for *Qu. L.* and that I will perhaps (probably) receive no more money.

Blok's misgivings were justified. As of August, his collaboration in *Questions of Life* was discontinued. The journal continued to exist with difficulty until the end of 1905.

We find a humorous memorandum on the editors of *Questions of Life* in Remizov's *Fiery Russia.* He writes, addressing Blok:

1905. The editors of *Questions of Life* in Saperny Lane. My duties are not those of a clerk, but of a house manager; the entire household I have in books for signatures (I myself signed!) and for the stamp of my master, Zhukovsky. You remember how the "VIP's" were insulted when I signed myself on business letters "the old Butler Alexei." Maria Alexeevna, the youngest clerk, was doubtful about your real last name — "Blok? A pseudonym?"

And when you arrived at the editorial offices, still in a student's uniform with a blue collar, the first thing I asked you was about your pseudonym.

Upon returning to Moscow from Petersburg, Bely again fell into the vicious cycle of the characters of the *Fiery Angel.* He had already succeeded in forgetting the unhappy Renata, but Ruprecht-Bryusov continued to take vengeance upon Count Heinrich-Bely. During that winter, the "magician" was in an especially aroused and gloomy condition. He picked quarrels with Bely; once he came to him, threw his galleys on the table, and began to revile Merezhkovsky. Bely wrote him a letter in which he announced that he could not attach significance to Bryusov's words because he was "a well-known gossip." In reply, Bryusov challenged him to a duel. The seconds — Ellis and Sergei Soloviev — smoothed the matter over. From that time until 1909, working together on the *Scales,* the poets often met and, in the presence of others, conversed very cordially. But when the two were alone, an uncomfortable silence took over; both lowered their eyes; the shade of the possessed Renata stood between them.

During that year, Bely often saw the patroness of art, Margarita Kirillovna Morozova, in whose private home on Smolensky Boulevard both public figures and religious philosophers and Symbolist poets would meet. A pupil of Scriabin and a friend of Prince Evgeny Nikolaevich Trubetskoi, she had a gift for uniting the most ununitable people, for speaking of the constitution with Milyukov and Prince Lvov, of mystical dawns with Bely and of the philosophy of Vladimir Soloviev with Lopatin and Prince Sergei Trubetskoi. She performed the service of creating a tone of unusual "cultured courtesy" between the professors and the Symbolists. Merezhkovsky and Bely gave lectures in her salon; Rachinsky, Bulgakov, Ern, Kisewetter, E. K. Medtner and Balmont visited her.

Bely writes in *The Turn of the Century*:

A comfortable white room carpeted in soft gray, where Morozova, huge, huge and radiant with smiles, issued softly from the bedroom; she seated herself softly, huge on the low little couch. The tea table was carried in, to her feet. Conversation about everything and nothing. She expressed her personal kindness, softness, in conversation. She had blinding eyes with a gleam now of sapphire, now of emerald.

In the same year, 1905, the Moscow Religious Philosophical Society was created. Meetings took place in Zachatevsky Lane, and there were as many as two hundred people: students, socialist revolutionaries, priests, members of sects, esthetes, Marxists. Moscow was seething; the intelligentsia was in a radical mood. Sventsitsky founded the "Christian Brotherhood of Struggle," uniting the Church and the revolution.

In May, Sergei Soloviev invited Bely to visit him in Dedovo, and in June, the two set out for Shakhmatovo. The poet at once sensed that both Blok and his wife had changed. Alexander Alexandrovich was gloomy and sat for hours by himself in the woods. Lyubov Dmitrievna locked herself in her room. It became clear to everyone at once that the "mystical triangle" had fallen to pieces. The friends' meeting ended dramatically. One evening, Sergei Soloviev went for a walk and remained out the whole night. On the following day, he appeared and said that he had gotten lost, found himself at the Mendeleevs' estate Bablovo, and spent the night there, Blok's mother said many sharp words to "Seryozha." He left Shakhmatovo insulted. This occurrence was the beginning of Blok's break with his cousin. Soloviev, Bely and Blok exchanged several cold letters. Then Lyubov Dmitrievna informed Bely that the correspondence between them would be discontinued; he replied that he was breaking off relations with her and Alexander Alexandrovich.

* * *

After returning to Moscow, Bely, in his habitual frenzy, gave himself up to a new passion: revolution. He went to meetings at the University, shouted in the crowd in front of the Duma, went to a sit-in at the University surrounded by Cossacks, hid from gunfire in Filippov's cafe. During those days, he was a Menshevik, Sergei Soloviev an Essar, Ellis a Marxist, L. Semionov an anarchist.

At a concert by Olenina d'Alheim, Bely made the acquaintance of a thin woman with graying, close-cropped hair and intent eyes. This was Sofya Nikolaevna Turgeneva, nee Bakunina. She introduced her daughters to him — Natasha and Asya — girls of sixteen and fifteen, nicknamed "little angels." The poet was struck by the almond-shaped, browless eyes of Asya and her "Giaconda" smile. This was Bely's first meeting with his future wife, Asya Turgeneva.

* * *

Bely was oppressed by the break with Blok: he suddenly went to Petersburg and arranged a meeting with him in the Palkin Restaurant. A joyful reconciliation took place: both Alexander Alexandrovich and Lyubov Dmitrievna were ready to forget about the "misunderstandings" between them. Bely was happy: in his mad imagination, he supposed that Lyubov Dmitrievna had guessed his love for her and was inclined to accept it; that Alexander Alexandrovich, sacrificing himself, was rejecting for him his "Lady Beautiful." He believed that they had explained themselves without words and that for the three of them a new life was beginning.

He spent two happy months in Petersburg in long visits with the Bloks. A cloudless azure filled his soul. The sudden outpourings of ecstasy sometimes put him in an awkward position. Once, at the Merezhkovskys, he made a "total mess;" first, taking Zinaida Gippius by the hands, he circled around the room with her, then twirled like a dervish in Merezhkovsky's study, overturned a little table and broke its leg. Dmitry Sergeevich decided that this was a mystical rite and admonished in fright: "Stop it, Borya, it's madness."

Zinaida Gippius took the lover under her protection and became his confidante. She assured Bely that he was acting correctly, that Lyubov Dmitrievna and he were created for each other. During this Petersburg visit, Bely became intimate with V. Ivanov, at whose Tower the famous Wednesdays began, and introduced him to Blok. At this time, V. Ivanov was preaching a new theater of mystery plays, Dionysian mysteries embodied in life. Blok was thinking of making a play from life and Lyubov Dmitrievna was dreaming of the stage. Their aspirations were in harmony and V. Ivanov enchanted the Bloks. They decided to create a group, a semi-studio, semi-society; Ivanov, Blok, Bely and Chulkov were included in it. The publishing houses Torches and Horae later arose from this literary collective.

At the end of the year, Bely went to Moscow. Blok said to him at their parting, "Move here with us permanently," and Lyubov Dmitrievna added: "Come as soon as possible; we'll all enjoy it." There were no explanations between him and Lyubov Dmitreivna. But he departed victorious, assured that she loved only him.

The end of the year was marked for Bely by a "thunderous" correspondence with Merezhkovsky, who was displeased with his articles in the *Scales*: "Fathers and Sons of Russian Symbolism," and "Ibsen and Dostoevsky." Bely had decisively turned aside from the religious paths of Merezhkovsky and rejected his "Solovievian" past. He called for "sobriety and a scientific outlook." In the first article, after rendering praise to "the fathers of Russian Symbolism" — Volynsky, Rozanov, Merezhkovsky and Minsky — "dear, unforgettable names," and noting the considerable significance of Dostoevsky in the history of the Russian religious regeneration, the author quite obviously hinted that the time to place the "fathers" in the archives had long since arrived. He concluded the essay with the words:

> While not rejecting religion (!?), we are urging away from the paths of lunacy to the cold clarity of art, to the histology of science, and serious austerity, as in the music of Bach, in the theory of knowledge.

With this announcement, Bely's first "mystical" period draws to a close. Criticism and theoretics also begin the second period — the "gnoseological."

The article "Ibsen and Dostoevsky" is even more arrogantly and provocatively written. Its thrust is directed specifically against Merezhkovsky, author of the book *Tolstoi and Dostoevsky*. Bely immoderately extols Ibsen, "the engineer and mechanic constructing the paths of ascent." His heroes are "chaste, responsible, decisive innovators." "The voice of Zarathustra," announces the author, "now calls us to the graves of Ruben and Brandt, those stern warriors for liberation." And Ibsen is contrasted to Dostoevsky, who is accused of all the mortal sins: in him "Philistinism, cowardice and dirtiness are expressed in the heaviness of the style; his abysses are spurious, his soul profoundly unmusical; he is a tasteless, intriguing mystic." With amazing undue familiarity, the author announces:

> We have heard many promises in the pothouses where the mystics fraternize with the police, where a particle has often passed for eternity, if only in the image of the "bath house with spiders."

And the pathetic conclusion:

> Is it not time for us to say farewell to such breadth, gather ourselves up, narrow ourselves, and go along the mountain path where stands the lonely image of Henrik Ibsen.

And thus — cold clarity, seriousness, scientific outlook, collectedness, responsibility — this is what Bely was preaching now. He was preaching what he lacked more than all else, what for his chaotic, spontaneous nature was most unattainable. Merezhkovsky could not restrain himself and, as Bely expressed it, "burst into a lion's roar." In his own hand (usually Zinaida Gippius corresponded with Bely), he wrote him a threatening letter, accusing him of "treachery."

72

Chapter Four: Tragic Love (1906-1908)

1906 was the most tragic year of Bely's life. He went to Petersburg in February; it seemed to him that Blok was not glad to see him, and he began to experience a hostile feeling toward the "unsympathetic" poet, the author of the "blasphemous" *Puppet Show*. Blok sensed his ill-will and avoided meeting him. Bely spent his days with Lyubov Dmitrievna, went with her to the Hermitage and to exhibitions; he introduced her to Zinaida Gippius.

The Merezhkovskys were leaving for Paris. Dmitry Sergeevich, having sold his *Trilogy* to the publisher Pirozhkov, was jovial, almost playful. Zinaida Nikolaevna "was bending over the trunks, packing bound notebooks with poems, flagons of perfume, bundles of manuscripts and elegant ribbons." Bely, Filosofov and Kartashev accompanied the departees to the Warsaw Station. Zinaida Gippius asked "Borya" to write to her about the Bloks.

Bely devoted two friendly articles to his departing friends. In the first of them, "Merezhkovsky. A Silhouette," the author produced an excellent portrait of Dmitry Sergeevich. In the Summer Garden at around one in the afternoon, one might encounter "a little man with a pale white face and huge eyes gazing into the distance. A waxen face with a thick chestnut beard growing out of its cheeks." But he also had another face. "Approach him, look closely at him: and this waxen, this cold, dead face will radiate for a moment the grief of a highly sensitive vitality, because the barely perceptible wrinkles around his eyes, and the curve of his mouth, and his peaceful eyes are illuminated by the hidden flame of wild ecstasies."

Now an unknown guest approaches Merezhkovsky.

In the study, from a table covered with books, from excerpts of Eckartshausen, from Dionysius Areopagus or from Isaac the Syrian (perhaps from Bakunin, Herzen, Schelling or even from Arabian fairy tales – he reads everything), with the aroma of the cigar in his hand, Dmitry Merezhkovsky would arise and, with a doubtful, cold gaze, stare at his visitor, stare through him – he always stares through a man. And then he would go into the living room with rapid steps and say to his wife: "Zina, someone has come to see me. Speak with him. I cannot speak with him."

This is one person. But here is another:

However, he meets anyone genuine, prfound, who is able to approach him, "embraces and kisses him," with such tender simplicity, such fatherly kindness.

The article concludes with a description of the Merezhkovskys' "salon:"

Here in the comfortable apartment on Liteinaya I was able to be present several times at the most significant, refined discussions, which have left a life-long impression. Here at the Merezhkovskys in truth they created culture.

In the second article ("Gippius"), Bely subtly notes in the refined poetess the disharmony between the thinker and the artist. Her work contains wit, taste and culture: but the sage does violence to the artist in her, while the artist weakens the seriousness of the religious appeals. But the contradictions in her poetry — order alternating with dissonance — attract like the music of Scriabin. 1906 marks the flowering of Bely's friendship with the Merezhkovskys — a luxurious flowering, but unusually frail. Soon Dmitry Sergeevich would be transformed for him into a "little domestic priest in slippers with pompoms," and Zinaida Nikolaevna into a wicked gossip.

* * *

In the meantime, the torment of Bely's relations with Blok had become unbearable. With the will-power of despair and passion, Bely succeeded in convincing Lyubov Dmitrievna to leave her husband and join her life with his. A decisive explanation took place between the friends. Blok magnanimously departed. But soon Lyubov Dmitrievna began to understand the insanity of her decision: she informed Bely that she herself was not sure of her feelings and asked him to give her two months to decide.

The Petersburg spring of 1906 left troubled, almost delerious memories. Tearing himself away from the tragic atmosphere of the Bloks' home, he sometimes attended the Wednesdays of Vyacheslav Ivanov. Mistrust toward the ambiguous sage, the author of *Transparencies,* grew stronger in him. He was repelled by discussions of the theses of the "mystical anarchism" which was arising then, of which Chulkov, Ivanov and to some extent Blok were guilty.

Thus the groundwork was laid for the bitter campaign against the "Petersburgians," which Bely conducted under the aegis of Bryusov on the pages of the *Scales.*

At one of the Wednesdays at the Tower, he read his essay "The Phoenix." Two forces are at war in the world and in the souls of men: the natural inert force of the Sphinx and the creative resurrecting force of the Phoenix. The revelation of the "word of the beast" is contrasted to the revelation of the "word of the eagle:" the artist is the creator of a universe, an eternal theomachist: in his fire he melts the "face of Sphinxes in our lives." The artist-Phoenix overcomes death with love; he "ascends to the bonfire, drunken with the wine of sunrises, and, having been consumed, is resurrected from the dead."

Thus Bely sometimes believed in the miracle-working force of creative work and love; he wanted to be resurrected to a new, happy life and to resurrect the soul of her who had agreed to become his companion.

* * *

At the end of May, Bely went to visit Sergei Soloviev in Dedovo. The summer was oppressively hot, and there were many thunderstorms. Russia was caught up in peasant disturbances; landowners' estates were burned; revolutionary agitation increased. Bely wrote a number of reviews on Bebel, Kautsky and Vandervelde under the pseudonym of Alpha Beta Gamma for the *Scales*. Together with Sergei Soloviev he became engrossed in reading Gogol, and it seemed to them that the wizard from "A Terrible Vengeance" was roaming over all Russia. Seryozha was gloomy: he had fallen in love with a peasant girl Elenka, who was a cook in the neighboring village of Nedovrazhino, he wanted to marry her in the name of merging with the people — and could not bring himself to decide. Therefore he went about disheveled — in boots and a red shirt, carrying a stake and crowning himself with a spruce branch. Bely rushed about: he went to his mother's estate, the Silver Well, where in twenty days he finished up his fourth symphony, *A Goblet of Blizzards*; from there he rushed to Moscow and wandered about barrooms proving to cabbies and debauchees that "it is better for us all to perish than to live this way." He wrote verses in the spirit of Nekrasov:

> Frightful hunger and cold are awaiting:
> Prison and ruin lie ahead.
> Ferocious, heady vodka
> Bursting like fire in the breast.

The correspondence with Lyubov Dmitrievna assumed a dramatic character: she wrote that she had been in agony all this time and understood at last that she had never loved him. Bely considered murder and suicide. In Moscow, in the Prague restaurant, a meeting took place between him and Blok. The latter tried to persuade him not to come to Petersburg. Bely ran out of the restaurant in a fury. He was on the verge of insanity. He sent Ellis to Shakhmatovo challenging Blok to a duel. Blok did not accept the challenge. In September, Bely was once again in Petersburg. Lyubov Dmitrievna wrote him that she was still not settled in her new apartment and asked him to postpone a visit. For ten days he sat in a semi-dark room on Karavannaya and waited; with despair in his heart, he wandered about the gloomy streets. Whole chapters of the novel *Petersburg* took shape then from the delirious impressions of this Petersburg autumn: the quay from which Nikolai Apollonovich Ableukhov sees the huge sunset and the spire of the Peter and Paul Fortress; the little restaurant on Millionnaya where the poet drank with some bearded coachman: he later led the hero of his novel into this restaurant. Once, from the corner of Karavannaya, he saw Blok: he was walking quickly, holding a walking stick atilt and raising his head high. His pale face cut into Bely's memory, and in the novel he transformed it into the face of Ableukhov-son: "swathed in his greatcoat, the cape flying in the wind like a long flapping wing, he resembled an armless hunchback." Unable to bear his loneliness any longer, Bely visited the Petersburg litterateurs: one evening at Sologub's he met the poet Mikhail Kuzmin, who amazed him with his supplicating eyes, his beauty mark and his huge beard. At a breakfast at E. V. Anichkov's he heard the "golden-tongued" Vyacheslav Ivanov reconcile Christ with Dionysius. He dropped in at Alexander Kuprin's where he met Osip Dymov, F. Batyushkov, and Sergei Gorodetsky. He had conversations with Chulkov, who proved to him that he too was a "mystical anarchist." In his reminiscences of Blok, Bely writes that the Petersburg literary world "gashed his soul," and that this gash was provoked by "his marauding attacks from the *Scales* on *Eglantine*, on *Horae,* on everything smacking of Petersburg."

Finally, an explanation took place with Lyubov Dmitrievna, after which he decided to kill himself. But on the following morning they met again and decided not to see each other for a year and then to "meet each other in a new way." On the same day, Bely departed for Moscow and after two and a half weeks went abroad. He tried to calm down and understand himself; but the correspondence with the Bloks continued, and the wound did not heal. He writes:

> The blood turns jet-black,
> Clotting in the wound,
> But the old pain —
> Is it really forgotten?

In Munich, he met his old university friend Vladimirov, and spent the mornings with him in the "Pinacothèque." He studied Dürer, Grunewald, Cranach, and visited a studio of engravings. The romantic Shwind enchanted him; but he began to be ashamed of his recent passion for Boecklin and Stuck. He and Vladimirov discussed problems of painting, of the culture of the arts, of the Middle Ages, and sought the roots of the Renaissance in Gothicism and scholasticism. The evenings he spent in the pub Simplicissimus and brought roses for its merry hostess, Katy Kobus. Here he made the acquaintance of Wedekind, the poet Ludwig Scharf, Sholom Asch, and the Polish poet Grabovski. A bald violinist with a resemblance to Beethoven played on a small platform; poets read their verses; the tables were lit by lamps with red lampshades. Bely wore a Bavarian outfit, drank beer, attended lectures and concerts; he liked life in Munich. He found that it moved in the light rhythms of a walse. He and Vladimirov dreamed of Italy: to put rucksacks on their backs and cross over the Alps on foot, Lugano, Milan. To be in Florence, to look at Giotto in Assisi, and from there to go to Rome.

But in December, he received a letter from Paris from the Merezhkovskys; they were concerned about his condition and summoned him to them. Entirely unexpectedly, Bely departed for Paris.

He wrote little that year: he reworked the *Fourth Symphony, A Goblet of Blizzards* and published a cycle of poems and several theoretical articles.

In the article "The Principle of Form in Esthetics," the author proposes a gradation of art on the basis of the elements of time and space. Music, the soul of all the arts, expresses time in rhythm: space is not presented in it. Poetry unites time (pure rhythm) with space (images); in it, the musical theme becomes myth. In painting, space predominates (the depiction of appearance) to the detriment of time. Thus, beginning with music as the highest art form, Bely arrives at the very arbitrary assertion that painting, architecture and sculpture are in essence lower forms of art.

Irritation at the "rites" at the Tower of Vyacheslav Ivanov, at the "mystical anarchism" of Chulkov and the Petersburg litterateurs in general, found an outlet for itself in sharp polemical attacks. In the article "Art and Mysterion," Bely inveighs against the contemporary pseudo-mystics. The author writes:

At one time, the narcosis of the mysterion assumed the aspects of an epidemic among the mystics, unexpectedly breaking out like a rash on the face. The Buddhist fraternized with the Christian in the name of the coming mysterion. The esthete turned to philanthrophy, while the social democrat was writing verses about the lofty nobility of the few. Here, verily, a molehill has become a mountain. One begins to understand that the word "mysterion" comes from the noun "mus" (mouse).... Someone in reply to the question of the mistress of the house — "Tea?" — shouted: "The tea of the resurrection of the dead." Someone unexpectedly proposed to clothe himself in white garments and crown himself with wreaths of roses, someone jumped up at a social tribunal announcing the approach of the end of the world, silencing a revolutionary with the Christian brotherhood of the struggle. Finally, in one theater a play was produced "with scents".... Many of us have the unenviable honor of turning our very dreams of mysteria into a goat dance.

An accurate diagnosis. The mystical theme of Symbolism had been degraded and vulgarized. After a momentary and frail flowering followed rapid decomposition. Blok was the first to speak of it in the *Puppet Show*.

Bely very humorously portrays a litterateur of by-gone days, "in a reddened little overcoat," and the contemporary Decadent in "an irreproachable dinner-jacket" (the article "The Litterateur Past and Present"). The writer of today, often a callow youth, raps out the form relatively well, makes books well. But he is not a man; he is marked by the fateful imprint of mortality.

After catching sight of the young, pale little corpse with the casual shaven face, the little corpse smelling of decomposition, but in an irreproachable dinner-jacket, you will say now: "A musical comedy singer." The contemporary writer is above all a writer, and not a human being. For him literary life is life.

Finally, in the sketch "Artist-Insulters," Bely adopts a tone of pathetic accusation. Notes of personal insult and annoyance are heard clearly in it. He exclaims:

Away from us, prodigal vampires that cling to us both in abuse and praise! It is not to you that we turn with a word of life, but to the children. We will to them our desecrated honor, our tears, our ecstasies; before them we are prepared to appear at the Last Judgment because it is in their name that we are created.

In reality, there were no "insulters" and "prodigal vampires," and the honor of the Symbolists was "desecrated" by no one. Thus opened the cannonade from the Moscow *Scales* against the Petersburg litterateurs. It continued for two years: in the center of the gun sight stood Blok.

* * *

Andrei Bely spent the winter of 1907 in Paris; he settled in a quiet pension on Ranelagh Street near the Bois de Boulogne; he breakfasted every day with Jaurès: the huge head, gray beard, sunburned cheeks and absent-minded bluish eyes of the famous leader impressed themselves on Bely's memory. Jaurès, with a napkin tucked under his chin, was absorbed in the newspapers and rolled little balls of bread; he asked about Russia, announced that the Russians were devoid of practical sense and that the Russian immigration was not making a good impression; he respected the French classics and loved to tell stories about animals. Bely introduced him to Minsky, the Merezhkovskys and Filosofov. The latter urged the head of *Humanité* to preside at a meeting protesting the despotism of Tsarist rule in Russia. Jaurès declined. This was at the time when the Merezhkovskys and Filosofov were preparing the book *Le Tzar et la Révolution* for publication. Bely's days began with a stroll in the Bois de Boulogne; he worked until breakfast; toward four o'clock he would set off for the Merezhkovskys. In the evenings he either worked some more or returned to the Merezhkovskys. Zinaida Nikolaevna seemed like a real Parisian to him in her black satin dress and white boa. Her salon was visited by I. I. Shchukin, Count Bucksgevden, Balmont, Minsky, the artist Alexander Nikolaevich Benois. Minsky was studying the night life of Paris in style, and took Zinaida Nikolaevna and Bely to La Place Pigalle, to the pub Enfer and to Bar Maurice. Bely frequented the cafe of poets where Moreas, Paul Fort and Charles Maurice sat in state. Alexander Benois, "gleaming like a polished parquet, elegant, gliding, a little round-shouldered, with a tidily trimmed beard and shining bald spot," took him around the Paris streets on the day of a

78

carnival.

This boisterous life was interrupted by a sudden illness. Bely developed an inflamation; he underwent surgery and was obliged to spend about a month in the hospital. The Merezhkovskys surrounded the sick man with tender care: Dmitry Sergeevich, who waited all morning for the conclusion of the operation, was affectionate and kind; Zinaida Nikolaevna wrote detailed letters to Bely's mother. Filosofov fussed over him like a nurse. The poet with grateful tenderness recalls the Paris spring (the book *Between Two Revolutions*):

> I fell in love with spring-time Paris: I was sorry to leave it.... Paris is a divide separating four years, the two years leading to it — storms of passions, the growth of despair; with the sweep of the knife bringing forth blood, all this poured out of me. Bloodless, with a face as gray as ashes, I gazed at myself for two years and everything that I saw was a farce: the union concluded with Valery Bryusov against Ivanov, Blok, Chulkov and my other recent friends — this is what I brought from Paris to Moscow.

In March, Bely was already in Moscow. He returned from abroad, in his own words, "cold, embittered, fanatical." Sergei Soloviev, forced to stay in bed by a sharp attack of rheumatism, greeted him with "tragic humor:" "Yes this is what we have come to; they cut you up there in Paris; you poured out your blood there, while here I was sick in bed. Yes, we have come to a point...." To both of them, illness represented a crisis: the past was finished; the symbol of this end was the fire in the little house in Dedovo where Vladimir Soloviev used to visit, and around which grew the white campanula transplanted from Pustynka. From the past remained... ashes. Thus Bely entitled his second book of poems *Ashes*.[1]

During the spring of 1907 the "Seven" of the literary department of the *Scales* were conclusively defined: Bryusov, Bely, Sergei Soloviev, Ellis, Baltrushaitis, Sadovskoi and Likiardopula. Bely became the head of the "theoretical/section": in almost every issue of the journal his editorials appeared under the general heading of "The Divide." Thus, for two years (1907-1909) Bely functioned as the official ideologue of Symbolism.

* * *

Bely's article, "The Meaning of Art," makes an attempt to construct a theory of Symbolist art on the basis of the contemporary theory of knowledge. The school of Windelbrand, Rickert and Lask acknowledges the primacy of art over knowledge. In order for a value to arise, the concept of necessitation must unite with one or another given. This unification lies in the free will of the personality, in its creative work. Therefore, scientific knowledge, philosophy, art and religion are all in essence different aspects of creative work. Art transforms the images of life into the images of values (symbols);

religion realizes them in life. What begins in art is completed in religion. Art has no meaning of its own other than the religious one: if we deny it this meaning, it must turn into science or disappear. The creation of symbols leads to the ultimate goal: to the transformation of the world, but only religion can attain this goal. Thus the Freiburg school of philosophy with its doctrine of value and creation helps the author to base his theory on the religious nature of symbol-values. But if art is only a path to the religious transformation of life, then the first task of the artist is to realize his own value, to create his own self.

In the article "The Art of the Future,"[2] the author writes:

> With art, with life, the matter becomes much more serious than we might think; the abyss over which we are hanging, darker and deeper.... We must forget the present; we must all recreate anew; for this we must create our own selves. And the only slope along which we can still clamber is our own selves. On the summit our "I" awaits us. Here is the answer for the artist: if he wants to remain an artist while not ceasing to be a human being, he must become his own artistic form. Only this form of creative work still promises us salvation. And herein lies the path of the art of the future.

The maximalism and moral force of this essay are entirely in the tradition of Russian religious thought. Here Bely echoes Gogol, the author of *Correspondence with Friends,* Tolstoi, the preacher of personal self-perfection, and Dostoevsky of the epoch of *The Diary of a Writer.* In Russia esthetics has always been perceived as lawlessness if it is not morally and religiously justified.

Bely's theoretical research was soon interrupted by the embittered polemics of the "Muscovites" against the "Petersburgians;" he took part in it passionately. The "seven" united around the *Scales* proved to be an army staff opening military action against the group of Petersburg writers, in the center of which were Blok, Vyacheslav Ivanov and Chulkov. It seemed to Bely that Blok had betrayed his theurgical calling, that "The Unknown Woman" and the *Puppet Show* were a desecration of saints. His irritation with his recent friend was inflamed by Ellis and Sergei Soloviev. The former had succeeded during Bely's absence in transforming himself from an enemy of the *Scales* into a collaborator; he proclaimed Bryusov the foremost poet in Russia and violently attacked anyone who would not acknowledge this supremacy. He could not bear Vyacheslav Ivanov and hated Blok for his "conciliation." The latter accused Blok of participation in "mystical anarchism" which was causing the decomposition of esthetics and religion. Bryusov cleverly guided "the political tactics of his unselfish henchmen, and with their help defended his 'primogeniture' from the Petersburgians." Bely vehemently attacked Vyacheslav Ivanov who had just published *Eros,* a small collection of verse; he thought that the sly Alexandrian was ruining the new art, preaching eroticism under the guise of religious symbology. He sharply attacked Chulkov, the ill-fated inventor of "mystical anarchism," and reproached Blok with the transformation of mysterion into "farcical buffoonery." The Petersburgians, uniting around the publishing house Horae, accused Bryusov's group of formalism, rationalism and reaction. They were disturbed by the indecent tone of the polemics, the crude tastelessness of the attacks. Thus was prepared the crisis of Symbolism leading to the decomposition and destruction of that movement.

Recalling this sad period in his life, Bely attempts to, if not justify himself, then at least to minimize his guilt; he succeeds poorly. "My nervousness," he writes, "exhaustion and very great weakness, the results of the operation, predisposed me to petulant pranks." During the summer, Ellis, left without a room and without money, moved into his apartment with him; they lived a "feverish and unhealthy life." "We inflamed each other's anger at the traitors to 'Symbolism,' sat up until morning, awakened half-starved and during the day scribbled impetuous manifestoes in the name of 'Symbolism'." And then again, "We continued to work ourselves up to the ultimate degree of bitterness; and it began to seem to us that Ivanov, Blok and Chulkov had made an agreement to ruin all of Russian literature."

These were the first symptoms of the persecution mania from which Bely later suffered so cruelly. He was obliged to confess: "The only secret figure of his polemics was Blok." Bitterness at the "loss of a friend" was transformed into vicious attacks. The tragi-comism of this literary strife lay in the fact that the author of "The Unknown Woman" was guilty of nothing; through him Bely hoped to wound the one who stood behind him and whom he hated and loved to the point of delirium. The first shot at Blok was Bely's review of the anthology *Unexpected Joy*. While acknowledging the author to be one of the most prominent contemporary poets and greatly esteeming his *Verses About the Lady Beautiful*, the reviewer emphasized Blok's betrayal of the past. He writes:

In the second anthology, instead of a temple there is a swamp covered with hummocks, amidst which protrudes a little hut where an old man and an old woman and "someone" for "some" centennial draw out beer. We begin to fear for the author. After all, this is not "Unexpected Joy," but "Unexpected Sorrow."

After pointing out that Blok's poetry, abandoning ideological ballast, has blossomed into a "luxurious double flower," the author concludes:

Through the frenzied charm, through the caresses squandered on imps, at times through the imitation of the child-like or simply idiotic, there is suddenly revealed the laceration of a soul, deep and pure, seeming to

81

ask fate with surprised humility: "Why?" "What for?"

In the following article, "Freedmen," the tone becomes sharply aggressive. The Petersburgians are represented as "conciliators" surrounded by literary rabble speculating on Symbolism. Bely writes:

At present, talent is surrounded by the oreole of slaves. And a slave knows that the patron will set free the most amiable of his friends. And the freedman in our days is the first pretender to the literary throne of the patron.

In *Reminiscences of Blok*, Bely confesses that by the "talent surrounded by slaves" he meant Blok, while the "freedman" in his eyes was Chulkov. He imagined that various "mystical anarchists" and "ecumenical individualists" were teeming around Blok, and he flung thunderbolts at the enemies he thought up. "We Symbolists," he shouted, "do not recognize the literary clowns, lascivious cats and hyenas devouring the corpses of their fallen enemies."(!)

In the article "A Child's Tin Whistle," Bely does battle with the contemporary Mitrofanushka,[3] announcing that Symbolism has ended and been replaced by Neo-Realism. He writes:

The artist-Symbolists acknowledge the right of the artist to be a leader and an architect of life. When we illuminate the problems posed in the light of psychology and the theory of knowledge, only then will we understand what the problem of Symbolism is. But on these summits of thought is heard the whistle of the cold hurricane which the modern Mitrofanushkas fear so much while they are whistling the funeral march to Symbolism.

The Mitrofanushka is of course Chulkov. And now there is also a direct attack on Blok:

Singing bird, rock yourself on your little branch, but, for God's sake, do not imitate Bach's fugue, which you could hear through the window, with a whistle. To be a musician of thought, it is not enough to blow: "to blow does not mean to play the flute; to play, it is necessary to move the fingers" (Goethe).

It is impossible to justify these malicious and insulting attacks on the poet, guilty of absolutely no "mystical anarchism," by an "irritability after the operation."

And again abuse for Chulkov and Vyacheslav Ivanov (the article "People with Leftist Tendencies"). Bely announces:

How many times closer to us are Belinsky, Pisarev, Mikhailovsky than these contemporary gentlemen preparing bad soup from their own nonsense, seasoned with Soloviev, Bryusov, Merezhkovsky, Nietzsche, Sturner and Bakunin. No, we have had enough of "leftist tendencies!" Silence, silence! Better socialism, better even kadetism, than mystical anarchism. Better individualism than ecumenical eroticism. Better empirical criticism than the occult breeding of nymphs.

Vyacheslav Ivanov espoused the transformation of the theater into mysteria and predicted that the spirit of Dionysian action would seize all of Russia, that Russia would be entirely covered with "orchestras." Bely wittily ridiculed him (in the article "Bryusov: The Poet of Marble and Bronze"). He exclaims:

Where is one to hide from Modernism? Everyone has become a Decadent. How many pale, exhausted faces have appeared! Go to the theater: pale youths, pale stylized heads. And everyone is speaking of the "spirit of music." A genius has appeared who performs symphonies on combs; one lecturer played the piano with his coat tails.... What if they proclaim the musical construction of social life with the transformation of the Duma into an orchestra? Let us imagine to ourselves a Duma in which the representatives of the parties, instead of making speeches, must sing arias; we will imagine a Duma in which, instead of voting, the deputies, crowned with roses, begin to dance around a statue of Dionysius led by choir-leader Vyacheslav Ivanov.

During the summer, the "half-starving and frenzied" Bely and Ellis went to the movies every night, but even the movies inflamed their bitterness against Blok. Bely writes (the article "The Movies"):

The movies are the democratic theater of the future, farce in the noble sense of this word. Whatever you like, only not the *Puppet Show (Balaganchik)*. Please, without the "chik."[4] All these "chiks" are a disgusting joke; as if it were sufficient to attach to any word the Manilov-like[5] "chik" and that word would gaze caressingly into the soul. The "puppet shows" transform mysteria into movies; the movies restore healthy life without the mystical "use of chik." The latest word in the most recent Russian drama is the introduction of the notorious "chik" into the most holy of places — into tragedy and mysteria.

These judgments about "chiks" and the "use of chik" are on the verge of delirium. The article concludes with low insinuations to Blok's address. The author continues:

If such blasphemy occurred because of a loss of faith in life, it would lead to ruin: but how is it that no one is ruined? How is it that blasphemous daring dawns in the breasts of clever people peacefully making their literary and other careers?

At his point Bely stopped; on this path it was impossible to go any further.

During the summer, Bely and Sergei Soloviev rented a little empty house near the village of Petrovskoe, two versts from Dedovo. There the poet finished his fourth symphony, *A Goblet of Blizzards,* and wrote the poems later included in the anthology *The Urn.* When he returned to Moscow, he again became absorbed in literary strife. He attempted to unite three journals, the *Scales,* the *Golden Fleece* and the *Divide,* in order to "fire from three batteries on the evil tower of Vyacheslav Ivanov," but the journals were quarreling among themselves: the *Scales* attacked the *Divide,* the *Divide* resented the *Scales* and furiously attacked the *Golden Fleece.* The misunderstandings between the *Scales* and the *Golden Fleece* ended in a complete break. A very wealthy merchant and patron of literature, N. P. Ryabushinsky, who published the *Golden Fleece,* somehow acted without tact toward one of the collaborators. The group at the *Scales* called a boycott on him, and when the publisher invited Bely to head the literary section of the journal, he replied with an ultimatum: Ryabushinsky must leave the post of editor as a person who did not understand literature. Unfortunately, Ryabushinsky did not have enough fortitude to do away with himself, and the post of head of the literary section he offered to Blok. Blok accepted. Bely flew into a rage: the Petersburgians had obtained their own organ in Moscow! Bryusov and Bely had broken off relations with the petty tyrant of an editor, and Blok agreed to collaborate with him! It was strike-breaking! In the book *Between Two Revolutions* the author caricatures the hated "exploiter" Ryabushinsky:

This handsome man looked like a hairdresser: no teeth but brilliance: lips purple, pearls for cheeks; eyes — prunes; his hair curled in a wave blacker than shoe-polish fell over his forehead; his beard — shoe-polish — was swollen; you couldn't pull it out — it would take years to pull out — it was very thick.

* * *

Finding fault with Blok's essay "On Realists," Bely wrote him an insulting letter, almost accusing him of being an informer. Blok challenged him to a duel. Bely brought him an apology, explained his resentment and perplexity, and insisted on a meeting. On August 24, Blok came to Moscow, and a twelve-hour conversation took place between him and Bely. The recent friends decided that "the ideological struggle must not stand in the way of trust and respect for each other."

During the autumn, in the newspaper *Dawn of Russia,* Bely's brilliant feuilletons, "The Symbolist Theater," appeared, written under the immediate impression of the tours of the Komissarzhevsky Theater. Symbolism in the theater is impossible, the author announced. Symbolist drama, if it were executed very strictly within the limits of the stage, would first of all destroy the platform dividing the viewer from the actor. Symbolist theater is mysterion, i.e., the abolition of the theater. We have not yet reached the heights of mysterion and are replacing it by stylization. The first result of this is the destruction not only of the personality of the actor, but of the very features of the man in man. The principles which govern Meyerhold inevitably lead to a theater of marionettes or even to a theater of Chinese shadows. The author attacks the staging of Blok's *Puppet Show*:

> The characters... Don't they really resemble marionettes here? They produce only typical gestures; if this is Pierrot, he sighs monotonously, waves his hands monotonously, to the accompaniment of the elegantly stupid and sad, sad music of Kuzmin, one, two, boom, boom. "Trakh!" pours into the window, the sky is torn asunder. "Boom!" the masks run off in different directions. The appearance of puppets would not be surprising in the *Puppet Show*. What is surprising is entirely different: "the announcement of the author through the mouth of Pierrot about the 'cardboard bride.' This bride is a symbol of Femininity. The announcement of Blok, the singer of Eternal Femininity, that the eternally feminine principle is cardboard, is amazing. The marionette-like character of the substance of Blokian symbolism in the *Puppet Show* — this is what is terrifying.

About this article by Bely, Blok wrote to his mother: "The best that has appeared during this time — Borya's feuilleton, 'Symbolist Theater;' I will send it to you shortly." The reproaches of the critic did not insult him; probably he considered them just.

Bely's feuilletons attracted the attention of V. F. Komissarzhevskaya and undoubtedly hastened her break with Meyerhold.

Bely's polemical ardor did not cool: he did battle with a group of writers united around the anthologies of *Eglantine,* accusing them of serving the reader a "vinaigrette of tendencies with impressionist sauce," inveighed against the "realists' " anthologies, *Knowledge,* and scolded the "moderate modernists" publishing *Literary and Artistic Week.* The latter demanded that he withdraw "his insulting expressions" and agreed to meet with him in their editorial offices at the apartment of V.I. Strazhev. Here, in the presence of B. Zaitsev, B. Griftsov, P. Muratov, A. Koiransky and Muni, the "battle" took place. Zaitsev tells about it in his memoirs of Bely:

> On that day Bely was very picturesque and talkative — he was all boiling and steaming; he revolved, spun about. On his pale face the eyes in the shadow of his eyelashes also darted about; apparently he was "striking" us with the "lightning" of his glares. He himself was profoundly

wounded by the tone of the letter: "Why did you not discuss it with me? I am a collaborator, you know. I am an honest writer! I am a man. You are not my superiors."

Thus, reconciliation did not take place. In *Reminiscences of Blok,* Bely admits that in this confrontation he "was wrong about a lot of things" and that it made a "depressing impression" on him.

The polemics of the *Scales* spread ever further; Bryusov's group was fighting with almost all Russian literature. And a "secretly prepared boycott" was called against the *Scales.*

* * *

On October 4, Blok and Bely met in Kiev at an "Evening of Art" given by the Kievan journal, *In the World of Art.* Bely had an attack of nerves before the performance. Lyubov Dmitrievna met him amiably and simply, and he understood that the past was over. Now she was for him no longer the Lady Beautiful, but simply a "doll." Bely set to work in his furnished room on Vasilevsky Island and burst forth into a venomous article, "The Theater and Contemporary Drama." Its thrust was directed against Vyacheslav Ivanov and his teachings on the theater-mysterion. He writes:

These sweet summonses to mysterion are suspicious in our time; they lull courage to sleep. When we are told now that the stage is a religious rite, the actor a priest, and viewing the play our communion with the mystery, we understand these words in an undefined, almost senseless way. What is a religious rite? Is it a deed of religious action? But of what sort? Before whom is this religious rite? And to what god must we pray? If so, give us a goat for the sacrifice. The "temple" will remain the Mariinsky Theater, and the restaurant a restaurant. We must not flee from life into a theater in order to sing and dance over the tragic dead goat and then, happening upon life, to be amazed at what we have done. This is how flight from Fate takes place.... Symbolist drama is not drama, but a homily of the great, ever-growing drama of mankind. It is a homily of the approach of a fateful denouement.

In his polemics with Vyacheslav Ivanov, Bely was thinking of Blok's destiny. He was also fleeing into the theater from Fate. But the Symbolist theater was not salvation; led itself to a "fateful denouement."

After several days, Bely returned to Moscow; he and Blok corresponded, then began to write more seldom and finally fell silent. Their relationship passed into a dead period. It continued for three years.

At the end of 1907, Bely wrote one of his most lyrical articles, "The Pearls of Life." In it, he bade farewell to his old friend the Argonaut, and assured himself that the former pain had passed, that before him was the spring of a new life.

Life is flying. Ever faster, ever faster, life is flying. Now the gold lace of foam drenches you with cold, and the winged Argo has begun to rock: it will capsize. "It will capsize!" your fellow argonaut, your best friend, initiated into the secrets of your voyage, whispers to you. Do not believe him. We will never know the minute when he is bitten by the vampire of death. Our life is a screaming swallow drowning in azure. He who has understood this has understood that there is neither pain nor joy. In both pain and joy is the suppressed quiet of the heavenly lake across which ripples of clouds are flowing.... Love life, love the springs — love them, do not cease to love! Look: there in the distance is a line of burning pearls!"

Blok has been bitten by the "vampire of death." What is to be done? The Argo will journey further!

* * *

Bely sums up the "results" of 1907 in the article "The Present and Future of Russian Literature." He examines the paths traveled by Symbolist art and predicts its subsequent fate: he speaks of the return of literature to folk sources and of the birth of a new all-people's religious art. The first Russian followers of Nietzsche, headed by Merezhkovsky, went forth to meet the religious discontent of the people: the students of Nietzsche and Ibsen, the Russian Symbolists, turned to Gogol, Nekrasov and even to Gleb Uspensky. The elemental force of the people has conquered the West in the Russian writer. And only now, perhaps, have we for the first time grown to understand the literature of our fatherland; it is all a continuous summons to the transformation of life. Gogol, Tolstoi, Dostoevsky, Nekrasov were not only artists, but preachers as well. The service of the Symbolists lies in the new profound perception of Russian literature from Pushkin to Dostoevsky. The western European individualist in Merezhkovsky and Gippius has approached Dostoevsky; in Bryusov it approaches Pushkin and Baratynsky; in Sologub — Gogol; in Remizov — Leskov; in Blok, Maeterlinck encounters Lermontov and Vladimir Soloviev. In their unconscious, vital elemental force, the contemporary writers are religious because they are of the people and are of the people because they are religious. The Symbolists are capable of saying a new and necessary word; in the depths of the people's soul they hear a genuinely religious truth about the earth. The author dwells on Blok's "oneness with the people." He writes:

There are those who have half-turned toward the people. For example, Blok. His disquieting poetry somehow approaches Russian sectism. He calls himself an "unresurrected Christ," and his Lady Beautiful is in essence the Mother of God of the Khlysty. The Symbolist Alexander Blok has created a strange fantastical world within himself. But this world has proven to be extremely similar to the world of the Khlysty. Blok is either still of the people or already of the people. On the one hand, he is tortured by problems of the people and the intelligentsia, although he has not yet risen to the heights of Nietzschian symbolism, i.e., has not experienced the Golgothas of individualism. Hence the people for him is a sort of esthetic category, while Nietzsche is a "foreign idol, not close or necessary to him."

Returning to Russian Symbolism, the author notes its two paths, its two "truths." There is the truth of the sermon in Merezhkovsky and the truth of art in Bryusov. Bely writes:

Merezhkovsky was a too early forerunner of the "deed" of Bryusov, who was too late a forerunner of the "word." In contemporary Russian literature, the deed and the word are not yet united.

And the article concludes with an unexpected, ominous announcement:

We have something in common within us, both writers and readers — we are all in the hungry, fruitless Russian plains, whither the evil spirit has driven us from time immemorial.

This is one of Bely's most significant articles. It precisely defines the cultural and historical meaning of the Symbolist movement. Starting from Western European "Decadence" and Nietzschean individualism, the Russian art of the beginning of the 20th century arrived at genuine nationality and religiosity and discovered anew the great literature of the 19th century. Its path goes from decline and fall to the Renaissance; it deserves the honorary title of the "Russian Renaissance." The observation of the resemblance of Blok's lyrical world to the world of sectism and of the Lady Beautiful to the "mother of God of the Khlysty" is among Bely's most profound intuitions as a critic.

* * *

1908

In January, 1908, Bely went to Petersburg and gave a lecture entitled "Friedrich Nietzsche and the Portents of the Present." Blok was not present at the lecture, but the poets met in a neutral place, in Palkin's restaurant, and spoke for several hours. "We established friendly pesonal relations and unfriendly literary ones" (Blok's letter to his mother of January 21). 1908 was a "dark pit" in Bely's life; Russia was oppressed by gloomy reaction; clubs of "those burning the candle at both ends" increased among the youth; Saninist[6] psychology reigned supreme; the hero of the day was the provocateur Azev; and society seemed poisoned by skepticism and cynicism. Bely continued to work at the *Scales*, but he felt that the journal was in its death-agony. He gave lectures in the Free Esthetics Society and in a literary and artistic circle, but there was none of the former enthusiasm. He writes in his memoirs:

> Spiritual darkness.... In solitude I composed the verses later included in *The Urn*.... "You cannot overcome" was the slogan of the day; you cannot overcome the past. The feeling of despondency was the result of the operation (anemia). I was even disappointed in the literary tactics to which I had recently wholly surrendered myself. I saw with bitterness that upon the movement I loved casual people placed the stamp of nonsense; and nonsense in the future will march under the flag of Symbolism.

Bely sought solace from loneliness and anguish in philosophy: he constructed the gnoseological foundations of Symbolism and became interested in the systems of Rickert, Cohen and Natorp; for this he was often criticized by his philosopher friends Berdyaev, Bulgakov and Schpet. They maintained that the poet was remaking Rickert in his own image, and that nothing of Rickert remained. The sharp and ironical Schpet made fun of his "Rickertian dress-coat:"

> Boris Nikolaevich will tear his dress-coat in a philosophical duel; that's nothing: he will go home and mend it without fail. And then he will appear once again, as if nothing had happened, in the mended dress-coat.

With the arrival in Moscow of Berdyaev and Bulgakov, the Moscow Religious-Philosophical Society came alive. Its chairman, G. A. Rachinsky, published Bely as a representative of the "leftist religious tendency," as opposed to Bulgakov, Ern and Prince E. N. Trubetskoi, who were too orthodox for his taste. Bely recalls:

> At about that time, Berdyaev entered my world of thought. This original thinker, who had passed through both the school of sociological thought and the school of Kant, impressed me as a great man filled with knightliness; in addition, the vital man in him was striking. I liked in him his straightforwardness, the frankness of his position of thought, and I liked the kind smile "from under his dogmatism" of maxims and the always mournful gaze from his shining eyes, his Assyrian head. Thus my warmth toward Berdyaev over the years naturally grew into a feeling of love, respect, friendship.

In 1908, Bely's old friend Medtner moved from Nizhni Novgorod to Moscow. This was the only person with whom he could speak frankly about his spiritual drama — the break with the Bloks. Medtner, the admirer of Kant,

Goethe and Beethoven, lovingly set about, as Bely expressed it, "harmonizing the world of his consciousness with the help of music, philosophy and culture." In the affair with Blok, he saw the "problem of an agonizing transition from Romanticism to Classical clarity." We have no evidence with which to determine whether this scholarly "harmonization" helped the poor poet, but Bely did not deceive himself. "My enthusiasm for philosphy," he writes, "was an expression of my inner loneliness." Blok sought forgetfulness in wine and passion, Bely in neo-Kantian logic.

In April, the Scorpion publishing house published *The Goblet of Blizzards. The Fourth Symphony,* with the following dedication: "With profound respect, the author dedicates this book to Nikolai Karlovich Medtner, who inspired the theme of the symphony, and to his dear friend Zinaida Nikolaevna Gippius, who resolved the theme." In the foreword, Bely tells the history of the creation of the symphony:

> The theme of blizzards came to me a long time ago — as early as 1903. At that time several passages were written (and later reworked). The first two parts in the original text were prepared as early as 1904 (later I revised them). At that time, I defined the basic motif of the blizzard precisely. Finally, the first part in its completed form was prepared in June, 1906 (there were two years when, for many reasons, I could not work on the *Symphony*); in rewriting, I inserted only a few satirical scenes, no more.

From the same foreword we discover the intention of the author so unsuccessfully emobodied in *The Goblet of Blizzards*:

> In finishing my *Fourth Symphony*, I find myself in a certain state of doubt. Who will read it? Who needs it? I worked on it for a long time and tried as much as possible to precisely depict several experiences underlying, so to speak, the background of everyday life and, in essence, incapable of being embodied in words. These experiences, clothed in the form of repeating themes pervading the entire *Symphony*, are represented as if through a magnifying glass. Here I encountered two types of doubt: should I, in the choice of the image for the experience, in essence not embodied in the image, be ruled by the beauty of the image itself, or by its precision (i.e., so that the image would accomodate the greatest amount of the experience)? Two paths defined themselves before me: the path of art and the path of the analysis of experiences themselves, their dissection into component parts. I chose the second path, and that is why I am in doubt: is the present *Symphony* an artistic creation or is it a document of the consciousness of a modern soul, perhaps curious for a future psychologist? I was interested in the construction mechanism of that dimly understood form in which my pre-

vious symphonies were written: there the construction suggested itself and I had no precise representation of what a "symphony" must be in literature. In the present *Symphony* I tried primarily to be precise in the exposition of the themes, in their counterpoint, unification, etc..... I looked at my *Symphony* while I was working on it only as a problem of structure. I still don't know if it has the right to exist.... Only the objective evaluation of the future will decide if my structural calculations have meaning or whether they are a paradox.

In conclusion, I will discuss the goal of the plot even though it is tightly bound to the technique of the writing. In the present *Symphony* I wanted to portray the entire gamut of that special type of love of which our age has a dim prescience, as did Plato, Goethe and Dante before — holy love. If, in the future, a new religious consciousness is ever possible, then the path to it is only through love.... I must stipulate that in the meantime I do not see reliable paths to the realization of this vague summons from love to the religion of love. That is why I wanted to portray the Promised Land of this love from blizzards, gold, sky and wind. The theme of blizzards is a dimly calling transport. Whither? To life or to death? To madness or to wisdom? And "the souls of the loving dissolve in the blizzard."

The foreword to the *Symphony* is significantly more interesting than the *Symphony* itself. The problem of the decomposition of experiences into their component parts and their transformation into symphonic themes, the attempt at the construction of a literary work according to the laws of counterpoint is a bold and attractive intention. The portrayal of "holy love" as a path to a "new religious consciousness" is a theme worthy of Plato and Dante. But these lofty intentions were not realized. *The Goblet of Blizzards* is the most forced, artificial and confused of Bely's symphonies. It was met with doubt and silence. The author tried to explain the failure of *The Goblet of Blizzards* by the fact that he "outsmarted himself." "From 1902 until 1908," he writes in *The Turn of the Century*, "I only split hairs on one work, mutilating it with new wording, so that in 1908 I published a quadrupally mutilated text." In the book *Between Two Revolutions*, he gives curious details about the work on the *Fourth Symphony*:

In 1906 in Munich, I dragged out the text of a symphony once already prepared, with the idea of revising it, dreaming of various technical feats such as: with the material of a sentence I wanted to act as Wagner did with a melody; I conceived of thematics as a strict line of rhythm; the secondary themes were two women, an "angel" and a "demon," merged in the spirit of the hero into one, not by the rules of logic, but of counterpoint. But the story did not submit to the formula: I saw the plot as a monolith, while the formula broke it into two worlds: the world of hallucinations of the consciousness, and the material world.... I was doomed to break the image into variations of storms of sounds and lusters. This was how *The Goblet of Blizzards* was constructed. It made evident once and for all the impossibility of "symphonies" in literature.

The idea of "symphonic" construction was suggested to Bely by the symphonies of Nikolai Karlovich and the musical theories of Emili Karlovich Medtner. To this was joined an ill-fated enthusiasm for Wagner's operas and an ever-growing interest in questions of form and structure in literary works. A year after the publication of *The Goblet of Blizzards,* Bely became involved in research into the "comparative morphology of rhythm and the structure of Russian iambic tetrameter," and through his work laid the basis for the Formalist study of Russian verse.

The Goblet of Blizzards begins with the exposition of the theme of the blizzard. It breaks into image sounds which, repeating, inter-weaving, growing more forceful and complex, comprise the counterpoint of the poem. Here are the basic themes: "snow, like lilies, began to swing over the city," "singing ribbons of silver were flying by," "snow scattered in handfuls of diamonds," "a white sleeve arose along the wall," "over the houses white sails were blown," "over the houses airy ships were flying," "a white corpse was rising at the window," "the moon was a shining dandelion." The theme of the blizzard is gradually transformed into the theme of a divine service. The deacon begins to wave the censer; the priest of the blizzard, the priest of the frost, in an icy mitre, begins the litany. Blasphemous "liturgical prayers" commence: "The Bride clothed with the snow approaches.... Let us pray to the snowstorm." In this whirling and clatter of the blizzard the visage of "holy love" arises; it is broken into banal reality and into mystical dreams, or rather, ravings. On the first plane, the heroine Svetlova languishes between her fat, puffy husband and her protector, the old colonel Svetozarovy; on the second plane, she is the Woman clothed with the sun, while the colonel is the dragon and serpent. The plot is developed in such a chaotic mixture of cynicism and mysticism, blasphemy and eroticism, that it is beyond one's strength to deal with it. The only lively places in this unhealthy confusion are the satirical attacks addressed to contemporaries. Here is Vyacheslav Ivanov: "The mystical anarchist meekly loved music; first listening to Wagner, it was as if his eyes burned green as a chrysolite.... Now he has become the prophet of superlogism, super-energetic eroticism, and pours forth mists understood by no one." Here is Chulkov:

Nulkov jumped out. He lay with his ear to the keyhole, listening to the prophecy of the mystical anarchist. He hastily made a note in a pocket notebook, seized by horror, and his hair stood on end in his excitement. "Now I will write a feuilleton about this!" he laughed into his sly moustache. "Who call tell it more ecstatically than I? Who can gather into a little jar, like honey, all the boldness, and cook it like mystical soup?

Here is Remizov: "Remizov ran out from the gateway. 'Do you want to play snowy Kriks Varaks[7] with me?' He looked at him from under his spectacles." Here is Blok:

> The great Blok went out and suggested making a snowy bonfire from icicles. Piece upon piece on the bonfire, great Blok; he was surprised that it would not ignite. He returned home and modestly said: 'I caught fire on a snowy bonfire.' The next day, Voloshin went around to everyone, celebrating the miracle of Saint Blok.
>
> Black crowds awaited Gorodetsky on Nevsky Prospect. The good people had been waiting for a long time. Gorodetsky acted like a knave. He snapped his fingers under someone's nose; thunderous howls accompanied the little boy. Zhorzhik Nulkov flew by in a smart cab, and shouted "We, we, we." Shestov sighed sadly: "I do not love idle chatter." "You are ours!" shouted the mystics, and bore him away to Vienna.

And finally, Berdyaev: "The black theocrat, like an Assyrian tsar, reconciled God and Man."

Immediately upon its publication, Bely sent it to "the great Blok." Blok wrote to his mother:

> Borya has published a symphony; he sent it to me with a tender inscription. I read it. While I was reading it, I received his anxious letter about the symphony. But there is nothing I can say to him; it is not just that I don't like it, but I have much against its spirit. And I will not answer him.

But after four days (April 21), he wrote to his mother again:

> I am angry with Moscow. Borya is writing me uneasy letters, but I don't have the strength to answer him. Because it is elusive... there are tricks against me in this symphony. The Moscow arrogance sickens me; they are annoying and tasteless, like turkeys. I go and spit as if a roach were in my mouth. The devil take them.

Blok's silence wounded the touchy author, and he took vengeance upon him with an ugly review of his miscellany, *Lyrical Dramas,* published in February, 1908. In *Reminiscences of Blok,* Bely tries to justify himself in reference to this insultingly scoffing review of a book by his recent friend. "How many times later," he writes, "was I ready to tear my hair over the fact that

93

it was published!" But he was not to blame: during that time, he was in the condition of "an hysterical medium; returning from conferences and meetings, I would lie prostrate on the couch in my study. I would see in the greenish mirror my 'worsening visage' and give myself up to anguish." Behind the wall, his mother was playing Mozart's *Requiem* and it seemed to him that he was being lowered into the grave to the accompaniment of these funereal sounds. Anguish leaned over him like a black double. Ellis, who loved to create nightmarish myths out of everything, assured Bely that he had a double — a black profile; this shadow had run away with him and was functioning somewhere beyond his will. The splitting of consciousness was expressed in the fact that the second half of his "I" suffered from attacks of "pain and polemical malice." In one of these attacks he had written his review of Blok's dramas.

It is called "Fragments of Worlds" and begins with a characterization of the poet:

Blok is a talented portrayer of emptiness. The beauty of his songs is the beauty of a perishing soul, the beauty of "chaos."

The development of Blok's poetry is depicted in the following poetic metaphor:

Like satin roses, Blok's verses unraveled; beneath them shone a "vision which knew no evil" for a few of his admirers. But when the shroud of his muse flew off (the roses opened), in each rose was sitting a caterpillar — certainly a beautiful caterpillar, but a caterpillar all the same. From the caterpillar were hatched all kinds of little priests and demons feeding on the petals of the heavenly (for us) dawns of the poet. From that moment, the poet's verse strengthened; however, he proved to be a sham mystic. And the Lady Beautiful proved to be the most venomous caterpillar of all (later decomposing into a prostitute and a sham quantity something like 1) the summons to life proved to be a summons to death. Blok's "dramas" are fragments of ruined worlds. In them, destruction is without rhyme or reason: thus destruction for the sake of destruction. The lyricism has vanished, that's all; and everything has been precipitated into the void. We read and admire, but, you see, a soul had perished here not in name, but in fact, saying: "Horror! horror! horror!" The force of the impression and the meaning of this "absurdity" is purchased by the sincerity of the downfall, collapse, bankruptcy. But... at what price?

This burial alive of his best friend showed Blok the entire depth of the abyss which had grown between him and Bely. After reading this maliciously consoling review in the May issue of *Scales,* he wrote to M. I. Pantyukh (May 22):

I feel increasingly the vanity of words with people with whom there have been so many conversations (and, to wit, mystical conversations) like Andrei Bely, Sergei Soloviev and others. I have gone another way, our relations have become muddled once and for all, and I strongly suspect that this is due to the systematic falsity of spoken thoughts.

Bely's article did not insult Blok; he understood that it was impossible to be insulted by such a "muddled person" (his expression). On June 14, he wrote to Chulkov:

Andrei Bely will come no more to make peace. But, you know, his article about me is clever and entertaining, although I do not agree with it.

In two articles, "Art," and "The Song of Life," Bely preaches his doctrine: "Art is life," and "Art is music," with great brilliance. He maintains that art is the art of living, and life is personal creative work exploding the world like a bomb, fusing necessity into freedom. What does it mean "to live?" To live means to have, to know, to be capable. To be capable means to be able to preserve every life (one's own, a stranger's, a friend's). To be capable means to be capable of resurrection — this is the goal of life. Therefore art is always tragic, while tragedy is always religious. An integrated personality is necessary for the creation of life: we have lost this and with anguish turn to the ancient past. Prehistoric man was integrated, harmonious, rhythmic: he was never crushed by the heterogeneity of the forms of life. He was himself his own form, and consciousness of life was defined by creative work... In this chain of bold aphorisms, suggesting the paradoxical doctrine of Nikolai Fedorov about the resurrection of the dead by the power of human creation, one is struck by the utopia of the "harmonious man" of the Stone Age. The poet's face, turned toward the future transformation of the world, suddenly pivots sharply toward the prehistoric past. It turns out that his ideal is "primordial man." In the article "The Song of Life," he develops the idea of the explosive nature of creative work. Creative work is a torrent of music which in our time explodes all forms of art. A day will come when this "fire-breathing lava" will also drown the old world. Creative work is a song which, like an arc, bears us over the waves of chaos. The word in song is incantation. Bely writes:

We have forgotten that a song is magic, and we will soon begin to understand that if we do not defend ourselves with a magic circle of songs, we will perish in a torrent of music... The song was the beginning of creative work in art. The song summons. The song lives; one lives by song — and endures. Endurance is Orpheus, an image evoked by song. The highest point of music is the symphony; the highest point of poetry is the tragedy... In deeds, in words, in feelings, man is the minnesinger of his own life; and life is a song.

The author pathetically concludes:

We need a musical program divided into songs (heroic feats), and we do not have a single song of our own. This means that we do not have our own pitch in our souls, and we are absolutely not ourselves, but someone's shades; and our souls are unresurrected Eurydices quietly sleeping on the Lethe of forgetfulness. But Lethe is rising from the banks. It will drown us if we do not hear the summoning song of Orpheus. Orpheus is calling his Eurydice.

These articles contain Bely's highest achievements in "Rickertian" criticism. It is true that he recarved Rickert's theory of the creation of values in his own image, but in his doctrine of the musical force of art creating a new beautiful reality and leading mankind to a universal resurrection, there is genuine depth and poetry.

In two historical and literary articles, "Symbolism" and "Symbolism and Modern Russian Art," the author asserts with new strength the necessity for the transformation of art into life: the artist must be made in his own image, art must be pre-embodied in the religion of life, "the word" must become "the flesh." There follows a survey of the different schools of Russian "modernism" from the group of writers at *Knowledge* to Bryusov's pleiad united around the *Scales*. In art, Bely maintains, there can be absolutely no realism, or estheticism, or impressionism: all these are extinct forms. Contemporaneity knows only one art — Symbolism.[8]

Bely spent the summer of 1908 at the Silver Well Estate and at Sergei Soloviev's Dedovo. He prepared the collection of poems, *Ashes,* for publication. In August, he visited the Merezhkovskys for ten days in Suid, near Petersburg. During the autumn in Moscow, the previous exhaustingly bustling life was renewed: the *Scales,* the Esthetics Society, the Religious Philosophical Society, meetings in the House of Song of the d'Alheims. At that time, the editor of *Russian Thought,* P. B. Struve, was reorganizing the journal. For a very brief period of time, Merezhkovsky headed the literary department; after his departure, Bryusov became the head of the department. The *Scales* was enduring an acute crisis. The official editor and publisher, S. A. Polyakov, wanted to discontinue publication. With difficulty, he was persuaded to continue the *Scales* for one more year. A committee was formed of Polyakov, Bryusov, Baltrushaitis, Likiardopulo, Soloviev, Ellis and Bely. Bryusov lost interest in the journal. Bely became head of the essay department and, in essence, of the whole "ideological tendency." Toward the end of the year, the decomposition of the group of "Scalians" was marked. Bely parted ways with Bryusov, quarreled with Ellis and with Sergei Soloviev. During the autumn, Bely went to Petersburg for several days: at the invitation of V. F. Kommissarzhevskaya, he gave a short lecture on Przybyszewski before the performance of his play, *Eternal Fairy Tale*. He recalls his meeting with the famous artist in the book, *Between Two Revolutions*:

> While I was shooting my lightning from the stage against Przybyszewski, my glance was attracted involuntarily by a small woman in black with a hat with a tremendous brim, sitting before me in the boxes; to judge by her figure, she was a young girl (pale, quiet), but the hat was a woman's; two blue-gray-green tremendous eyes electrified me from their dark orbits.

After the performance, Bely visited her in the dressing room:

> She stood before me austerely and timidly, gazing expectantly, without words: teachers at the gymnasium stand like this before the inspector, in expectation of a question; her little face pale, lips pressed together like a child's.

The end of the year was marked for Bely by a quarrel with the Merezhkovskys. Dmitry Sergeevich came to Moscow and gave lectures at the Morozova house, at the University and in the Polytechnic Museum (on Lermontov). Bely came to the defense of Merezhkovsky's ideas, although he was not fully in agreement with them; therefore his tone was forced, and his defense came out unconvincingly. After the departure of the lector, he felt that "everything had fallen to pieces" between them. Thus, the year ended in a breaking off of almost all relations with friends. Bely locked himself in his green study; he did not respond to callers and went nowhere. He felt an ebbing of his powers. Often he would say to Medtner: "It's impossible to live this way." He was swallowed up in anguish — the old anguish of unhappy love. During these dark lonely days, a pamphlet by Anna Bezant came into his hands; it interested him, and he began to study the Doctrine Secrèt of H. Blavatsky and to visit the theosophical circle of K. P. Khristoforova. At the end of 1908, Bely entered a new occult period in his life.

The Eglantine publishing house published the second collection of Bely's poems, *Ashes*, at the end of 1908, with the designation of 1909 on the cover. The book is dedicated to "the memory of Nekrasov." In the introduction, the author writes:

> Yes, the pearly dawn, and the pot houses, and the bourgeois cell, and the heavens above, and the sufferings of the proletariat — all are the subject of artistic creation. The pearly dawn is no higher than the pot house, because both one and the other in artistic depiction are symbols of a certain reality: fantasy, everyday life, tendentiousness, philosophi-

97

cal meditations are predetermined in art by the artist's relationship to life. And therefore, reality is always higher than art, and therefore the artist is a man before all else.

The author emphasizes the historical significance of his poems:

The picture of the ravines overgrown with weeds and little villages is a living symbol of the destruction and death of the patriarchal way of life. This death and this destruction are washing away villages and estates in a sweeping wave; the delirium of capitalistic culture is growing in the cities.

In the first section, entitled "Russia," a long poem grows from the verses "On the Remote, Unawakened Expanses of the Russian Land." From mystical dawns and prayers inspired by the lyrics of Vladimir Soloviev, Bely passes into the world of Nekrasov's "sobbing muse." He tries to free himself from the traces of his former Decadence, to mold severe and firm verse. The Nekrasovian lament for the people's sorrow is transformed in him into funereal sobbing. This is no longer the narodnik's[9] grief, not the tears of a repentant nobleman, but the ominous song of the ruin of the native land, of its "accursed" destiny:

> Fateful land, icy land,
> Damned by an iron fate —
> Mother Russia, oh evil native land,
> Who could play you such a trick?

The verses on Russia are suggested to the poet by an infinite, endless despair. And here the point is not at all in the "destruction of the patriarchal way of life"; Bely sees Russia not on an historical, but on a metaphysical plane. For him Russia is the symbol of death and destruction. There is unique tragic majesty in this monstrously gloomy prayer for the dying to his motherland. The section begins with the famous poem, "Despair:"

> Enough! Do not wait, do note hope, —
> Disperse, my unhappy people!
> Vanish into space and be shattered
> Year after agonizing year.
>
> * * *
>
> Ages of poverty and bondage...
> Give me leave, oh native motherland,
> In the damp, in the empty expanse,
> In your expanse to sob and sob.

* * *

Where out of the night there gaze at my soul,
Hovering over a web of hillocks,
The cruel yellow eyes
Of your crazy taverns.

* * *

There — where the dashing track
Of death and illness has passed —
Vanish into space, vanish,
Russia, Russia mine!

The frenzied, sobbing sounds speak of the "fateful inheritance" of the
soul of the Russian people. The Raskolniki[10] who immolated themselves
were seized by such a passion for destruction.

The poet finds thorny, grinding sounds for the depiction of country
life:

There bristles the peasant hut
Of crooked-mouthed construction,
Like gray old women
In a half-witted crowd.

Their backs "bristle up like dry wool"; there is dead silence here; "nothing is expected" here.

Days after days, year after year...
Again: after a year, a year...
Crop failure after crop failure...
Here is the god-forsaken people.
("The Country")

God-forsaken expanses, an empty road; a wanderer with a bundle on a
stick over his shoulder, a striped post...

Shaggy clouds of smoke fly up
Over the tops of stunted birches.
("On the Rails")

The poem, "From the Window of the Train" rings in lacerating song,
broad and mournful:

They fly by: so emptily, so nakedly —
They fly by — over there and now over here —

99

They fly by — after villages, villages...
They fly by: after everything, everything.

This four-times repeated single beginning "they fly by" gives to this
phrase a special plaintive slowness... And once again — Russian "squalor":

And a graveyard, and a pot house, and a child
Sleeping there at the breast:
There are squalid flocks of huts,
There are squalid flocks of people.

Again the repetitions strengthen the dreary monotony of the melody.
And finally, the "sobbing" address to Russia:

Mother Russia, my songs are for thee,
Oh mute, severe mother;
Here let me more god-forsakenly and more obscurely
Sob out my good-for-nothing life...

The poet has divined the lyrical manner of the folk lament.
The notes of the traveler are very expressive: the strip of the railroad,
the green needle of the semaphore:

The shabby form of a soldier,
Porters, tears, a whistle.
                    ("In the Train")

The station:

The station: in the fires of the buffet,
An old man of respectable age
Over a fried cutlet,
Waves his epaulette.
                    ("The Station")

In the window, the telegraphist chirrs with dispatches; he has little children, a pregnant wife, twenty-five rubles for a salary.

Extended in eternal sleep
Is the space, the time of God
And life and life's goal
The railroad
A cold bed.
                    ("The Telegraphist")

100

And in the woods, in a scarlet sunset, lies a run-away convict; he caresses his native soil and the "rusted chains on his legs"; he drearily gazes from the slope at his native village ("The Convict"). On the steppe, prisoners are walking and they sing a jail song:

> They have shackled our legs for us
> in chains,
> In the mornings we remember
> the steppes.
> ("The Prisoner")

Wanderers, beggars, solitary pilgrims, convicts, prisoners, bandits — all of dark, wandering, luckless Rus' moves in the darkness along unawakening expanses; the tenacious weeds extend beyond Rus' like relentless "Sorrow-Misfortune":[11]

> Behind me rustles up to the village
> The thorny, malicious undergrowth...
> I drink, I stroll in the cook-shop.
> My rags are covered with mud.
> ("The Weeds")

In resinging folk songs, Bely attempts to make his verse similar to the rhythm and quality of folk lyrics. A peasant youth does not depart for a "wandering," but for a "little wandering," speaks not with "sorrow," but with "sorrowing sorrow." The "solitary little orphan" goes to holy places in order to cure himself of drunkenness and, while going, keeps repeating:

> On the path — on the little road
> Carry me, dear legs —
> Along the fields, along the bushes,
> Along the holy places.
> ("The Aspen Grove")

This folkishness, however artistic, nevertheless remains a stylization. More successful are the experiments at a rhythmic transmission of the dancing tunes. The poem "Making Merry in Rus' " is masterfully "rendered."

> As we carried in flask after flask —
> We drank the fiery liquid.
> And I
> Drank my fill,
> And I
> Danced my fill.

101

The deacon, the scribe, the priest, the sexton
Flocked to the meadow.
Ekh,
A sin for men!
Ekh — a laugh for the hen!
In a trepak-trepak we went boldly,
In a trepak, my soul, go, go to it, pour forth!
What is there to think, what to expect:
To puff, to spit, to not give a damn;
To not give a damn, and trample about,
To make merry, to live and guzzle.

After the trepak comes the komarinskaya:

You are such a komarinsky fool,
You go and go from the little road to the pot house,
Ai, liuli-liuli, liuli-liuli, liuli:
The pot houses have gone all over Rus'!
("Komarinskaya song")

The "Poems on Russia" conclude with the dreary question:

The ranging array of expanses:
In the expanses, expanses are hidden.
Russia, where am I to run,
From hunger, pestilence and drunkeness?
("Rus' ")

In one and the same year both Blok and Bely were writing poems about Russia; their lyrical themes are similar: a dark, poor, fateful country, limitless expanses, wretched huts, vagrant and wandering elemental force. The paths of the two poets again mysteriously crossed: both, from the "dawns" of Soloviev, had moved on to the "groan" of Nekrasov. Bely's populism echoes Blok's populism. Once again, their mystical connection is revealed. And again, in this similarity, there is so much difference. Bely's poems about Russia are perhaps the best of his poetic creations: in form and mastery — rhythmic diversity, literary ingenuity, the wealth of sounds — they perhaps surpass Blok's poems. And yet, they are incommensurate with Blok's artistically. In Blok, a light shines in the darkness, the beautiful face of the Woman — native land is radiant; in Bely the motherland is lying in a coffin. Blok loves and admires, trembles with ecstasy and torment; Bely recites a funeral prayer and revels in decay. For the former — a burning wind, air torn by the leap of the mare of the steppes; for the latter — the asphyxia of the crypt, the pot house and the jail. Blok sees Russia through the "tears of his first love;" Bely adjures:

102

Vanish into space, vanish
Russia, Russia mine!

* * *

The second section of *Ashes* is entitled "The Country." In the meter
and style of Nekrasov's *The Peddlars*, the author tells an artless story of love
and death. A merchant says to a maiden:

> Stroll with me for the summer:
> I, little friend, on you
> A scarf of canary color
> Will tie.

But the maiden loves another:

> He is tall, black-browed,
> A trim young man —
> For a ruble
> He brought her a carpet scarf.[12]

The rejected merchant sharpens a knife against his rival in the thick rye:

> I will carry you off, my love,
> To the ditch by the sea,
> Days will pass: at peace, sinful,
> I'll drag myself to Sarov.

The youth goes to the rural district office. He pushes his cap gaily back
on his head. Happily he remembers how he and his girl love each other.

> In the lilac bluebells,
> Hugging each other tight,
> Among the honey-bearing lilac bluebells,
> Among the silken grasses.

On the steppe, the merchant finds him and stabs him "in the breast with
a sharp knife up to the handle." The murderer runs to the town "along
crooked alleys straight to the pot house." The poem "In the Little Town" is
very expressive.

> Hands at my sides: hey, my swans,
> It's time for you to dance.
> Pour some vodka into a glass for me —
> Caress me, sister.

* * *

Somewhere there is a sobbing sound —
Somewhere there is an organ...
Give me herring with onions!
Unlace your girdle.

* * *

Hey, from where, hey, do you know
Have I appeared?
Tryndy — tryndy, balalaika,
Trykalka[13] mine!

* * *

And the merchant ends his life on the gallows:

They twirled the noose cleverly.
The blood turns to ice.
The rope swung.
"Hey, don't argue!"

The third section is "The City." In a number of poems, the poet depicts
the illusiveness of the contemporary city. People are masks; life is a masquerade. Among the dancing corpses appears the red domino, Fate.

The guest enters, click the dice,
The shroud blows back: the guest is death.

* * *

The guest: — the mute, fateful,
Fiery domino,
His unliving head
Inclined over his hostess,
Waits. And aside, in a light lilt:
"You are destined to perish!"
Over the hostess, inadvertently
The domino rustled.
("The Masquerade")

And again the red domino:

Who are you, who are you, stern guest? —
What do you want, domino?
But, covering himself in his crimson cloak,
He moves away.
("The Holiday")

104

In a restaurant, in a separate room, an old man caresses a horsewoman; the red domino breaks in and stabs him with a dagger.

> The mute domino bent
> Over him; he spilled forth
> Satins in a scarlet radiance —
> And again, waving a wing of the satin mask,
> Wiping the bood from the dagger,
> He circles around the garden in a dance.
>   ("In the Summer Garden")

And finally, the "Satanic depths" of the red domino are revealed.

> He is in a black mask, in a light red toga
> And the toga flies up like swishing silk.
> He proclaims: "You will be like gods."
> He has come. He stands. But the square has emptied.
>   ("On the Square")

Thus, in the midst of the city madness — at balls, masquerades, banquets, on the squares and streets — the devil passes. Bely's red domino, connecting the themes of *Ashes* with the theme of the novel *Petersburg*, is connected with Gogol's "Red Jacket,"[14] which haunted the poet's imagination during the years of revolution.

The year 1905 is reflected in the poems: "The Banquet," "Reproach," and "The Funeral." Crowds of workers go from the factory; barricades are erected; red banners wave. But the poet and his friends make merry in the "Aquarium." The guitar resounds; a Hungarian dances wildly.

> Leaning on the table, I began to cry,
> Forseeing the finger of iron fate:
> "Rejoice, drunken friends,
> Over the gaping abyss."
>   ("The Banquet")

The poet reproaches a beauty in silks and laces:

> There my people is without shelter; my
> Stern people is in poverty and captivity.
> My leaden gaze troubles you.
> You will drown in expensive Valenciennes.
>   ("Reproach")

And again a crowd of workers, dragoons, the clatter of revolvers:

105

The melody of the funeral is more remote.
Bullets both cry and cut down.
New clouds of bloody banners
Are carried into the distance there.
("The Funeral")

The fourth section of *Ashes*, "Madness," with its delirious stammering, resembles the symphony, *A Goblet of Blizzards*. A prophet, driven from the cities and stoned, performs religious rites in the fields, among the thistles; he has a "grass Bible"; his clergy is turnips, his congregation flowers; he is a free priest, hand-picked by a "porphyritic bush." This blasphemous bad taste the poet proudly called "esoteric"; his contemporaries considered it pathological.

The leit-motif of Bely's poetry during the period of his tragic love for Blok's wife is the theme of death and burial. He sees himself in the coffin, mourns, performs a requiem for himself, buries himself and gives the funeral sermon:

...around
Are the bride, the mistress, the friend,
And a crimson bunch of flowers,
While with me, no one,
Nothing.
("Funeral Service")

The thought that the one who had tortured him during his life would have pity on him as a dead man is especially sweet:

My bride began to sob;
Making the sign of the cross on my pale forehead

* * *

She bent toward me;
I scorched her with ice.
The ring shone
On my finger.
Dilino — bimbom.

And now the coffin is carried out:

And the silver of the
Catafalque floats.
They are singing
But I do not heed.
And I

Pity
Pity
Pity
The earth.

* * *

They carry me
To the Last Judgment:

* * *

("The Removal")

From the funereal cycle, the poem "To Friends," which it is impossible to read without agonizing pity, stands out. There is so much sincere sorrow and anguish for love in it that we forget about the insanities and blasphemies and see only an unhappy human being.

I trusted the gold brilliance,
But died from the sun's arrows[15]
I measured the centuries in thought
But could not live my own life well.

* * *

Do not mock the deceased poet;
Bring him a wreath.
On the cross during summer and winter
My porcelain wreath will wave.

* * *

I loved only the ringing of the bells
And — the sunset.
Why am I in such pain, such pain!
I am not to blame!

* * *

Have pity on me. Come to me;
I will wave the wreath toward you,
Oh, love me, come to love me —
I perhaps have not died, perhaps I will awake —
And return...

The touching, child-like helplessness in the words: "I perhaps have not died..."

In the last section, "Gleams of Hope," there are several lyrical poems dedicated to love departed. Despair and rapture over ruin are replaced by reconciled sadness. The poet recalls a summer day, a whirling field, cornflowers in the rye; wrapped in a shawl, he admires the "gold fountain" of the ears of

107

corn.

> I said: "Do not forget,"
> Giving you a little azure bouquet.
> You — resting your head on my breast.
> You kissed flower after flower.
> ("A Stroll")

> And everything passed. From the gold fire, ashes remained:
> On the road the dead flowers
> Soared upward in the wind.
> You do not love me; you have forgotten
> You have forgotten everything!
> ("Remember")

And *Ashes* concludes with the sorrowful verses:

> I raise my sleepless eyes,
> Eyes,
> Full of tears and fire,
> Into the gaps of gaping night,
> In the evening reflections of day.
> ("Calm")

Such is the complex, diverse and multi-styled content of the collection. In comparison with *Gold in Azure, Ashes* is a book more mature and technically perfect. Bely often achieves a high level of stylistic mastery. In his poems, blinding lines ignite suddenly, captivating strophes resound, but he rarely succeeds in completed poems. He is an improvisor of genius and a bad composer; his verses are complex, conglomerate, but never not constructed. Hence his formal research: the sound orchestration, the rhythmic approaches, the overload of images and metaphors. He attempts with these technical methods to hide the internal disharmony of his lyrics.

Chapter Five (1909-1912)

In January, 1909, Bely went to Petersburg for several days and gave a lecture on "The Present and Future of Russian Literature." Zinaida Gippius and Vyacheslav Ivanov were present at the lecture. Ivanov approached the lector, told him that his collection, *Ashes,* was a major literary event, and asked him to come for a visit after the lecture to talk about it. Zinaida whispered, "Listen, if you go to Vyacheslav, I will never forgive you." But Bely went nevertheless. After the death of Ivanov's wife, Lidia Dmitrievna Zinovieva-Annibal, in 1907, great changes had taken place at the Tower. The mistress of the house was M. M. Zamyatina, a friend of the deceased; an unusual and puzzling being, the occultist Anna Rudolfna Mintslova, moved in at the Tower with her. Bely describes her:

> Large-headed, corpulently clumsy, cut off from everything, as if in cosmic space with its Torricellian emptiness of huge dimensions, in her black shift, she loomed up before me momentarily.... She thrust her heavy head between us. Her yellow mane stuck up above her; and however much she tried to comb it, it stuck out like snakes, tufts, over the immense forehead without eyebrows; and her small, half-blind, liquid-blue eyes squinted.

Vyacheslav Ivanov, Minstlova and Bely struck up a conversation which lasted all night. From those with whom he was speaking, the poet found out that in *Ashes* he had unconsciously portrayed the witchcraft pouring out all over Russia; that, in reality, there exist "enemies" poisoning Russia with bad fluids. Eastern occultists were acting on the subconscious of the best Russian people, shooting poisoned arrows at them from the dark world. Therefore, the respresentatives of culture, "the princes of the destinies of culture," as Vyacheslav Ivanov put it, must forget their differences and form a noble brotherhood to serve the Spirit and the Truth. Then powerful forces of light will arise, saving Russia from the destruction which is moving in from the East. These thoughts amazed Bely with their resemblance to the idea of the dying Vladimir Soloviev about "panmongolism," and completely corresponded to the persecution mania growing within him. The idea of a new order drew him close to Vyacheslav Ivanov, with whom he had so recently engaged in cruel polemics. On the following day, the conversation was resumed. Bely did not return to the Merezhkovskys; they appeared to him now as "possessed by evil powers." Upon his return to Moscow, he wrote frankly of this to Dmitry Sergeevich; their relations were discontinued.

In the same January, in a literary and artistic circle, an "incident" occurred with Bely, described by Boris Zaitsev in his memoirs:[1]

After the lecture, receptions began, attended, among others, by the bellettrist Tishchenko, known by the fact that Lev Tolstoi had proclaimed him to be the best contemporary Russian writer. This Tishchenko was quite an undistinguished person, plain, not at all belligerent — how he happened to excite Bely I do not know. But the argument on the platform before hundreds of listeners came to the point where Bely drew himself up and "screamed": "I will fight you physically!"

What happened further, Bely himself relates:

An indescribable scandal began; Berdyaev seized me; water was brought for me, and the writer I had insulted was surrounded and soothed; there were shouts of "Curtain! Curtain!" The audience jumped up. Chairs were overturned in the hall. Anna Mintslova led me away; the excited Gershenzon caught up with us.

Again, according to Zaitsev's account:

A picture on the huge stairway: Andrei Bely descending from the top in a crowd of friends. All around — noise, uproar. Bely, in a half-faint, leaning on his companions, hardly able to move his legs, slumped completely down like a Pierrot. They got him downstairs and took him away. The duel was to be the next day.

The following morning, Zaitsev and Sokolov, the publisher of Griffon, went to Bely in Denezhny Lane. Zaitsev writes:

On that morning, Bely was absolutely white ["belyi"], almost in hysterics; he had not undressed or gone to bed, and paced around his study all night.... Giving vent to his feelings in front of us, as it appears, he admitted that the preceeding evening he had gone too far. He said words to the effect that "Tishchenko is nothing! It is not Tishchenko. There is no Tishchenko; he is a likeness, a mask. I didn't mean to insult him. Tishchenko is even likeable... but through his features, something else shone out at me, you see: the force of chaos, the force of darkness, you see" (Bely rolled his head back, his eyes grew wide, he somehow gurgled in his throat, making a sound like m... m... m..., as if it were they, these forces). "The enemies were using the inoffensive Tishchenko; he is innoffensive. A pocket-sized little man, a dear dwarf; yes, I even love Tishchenko.... Tishchenko is modest.... Tishchenko is good...." At our insistence, Bely wrote a letter, an apology, which Sokolov transmitted to the necessary quarters.

The incident "crushed" Bely. A. S. Petrovsky took him to the Rachinskys' estate, Bobrovka (in Tverskaya Guberniya). There he lived alone in the gloomy old house of many rooms decorated with pictures of ancestors, with a huge library. Around the house a pine forest (with owls and eagle owls) showed black. A deaf-mute old man was his servant. Bely worked with enthusiasm on the morphology of iambic tetrameter and collected materials on rhythm. In the evening, he read books on alchemy, astrology and the Cabala. It was here, in the estate buried in snow-drifts, that he began to write his first novel, *The Silver Dove.*

Bely ascribes a special mystical significance to his presence at Bobrovka. It is the watershed of two periods in his life: one from 1901 embraces seven years; the other, from 1909 to 1916, is another seven-year period. The first period is the path from pessimism to the problems of Vladimir Soloviev and Symbolism; it ends with the attempt to substantiate Symbolism. The second period is the path from Symbolism to the symbology of secret knowledge, the path of self-knowledge. He writes:

> The first epoch is the epoch of the "symphonies," the second — of novels. The first seven-year period is connected with Scorpion and Griffon, the second — with Musaget and *Spiritual Knowledge.* The first seven-year period I was in Russia, the second is adorned with travels; the first — in a circle of friends, the second — with Asya. The first seven-year period — a heart-felt friendship with the Merezhkovskys, the second — various encounters with Vyacheslav Ivanov.

After returning from Bobrovka to Moscow, in the home of Maria d'Alheim, Bely met her niece, Anna Alexeevna Turgeneva, who had arrived from Belgium where she was studying engraving. She made sketches of him and soon a great friendship sprang up between them. Bely paints a picture of his future wife:

> The appearance of a little girl with drooping ashen curls: she was eighteen years old. Her eyes could gaze into the soul. A little wrinkle would cut into her large masculine forehead hidden in hair: you wouldn't want to cause it to appear again; and suddenly she would smile, smoking a cigarette: the smile of a child.

In May, Bely fled from Moscow to the Savvinsky Monastery near Zvenigorod with Asya, her sister Natasha, A. M. Pozzo and A. S. Petrovsky; they stayed there for five days. They sent Petrovsky to Moscow for money in order to pay the hotel bill. Then Asya left for Volyn to visit her dying grandmother, and from there to Brussels to finish her engraving school. In Moscow, Bely met Mintslova, who strengthened him in his intention to create a "Brotherhood of Knightly Armed People;" he began to agitate in youth circles. His idea was taken up by Medtner, Ellis and Petrovsky. As was his custom, he spent the summer with Sergei Soloviev in Dedovo, but the friends began to have differences: Sergei Mikhailovich had no sympathy for theosophy and occultism. Bely was writing *The Silver Dove* and corresponding with Asya assiduously.

During the autumn, a new publishing house, Musaget, was organized in Moscow. Rachinsky, Petrovsky, Sizov, Kiselev and V. Nilender were affiliated with it; the editorial trinity was composed of Medtner, Bely and Ellis. Medtner became haughty and peremptory in his role as editor. "The appearance and tone of editor," writes Bely, "did not suit Medtner, while the stubbornness with which he tried to force his new aspect upon me led only to the result that after a year I lived with the single thought of flight from Moscow."

That same autumn, the philosphers F. A. Stepun and S. I. Hessen arrived from Freiburg; they were seeking publishers for a Russian division of the international philosophical journal, *Logos*. Musaget offered them its services. Soon Musaget broke into three publishing companies: Musaget itself, with literary goals; Logos, attempting to find a philosophical basis for problems of culture, and Orpheus, devoting itself to mystical matters. These three tendencies — esthetic, philosophical and mystical — were in a state of inner conflict.

But three new publishing houses did not exhaust the Moscow abundance of 1909. In addition to Musaget, Logos and Orpheus, a fourth religious-philosphical publishing house, the Path, arose, supported by M. K. Morozova and uniting around it Berdyaev, Bulgakov, Prince E. N. Trubetskoi, Gershenzon and Rachinsky. The old strongholds of Symbolism, the *Scales* and the *Golden Fleece*, ceased publication.

Bely spent the end of the year in intense work: he finished writing *The Silver Dove* for the last issues of the *Scales* and prepared for publication two collections of articles: *Arabesques* and *Symbolism*. He was obliged to select and edit a number of articles and notes. With *Arabesques*, the matter was relatively simple: everything concrete, graphic, aphoristic, was selected for them. With *Symbolism*, it was more difficult; only theoretical articles were intended for this collection. In the book *Between Two Revolutions*, Bely writes:

I wavered more than once: was it worth it to publish this loose, awkward book? Its chapters were written by me in different years, embracing articles with an obvious surplus of Schopenhauer, and articles written under the influence of Wundt-Höffding, and articles reflecting the style of neo-Kantian treatises. None of these could reflect my theories of Symbolism.... The theory of Symbolism has not been written, but in return, the clay colossus (500 or more pages), *Symbolism*, whose looseness I sensed even then, lives as a monument of the epoch; the heap of shouting, contradictory articles is the reflection of my stormily agonizing life.

Bely would rush home from meetings at Musaget and feverishly scribble the 250 pages of commentary to *Symbolism*, outlining with the speed of lightning the plan for the theory of Symbolism, together with articles on rhythm (calculations, tables). He writes:

The dawn would find me at work. After sleeping until two in the afternoon, I would rush to work, not even going out to the dining room for tea (it was brought in to me) and at 5:30 would rush out to do my duty: to serve time at Musaget and give courage to the staff of collaborators, so that, running home at midnight, I might again calculate and write until morning. For weeks, my study presented a strange sight: the arm chairs pushed together in order to clear the space of the rug; on it, like a fan, were two dozen open books (references, excerpts); in the middle of the fan, lying on my stomach on the rug, I spent hours scribbling commentaries; my hand flew along the books; I worked furiously.

In 1909, the second and last meeting of Bely and Kommissarzhevskaya took place. She arrived on tour in Moscow. After the performance, Bely delivered the speech of welcome for her. She asked him to visit her at the theater. They went to Petrovsky Park in a cab, and she told him about her idea of creating an actor; but for this, it would be necessary to create a new man. Kommissarzhevskaya had a grandiose pedagogical plan: nurseries, schools, a theatrical university. She asked for Bely's assistance:

"Understand." She took me by the hand and gazed up and down into my eyes. "I am bringing you my infant." And she brought her two hands to my chest. "Can it be that you will not smile at him, that you will turn away and pass by?"

They spoke excitedly for a long time. They accompanied each other endlessly... Several months later, Kommissarzhevskaya died suddenly in Tashkent.

In 1909, Bely wrote his most significant articles on Symbolism: they sum up his intense meditations of many years about the new art, and make a final attempt at a philosophical basis for the theory of Symbolism. A number of these investigations are revealed in the articles in *Symbolism*. Where are the sources of contemporary art to be sought, the author asks. Some find them in Classicism, others in Romanticism. But both are immaterial. The new school is inspired by the consciousness of the uncrossable boundary between it and the recent epoch. This finds expression in a crisis of world-view. Contemporary artists are dimly aware that they stand on the border of two major periods in the development of mankind. Bely writes:

We are corpses corrupting the old life, but we are not yet born to the new life.... Over us sounds the categorical imperative of inevitable death or creation during life.... The sunset of the analytical period benumbs us, and we are revivified by the dawn of a new day.

The next article, "The Problem of Culture," refines the definition of Symbolism. The new art proclaims the primacy of creative work over knowledge, affirms the possibility of transforming reality in the artistic act. The goal of Symbolism is the re-creation of personality, the discovery of more perfect forms of life. Symbolist art in essence is profoundly religious.

In the large treatise, "The Emblematics of Meaning," the author constructs a system of Symbolism on the basis of Rickertian philosophy. In the foreword we read:

In "The Emblematics of Meaning," I give a negative foundation to the doctrine of Symbolism: its positive delineation I am postponing. I consider it necessary here only to say that Symbolism for me is a kind of religious creed having its own dogmas.

Here are the basic theses of Bely's "system." There is no scientific world-view, nor can there be any; science goes from lack of knowledge to lack of knowledge; science is the systematization of all lacks of knowledge.

According to Rickert, knowledge is also the transformation of reality; it occurs by means of the creation of idea-images, by means of symbolization. All reality flies by like a dream, and only in creation do reality, value and the meaning of life remain. The artist creates values from his inner experiences: their emblems in art are the images of the über-menchen and gods. Thus art naturally moves into mythology and religion. The more profound and powerful the personal experience, the sooner it is perceived as a value. Then the individual experience becomes individually collective (the experiences of artists, poets); the individually collective experience later may become universal as well (the experience of Christianity). The personality is rendered a symbol of a value, i.e., the visage, the living image of Logos.

The meaning and value of our activity lie in the creation of life. We are obliged to throw ourselves into the chaos of life and, when we have done so, we begin to understand that it is not chaos, but cosmos.

The musical elemental force of the world resounds in the roar of the chaotic waves of life.... In our own selves we must find the strength to say to this life our "yes" or our "no." If we say "no," we have perished. If all our being, opposing the meaninglessness, against common sense, pronounces "yes," the light of the final affirmation bursts out before us, and we hear the eternal hosannah of the universe. Thus experience creates values; in personal experience, the given is transformed into the necessary and the necessary into the true. The Freiburg school advances two fundamental judgments: "the true is the necessary," and "the necessary is a value." In reality, the condition upon us seems to be chaos; but as soon as we begin to experience it, it seems to us that the world is filled with "gods," demons and spirits. The chaos we have experienced is no longer chaos; we become the image of Logos, organizing chaos. We gain knowledge in experiencing. This knowledge is not knowledge; it is creation.

A symbol is the unity of form and content, the given in individual experience. The symbolic image is experienced more like religious symbolism than esthetic symbolism. The article concludes with the following prediction:

The future theory of Symbolism will have to base the very theory of knowledge on metaphysics, and deduce metaphysics from creative work. Most likely, the theory of Symbolism will not be a theory at all, but a new religious and philosophical doctrine predetermining the entire course of the development of Western European thought.

Neo-Kantian idealism is carried to the ultimate extreme in Bely's system. Outside of the creative spirit the world is chaos; consciousness ("experience") creates reality, organizes it according to the categories of the necessary, the true and the value. There is no ontology behind these concepts other than personal experience. Therefore, the artist is not only a creator of words and images, but also a demiurg, creating worlds. Art becomes theurgy. This theory is the Luciferian summit on which any art is ended. Bely believes that Symbolism is no longer art, but religious deed. Culture is exhausted, mankind stands before the transformation of the world and the new appearance of God.

The daring hope of the poet was not fated to come true. But in the hasty syntheses of Bely, this "too early forerunner of a too slow spring" (Merezhkovsky's words), there were flashes of genius. The affirmation of the primacy of creative work over knowledge, the definition of a symbol as an "individual image of experience" and as the unity of form and content, the delineation of the religious basis of art and the declaration that its ultimate goal is the transformation of the world — all these ideas entered the Russian esthetic consciousness forever. The theory of Symbolism was not constructed, for a "religious creed" is not "constructed." And all the same, Bely laid the path to a future "theory of art."

After the cycle of theoretical articles, there are a number of articles devoted to an experimental study of rhythm. Here Bely is in truth a discoverer of new lands and the teacher of a brilliant pleiad of young researchers. His still very incomplete attempts at the formal analysis of verse created an entire school of so-called "Formalists." He called into being the "science of verse," the study of Russian metrics, rhythmics, sound orchestration, the eidology of thematics, composition. Russian "poetics," the youngest of all the philological sciences, is indebted to him for its birth.

In the article "Lyrics and Experiment," Bely maintains that esthetics is entirely possible as a precise science: its material is the form of the artistic work. Let us take, for example, Nekrasov's "Death of a Peasant." This poem may be studied from the point of view of 1) the length of the words; 2) the symmetry of the words; 3) the arrangement of the verbs, nouns and adjectives; 4) the combination of vowels; and 5) rhythmics.

Rhythm is the basis of poetry, the most important and least studied sphere of esthetics. The author defines rhythm negatively, as the totality of deviations from the meter. For example, in iambic tetrameter, according to the metrical scheme, there must be four accented syllables.

> Moi *dia*dia, *sa*mykh *che*stnykh *pra*vil
> (My uncle, of most honorable principles)

But in poetic practice, we constantly encounter the ommission of one or even two accents. Thus, in the line

> Kogd*a* ne v *shu*tku zane*mog*
> (When he became seriously ill)

there are only three accented syllables; it falls not into four iambs (u$\acute{-}$/u$\acute{-}$/ u$\acute{-}$/), but into two iambs and into a quadrange with one accent and three unaccented syllables:

> ku zane*mog*
> /u   uu $\acute{-}$/

The quadrangle with the accent on the fourth syllable is conventionally called the fourth peon. In the line

> i *lu*chshe *vy*dumat' ne *mog*
> (and he could think of nothing better)
> u$\acute{-}$/u $\acute{-}$ u u / u $\acute{-}$

the accent is omitted on the third foot; the quadrangle with the accent on the second foot is conventionally called the second peon.

> chshe vydumat'
> / u $\acute{-}$ u   u /

Thus, in Russian iambic tetrameter, we find, instead of a monotonous repetition of four accents, a complex combination of lines with four and two accents, variations of iambs with a second peon and a fourth peon.

116

Bely goes further. He studies the figures of rhythm. Let us take, for example, the following two lines:

Ikh zhizn', kak okean bezbrezhnyi,
Vsia v nastoiashchem razlita.
(Their life, like a boundless ocean
Is all poured into their present.)

Rhythmically, they are portrayed in the following manner:

u ´ / u u u ´ / u ´ / u
u u u ´ / u u u ´ /

That is, the first line consists of an iamb, a fourth peon and an iamb, and the second of two fourth peons. By noting with points the omitted accents and joining them with lines, we obtain the figure of a roof.

Ikh zhizn', kak okean bezbrezhnyi,
Vsia v nastoiashchem razlita.

Let us take another two lines:

V khronologicheskoi pyli
Bytopisaniia zemli.
u u u ´ / u u u ´
u u u ´ / u u u ´
(In the chronological dust
Of the earth's history.)

The lines are rhythmically symmetrical: each consists of two fourth peons. By joining the points of the omitted accents, we obtain the figure of a quadrangle.

V khronologicheskoi pyli
Bytopisaniia zemli

By means of the same method, the author obtains the figures of an overturned roof, a trapezoid and a rectangle of three sides.

Further, Bely moves into a study not of two, but of three complex lines. Of the figures he found, we will note only two: the figure of the rhombus and the figure of the cross.

The figure of the rhombus:

Privychka usladila gore

117

Neotrazimoe nichem
Otkrytie bol'shoe vskore
(Habit sweetened sorrow
Irresistible is
The great discovery soon after)

In the first line, the accent on the second foot ("us") is omitted; in the second line, the accents on the first and third foot ("neot" and "moe") are omitted; in the third line, there is no accent in the second foot.

Privychka usladila gore
Neotrazimoe nichem
Otkrytie bol'shoe vskore

The figure of a rhombus is obtained.
And finally — the figure of the cross:

Kak by prorochestvu nazlo
Vse schastlivo shlo
Za otdalennymi gorami
(As if in spite of the prophecy
Everything went well
Beyond the distant mountains.)

As a result of his research, the author arrives at the conclusion that the more deviations from the meter in a given poem, the more rhythmic it is; rhythm is in inverse proportion to the meter. On the basis of the figures he found, he establishes four rhythmic categories for Russian poets.

In the first category by wealth of rhythm are Tyutchev, Zhukovsky, Pushkin, Lermontov, Baratynsky and Fet; in the second — Yazykov, Polonsky, Karolina Pavlova. To the third belong Nekrasov and the poets of the 18th century; finally, in the rhythmically poorest category are Maikov, Sluchevsky, Alexei Tolstoi and Benediktov.

The author concludes his work with important methodological instructions:

Deviations from meter must be described, studied, systematized. The working of such deviations would lie at the basis of the workings of rhythm in Russian verse. The laws of the deviations would be the laws of poetic rhythms; the laws of poetic rhythms must be compared with the laws of musical rhythms.

In the following article, "An Attempt at a Characterization of Russian Iambic Tetrameter," the author, continuing to draw figures and make calculations, refines his terminology in the process. He defines rhythm as a "certain unity in the sum of deviations from the given metrical form," and the omissions of accents he prefers to call "accelerations." Thus, about the line

Vzryvaia vozmutit' kliuchi
u -́/u u/ u -́   u -́ /
(In exploding to disturb the sources)

it must be said that it bears an acceleration in the second foot.

The presence of accelerations in the second foot we first observe in Batyushkov; the first comparative wealth of accelerations on the first and third foot is noted in Zhukovsky. This allows the investigator to draw an important conclusion: "Not Pushkin," he announces, "but Zhukovsky and Batyushkov are the reformers of Russian iambic tetrameter. Pushkin only normalized the boundaries for all of the following epoch."

The article "A Comparative Morphology of the Rhythm of Russian Lyricists in Iambic Dimeter" is devoted to the first attempt in Russian literature at a rhythmic characterization of the Russian poets, beginning with Pushkin and ending with the Symbolists. The conclusions concerning modern poetry are very interesting:

In almost all headings, Blok is more rhythmic than Vyacheslav Ivanov, while Ivanov is more rhythmic than Bryusov. The most prolific in the sum of concurrences with the best rhythmics is Blok, then Sologub, then Vyacheslav Ivanov, then Bryusov, and then Gorodetsky. In the modernists, neither a revolution in rhythm nor a sharply expressed evolution is observed. In Sologub and Blok, rhythm rises from the Pushkin-like versificatory smoothness of the heritage of Maikov and Alexei Tolstoi to genuine rhythmic breathing.... Bryusov in the best lines of his rhythm approaches Zhukovsky; Blok in the rhythm of his iamb is an original combination of Pavlova and Lermontov; Sologub's iamb is a renewal of the rhythms of Lermontov, Fet and Baratynsky.

The following article is entitled "A. S. Pushkin's 'Sing Not Before Me, Fair Maid' (An Attempt at Description)." Bely gives an exemplary analysis of the artistic form of the poem. This remarkable investigation had huge methodological significance; it opened the eyes of contemporaries to the question of the form of an artistic work.

The author studies the Pushkin poem he has selected from the point of view of meter, rhythm, word instrumentation, architectonics and descriptive forms of speech (epithets, metaphors, metonymy). Enthusiastic over his method, Bely in the concluding words of the article falls into absolutely unjustified, extreme formalism. His imitators and followers go even further along this dangerous path. "The poem does not have its own content," Bely an-

119

nounces; "it arouses this content in us; by itself it is complete form plus naked thought, quite pale and unoriginal." A conclusion unexpected and of small comfort.

An epilogue to Bely's "formalist" investigations is the article "The Magic of Words," in which he summarizes his theory of magical idealism. Neo-Kantian ideas of the value of experiences and creation arrive at completion here. The word is the only reality; around it is emptiness. There is neither God, nor man, nor nature — there is only the Word. It creates the world, objectifies space and time. Creation is designation, i.e., the magic of incantation and exorcism. Bely has an original cosmogony and theogony. He maintains:

> All knowledge is a fireworks of words with which I fill up the emptiness surrounding me. Before, the emptiness was kindled by the fires of images: this was the process of mythological creation. The word gave birth to the image symbol — the metaphor; the metaphor was represented as really existing. The word gave birth to the myth; the myth gave birth to religion; religion to philosophy.... We are still alive, but we are alive because we cling to the word.... Our children will forge from the words which have arisen a new symbol of faith; the crisis of knowledge will seem to them only the death of old words. Mankind is alive while the poetry of language exists; the poetry of language is alive. We are alive.

This is not the religion of Logos, but the religion of the artistic word; in it the "magical idealism" of the Jena romantics (Novalis, Tieck, Wackenroder) is reduced to "magical verbalism." Art occupies the ruling place of religion, and the artist supplants the Creator.

Bely's "formalist" method was subjected to stiff criticism many times. The author's negative definition of rhythm, the schematicism of his tables and drafts, which did not exhaust the living verbal-ideological weave of the poem, were demonstrated to him. The abundance of rhombi, crosses and overturned rooves is only the external sign of rhythm. The rhythmic design is more complex and spiritual than it seems to the investigator. But however the words of the first rhythmologue have aged, their historical significance is tremendous. After the noisy appearance and ignominious disappearance of the "formalists" (S. Bobrov, Brik, Shklovsky), there appeared a school of serious scholars working on questions of Russian poetics (Zhirmunsky, Tynyanov, Vinogradov, Tomashevsky, Yakubinsky, Slonimsky et al.).

On the hundredth anniversary of Gogol's birth, Bely came out with a brilliant article ("Gogol"). The author considers Gogol and Nietzsche "the greatest stylists in all of European art." The poor Symbolists have before now been reproached for their "blue sounds." But neither in Verlaine, nor in Baudelaire, nor in Rimbaud is it possible to find images so unbelievable in their boldness as in Gogol:

All these mincing, snooping and shuffling Perepepenkas, Golopupenkas, Dovgochkuns and Shponkas are not people, but horse-radishes. There are no such people! But to complete the horror, Gogol forces this beast or radish (I don't know what to call it) to dance the mazurka, to offer tobacco.

And the author continues:

> Gogol did not know people; he knew giants and dwarfs. And Gogol did not know the earth: he knew the fog "illumined" by the shine of the moon, or a black vault. Gogol is a quagmire and a summit, mud and snow; but Gogol is no longer earth.... The ecstasy of Gogol is not resolved in the mystery of love, but in a wild dance; everything is transformed not in love, but in a dance of madness.

After Merezhkovsky's work on Gogol, Bely's article is the most remarkable of all that was said in Russian literature about the "Ukrainian wizard." The grade-school legend of Gogol as a realist and depictor of ordinary life was forever destroyed by the Symbolists. This reexamined, fantastical and dreadful Gogol cast a spell on Bely, the author of *The Silver Dove* and *Petersburg*.[2]

In 1909 the Griffon publishing house printed Bely's collection of poems, *The Urn*. The book, dedicated to Valery Bryusov, bears an epigraph from Baratynsky: "All the charms of by-gone days are foreign to one who has been disappointed." Its contents are precisely defined by this melancholy sentiment. *The Urn* is a poem about the poet's unhappy love for Lyubov Dmitrievna Blok; it contains reminiscences, complaints, reproaches, sad reflections, philosophical consolations... The period of embitterment and ferocious rebellion had passed; langorous melancholy and quiet reconciliation remained.

When Bely was preparing his collection for publication, he had already entered upon the path of "initiation" and "secret knowledge." The enthusiasm for occultism is reflected in the foreword to the book:

> In calling my first book of verses *Gold in Azure,* I absolutely failed to connect the symbolic meaning its title bears with this youthful, very imperfect book. Azure is the symbol of lofty initiations; the gold triangle is an attribute of Hiram, the builder of Solomon's temple. What is azure, and what is gold? The Rosicrucians answer this. The world, for a time perceived in gold and azure, throws the one who understands it thus into an abyss, avoiding the path of occultism. The world is consumed, crumbling into ashes; together with it, the perceiver is consumed as well, in order to be resurrected from the dead for the active path. *Ashes* is a book of self-immolation and death; but death itself is only a curtain covering the horizons of the distant, in order to find

them in what is near. In *The Urn*, I am collecting my own ashes so that they do not hide the light from my living "I." The dead "I" is contained in *The Urn*, while the other, living "I" is aroused in me toward the truth. *Gold in Azure* is still far from me... in the future. The sunset azure is sullied with dust and smoke, and only the night-time blue washes the dust with dew. Toward the morning, perhaps, the azure will be cleansed.

The author considers the leit-motif of his book "reflections on the frailty of human nature with its passions and frenzies."

The first two sections of the collection are entitled "Winter" and "Loss of Faith." They contain, in the words of the author, "intense sadness, sometimes deepening into despair, sometimes enlightened by philosophical meditation." The poet experiences bitter disappointment in love; and love, replaced by passion, is scattered in a blizzard. The remembrance of lost happiness is accompanied by the motif of winter, snow, blizzard. The beloved takes on the features of the Snow Queen, cold and merciless; all of life is transformed into a snowy, pervasive maelstrom. This section is connected to the symphony *A Goblet of Blizzards,* on which Bely was working at the same time.

Gold in Azure was written under the influence of Vladimir Soloviev and Fet, *Ashes* was inspired by Nekrasov, and *The Urn* reflects the poetic style of of the beginning of the 19th century; its classical, light and lucid iambs resurrect the traditions of Batyushkov and Baratynsky. The poem "Winter" sounds like Pushkin:

> More powerful than snow, more misty than snow:
> More freshened anew, we breathe.
> I love the country, the early evening
> And the sadness of silver winter.

* * *

> Again I drink in, without sorrow,
> The quiet of the country;
> In my hand a crystal goblet
> Plays with lacey foam.

The poem "The Quarrel," dated 1908, marks the anniversary of the "fateful meeting." The poet addresses the unfaithful one:

> With your mouth was it long ago that you burned
> My mouth to the point of pain, was it long ago,
> You were all toppled over in flowers,
> Wallflowers, roses and magnolias?

* * *

122

And you went away... And evil gazes
In the shadows after the fiery trace.
The pale forehead is bathed
In a wave of hair, a wave of gold.

A voice drones to him "Love has departed!" He goes away into an icy field:

I will lie in a snowy grave
The tortures of unshared love:
You jumped up, above your head
Wringing your hands.

The verses "I Knew It" are just as romantically melodic. The poet dreams of a quiet house; he hears her words: "I will not break the oath." But he knows that this is the silver maiden, a snowstorm come to freeze his heart.

I have known everything by heart for a long time.
Come to an end, fateful fairy tale!
Immeasurable, mute sorrow,
Cold, mute caress!

And here is another remembrance: snowy distances, an empty field, fir trees ("In the Field"). The two are alone. A charming stanza:

I recall/my incorrigible past...
I recall/her face cold and bitter...

A year passes. Now she is alone in a cold home; she approaches a frozen window, sees wolves and a dead moon:

And she orders the shutters to be closed...
Like an aroused conscience,
The midnight wind drones to her
The story of my solitary destiny.

In the poem "Conscience," the poet's complaints, shackled in the armor of Pushkinian style, resound with unforgettable injury:

I gave them all that I had brought:
The doubts of my defeated soul,
The crystals of thought, the pearls of tears,
And the heat of love and song-singing,

* * *

123

And the morning of the living day.
But I became a hindrance to their leisure:
They so tenderly into the snowstorm
Drove me from their home.

The anguish of love whispers thoughts of death:

Can I live? Can I exist? But why should I exist?
Death, strike me down!
("The Path")

or:

Be blind,
Blind death!
Be mute,
Mute night!
("Night")

Now he is in the country; the sounds of Hayden are heard from the house:

What quiet! How ordinary it is all around!
What scanty, fireless sunsets!
Like everyone, even you will pass on, my friend,
my poor friend,
Why does the sea of excitement froth again in my soul?
("Night")

In order to escape the "astringent pain," in order to experience the "priceless loss of priceless days," one must withdraw into himself and reject the "world of phenomena." We move on to the third section of *The Urn* — "philosophical sorrow." "Loss of faith" in love leads the poet to absorption in philosophy. But neither Cohen, nor Natorp, nor Rickert give him consolation. Later, redoing his verses for the Berlin edition of 1923, *Poems*, Bely prepared this section with the following introduction:

After devoting himself to intense occupation with philosophy during 1904-1908, the author came more and more to a consciousness of the ruinous results of a reevaluation of neo-Kantian literature: the philosophies of Cohen, Natorp and Lask influence the world-view, producing a rupture in man into callousness and sensuality. Callous sensuality — that is the result at which the philosophizing gnoseologist arrives: and to him is revealed in grandiloquent flights of thought the visage of Lucifer. Hence the influence of Vrubel in the present verses.... These poems paint the action of abstraction on life: this abstraction acts as a subtle and tempting poison, leaving the entire being of man unquenched and hungry.

In *The Urn*, "philosophical sorrow" is colored with irony:

> Already for a year there has trailed me
> Everywhere a Marburg philosopher.
> My mind he submerges in the night-time gloom
> Of metaphysical questions.
>
> * * *
>
> "Life," he whispers, pausing
> Among the greening graves,
> "Is the metaphysical connection
> Of transcendental premises."
> ("Wisdom")

In the poem "The Tempter," dedicated to Vrubel, a strict and cold guest visiting the poet after a reading of Kant is described:

> Oh, let reason wander anxiously
> Over the heap of faded books...
> And the visage of Lucifer arises
> Like the mirror visage of the moon.

The sections "Tristia" and "Thought" are inspired by the philosophical poetry of Tyutchev and Baratynsky. Bely very artistically imitates the older poets.

Here is a melody in the voice of Tyutchev:

> And ever in mortal vanity
> Prophetic dreams disturb us
> When we stand before the universe
> More profound, shaken.
> ("Life")

Or again:

> Here the abyss appears in anguish,
> Here in the beginning the world pulled apart...
> Over this abyss I, by a hand
> Not human, am abandoned.
> ("Enlightenment")

125

Here is Baratynsky:

> The soul is full; it is lucid.
> You are both consoled and heightened.
> The silence breathes with portents.
> As if the old cry is audible.

The Urn is a book of skillful stylizations. While working on the history of Russian verse, studying the development of rhythmic lines from Derzhavin to Blok, Bely verified his theories in practice and, parallel to the articles on rhythm, he was writing the verses of *The Urn*. Batyushkov, Pushkin, Tyutchev and Baratynsky clothe his unhappy love for Lyubov Blok in the solemn folds of the classical style. But the lofty and noble simplicity of this clothing rarely corresponds to the inner significance of the poems; more often, it "overwhelms." It is presented as a stylistic masquerade. The author of *The Urn* is a magnificent versifier, but not a great poet.

* * *

The beginning of 1910 passed for Bely under the sign of theosophy. In Moscow, Anna Mintslova aquainted him with the intimate courses of Steiner, warning, however, that she had ceased to be his student. She spoke mysteriously of the fact that she now had other teachers.

On her insistence, in January of 1910, Bely went to the Rachinsky estate, Bobrovka, and there, for several weeks, devoted himself to occult "exercises." From there, on the summons of the same Mintslova, he went to Petersburg and settled at Vyacheslav Ivanov's Tower. For six weeks he lived in this hospitable "encampment" (Merezhkovsky's expression). At night, when the numerous guests dispersed, Vyacheslav Ivanov, rubbing his cold hands and pulling on a cigarette, would say to Bely, "Well you little Gogol, begin the Moscow chronicle." Vyacheslav Ivanov saw in Bely a resemblance to Gogol — and laughed merrily when Bely, standing on the rug, would tell about his childhood, his father, the professors, imitating the persons of the Moscow eccentrics and performing parody scenes. Bely's memoirs, *On the Brink of Two Centuries, The Turn of the Century*, and *Kotik Letaev* later grew out of these improvisations. At five o'clock in the morning, Ivanov would lead his guest into the study: there long conversations about God, Symbolism, the destinies of Russia would take place between him, Bely and Mintslova. At seven o'clock in the morning, an omelette and samovar would appear. At eight, the tired host and his guests would disperse to their rooms to sleep. Thus, day after day: a "mad," but "agreeable" life — outside of time and space.[3]

But the more closely Bely examined his "inspiration" — Mintslova — the more she disturbed him. He began to understand that she was a confused and sick being; she suffered from hallucinations; she feared the persecution of the forces of darkness and lived in the fantasies she created. Her pompously prophetic tone irritated Vyacheslav Ivanov and between the three "initiates"

126

difficult scenes took place.

In Petersburg, Bely gave a lecture on rhythm in the Society of the Zealots of the Artistic Word at the Apollo, and a speech on "The Dramas of Ibsen" in the town of Solyani.

At the beginning of spring, he brought Vyacheslav Ivanov to Moscow to celebrate his entrance into the group at the Musaget publishing house. The Petersburg poet made the acquaintance of Sizov, N. K. Kiselev and V. O. Nilender; he was honored at the Prague and Musaget. Bely organized a circle for the study of rhythm; it included V. Shenrok, Sergei Bobrov, V. Stankevich, A. Sidorov and the young poet Boris Pasternak. The circle collected materials for the description of Russian iambic pentameter.

A part of the summer was spent at the estate of V. I. Taneev, Demyanovo, where he earnestly studied rhythm and wrote the article "The Crisis of Consciousness and Hendrik Ibsen," and at the end of June he went to the village of Bogolyuby in Volynskaya Guberniya for a meeting with Asya Turgeneva. In a white house surrounded by an oak grove lived the family of the forester V. K. Campioni: his wife, by her first marriage a Turgenev, his children and his three step-daughters: Tanya, Natasha and Asya Turgeneva. Here, perched with Asya in a tree and rocking on the green branches, Bely spoke about his life, his projects, his desire to break with the past and begin to build a new life. "Those hot June middays," he writes, "in the branches, amidst the wind embracing us, have remained some of the most significant moments in my life." Finally, a decision was adopted: Bely proposed that Asya become his wife; she agreed, but "knitting her brows," announced that she had taken an oath not to be married in a church. Bely recalls:

> On the night of the decision, a number of initiatives, all of which were accomplished, rushed like lightning through my head: toward September, Asya and her mother came to Moscow; I found them a place to stay. I appealed to Musaget, giving them the right to print all my books long out of print, the four *Symphonies*, three collections of verse, the volume *Travel Notes* which I would write while abroad. I gave them everything I would write in the future; but I begged them to give me at once three thousand rubles for a revolution in my life.

In Bogolyuby, Bely read Blok's poem "On the Field of Kulikovo" and wrote him an ecstatic letter. Blok answered it cordially. Thus their quarrels were ended. Bely rejoiced that after all the difficulties and ordeals, they had found each other in spirit at last. The emotional brotherhood had dissolved at some point; now a spiritual brotherhood had grown up, and this time forever.

After returning to Moscow, the poet held his final farewell conversation with Mintslova. Heavy, corpulent, in a loose black shift resembling not a dress but a sack, she sat in a deep armchair, leaning her puffy head on the back of the chair and gazing about with swollen, glassy eyes. From her disconnected, half-mad speeches, Bely understood that she had not fulfilled her "mission:" to create in Russia a brotherhood of the Spirit; therefore, the unknown teachers were punishing her for breaking her oath, and she must disappear forever. The most surprising thing in this mysterious story is its end. In 1910, Mintslova disappeared in reality; no one ever saw her again. For some time, dim rumors about her were heard; then she was forgotten.

September, October and November passed for Bely in feverish activity; he prepared for his departure abroad. Finally, after many complications, at the end of November, he and Asya went to Sicily. Gershenzon and Berdyaev accompanied them to the station: Berdyaev brought Asya an armful of red roses.

Marina Tsvetaeva recalls Bely's companion, Asya Turgeneva:[4]

I saw Asya for the first time in Musaget. Erect, with a little head taken from nature in the setting of Lamartine Anglaises engravings, with an eternally smoking cigarette in her tapering fingers..... I never saw more beautiful hands — she was entirely out of an English engraving and was herself an engraver. She had already done the cover for Ellis' book of verse, *Stigmata,* with some temple.... Her charm lay in the mixture of masculine, youthful habits, I would even say of masculine efficiency, with extreme lyricism, maidenhood, the virginity of her features and form.

Marina Tsvetaeva approached Asya to talk about a cover for the second book of her verses. They spoke for a long time.

Not a word about Bely.... The word "fiance" then, during the age of Symbolism, was considered indecent, while "husband" (the word and the thing) was simply impossible.

Bely and Asya departed. "At the station," writes Marina Tsvetaeva, "Asya was all huddled up, rolled up in a braid, like her own scarf, and not a tear. While he — was simply happy. He shone."

His travels with Asya Bely described in the book *Travel Notes. Sicily and Tunis* (Moscow-Berlin, Gelikon, 1922). In it he sought to retain the immediate freshness of impressions, to transmit the rapid change of images and thoughts. He writes in the "afterword:"

I had as my goal: to give a precise account of the flying spots on the way, the change of flying thoughts, the dance of chance.... The bazaar of trifles taken as they first entered my consciousness in all their immediate presence: this is the aim of the *Notes.* Like a multi-colored rug, I spread it out "under my feet."

The *Notes* are written by one in love; they possess the "gaiety of spirit," joy of life, sounds, colors, the hot wind of the south. This bright book is unique in Bely's agonized creative work.

The train left from the Moscow platform.

My wife and I smiled. Asya, in a brown, light coat, in a somehow strangely cocked hat, was smoking a cigarette. It was not to be believed: the arguments, circles, the dusty chairs at the editorial offices, conversations about rhythm and meter, sonnets, esthetes, dreamers, god-seekers — all had flown away.... Asya looked about trustingly; she questioned me: after all, you wanted to travel yourself — don't blame me.

The first shining vision: Venice. "The murmur of Adriatic streams, a red sail in the green distance." Bely writes of St. Mark's Cathedral:

The flowering of the Byzantine style in Venice is a sailor's dream of the East, from which he had sailed, letting out a red sail.

The travelers parted sadly with the fairy-tale city. Venice accompanied them with a "faraway desposit of white and red fires." "She poured out streams of her diamond tears beyond the foggy haze of the sea; and the phosphoric column of the moon splintered into scales of brilliance."

In Naples, he began to sense evil subterranean forces hidden at the feet of the gay and multi-colored city:

In Naples, the eruption was thrown more obviously at me; this eruption was the brilliance of the colors: an indefatigable brilliance; not the brilliance of health, but the brilliance of sickness.... This city remained in my impressions as a multi-colored jester lying at the sea, after putting down Vesuvius, its nose to the shores.

From Naples they went to Palermo and settled in the Palm Hotel, the manager of which, the entomologist Ragusa, was made famous by de Maupassant in his book *La Vie Errante.* In this hotel, surrounded by a "paradaisical" garden, Wagner had completed his *Parsival.*

And, suddenly interrupting the story, the author returns to the past, to his first meeting with his companion:

I met Asya a long time ago; I saw her in some house. I saw in her even then her almost unnoticeable half-smile; you encounter it in Egyptian statues. It is the smile of a soul, which sees through the threshold the riddle of the prophesying sphinxes. With this riddle, Asya approached my sufferings, when, hanging over a dark well, I was losing hope. She was also hanging; leaning over the well together, we saw a strange visage.

After Palermo, Bely and his wife settled in Monreale, a little town on the summit of a mountain, famous for its ancient cathedral. With inexhaustible ecstasy, they viewed the Byzantine mosaics. For Bely, "All Sicily is a luxurious ornament of the East woven into Italy.... The nature of Sicily is a song someone sings; and the fruit poured within it is the song of Sicily...." And this song accumulated in the mosaics. "The mosaics," he continues, "are photography and absolutely not painting: in them the colors are light. The triumph of all flowering nature is created from the refraction of light."

In Monreale, they lived in the wretched Ristorante Savoia; the winter was rainy and cold. "We lived in a world of fog for twelve days; again we grew warm after the cold: the mosaics gave out warmth like wood. We met the holidays." Finally, they could take no more and decided to go to Tunis "to get warm in the sun." Tunis blinded them with its whiteness, deafened them with the noise of street life. The poet observed the eastern crowd:

The stormy white flood of cackling voices flew by, breaking up into thousands of struggling bodies along the little bazaar passageways. It swelled like an avalanche, flowed like an avalanche, rumbled like an avalanche, sang like an avalanche, deafened and pursued and drowned.

In Tunis, European and Arabic culture collided sharply; in the ancient noble East, the poet discovered his spiritual native land. He writes:

The culture of Tunis is warmed with memories of complete, whole knowledge of life, even though the spirit of the times has outgrown this wholeness. The spirit of our time is not divined by us, by Europe, yet.... The European man on the street, standing at the level of all the contemporary work of the beginning of the 20th century, of course, is only a pathetic clown in comparison with the village Arab.

Upon settling in the Arab village of Rades, Bely became absorbed in the blissful, timeless quiet of the East:

These are strange, quiet, magnificent days. I forget whence I have come. I am a Russian; and I am a European. Europe? I am forgetting it; I don't want it. I know that in England, I know that in Germany, I would have missed my native land. Here, I don't miss it: it is as if I were born here; and as if I will die here. These are clear, magnificent days. I am without kith or kin, and I want to say to the moments: stand still, beautiful moments.... Here I have recognized that my former paths are exhausted; that my return to my native land which awaits me will be an arrival for the first time.

In Rades, they lived in a strange, five-sided room. Along one of the walls was a low seat, another — a continuous window; from it, beyond the multi-colored rug of roofs, fences, flowers, beyond the little tower of a white minaret, the Bay of Carthage was visible in the distance. Asya was cold and used a hot-water bottle, reading Arabian fairy tales; warm tea was on the rug; from afar, the song of an Arab, dejectedly gutteral, was heard. In February, it warmed up. The poet and his wife loved to wander along the narrow streets of Rades with their sparkling tile water fountains, piers and verandas. They loved to look at the vari-colored cloaks of the Arabs, turquoise, green, olive, chocolate brown. They made friends with a sheik, a postmaster and workers.

The *Notes* conclude with meditations on the "black flame of culture," on the secret of Nigerian culture. The author is right in calling his book a "multi-colored rug." It is written in the broad impressionist manner: impressions, descriptions, meditations, philosophical digressions and lyrical flights alternate in it in delightful disorder. The promised second part of *Travel Notes* was not written. But in the last years of his life, while working on his memoirs, the author briefly told about the end of his travels.[5]

From Rades, the Russian travelers went to Egypt. The ascent of a pyramid had great mystical meaning for Bely. He says:

We suddenly felt wild horror from the unprecedentedness of our position. This strange physiological sensation, turning into a moral feeling of being turned inside out, the Arabs of this territory call the pyramid sickness, the medicine for which is hot coffee. While we were "being cured" with it, the guide, sitting beneath us on the lower steps, was ready to grab us if we fell. And we wanted to rush down in spite of everything, because everything there seemed to be shouting: "Horror, the pit and the lash await you, man!" ... For me, this being turned inside out was connected with the turning point of my whole life. The result of the pyramid sickness is a change in the organs of perception. Life was adorned with a new tonality, as if I had ascended the pitted steps as one person and descended as another. The altered relation to life soon told upon *Petersburg*, which I had begun to write; there the sensation of standing before the sphinx is transmitted throughout the entire novel.

The high point of the journey — the pilgrimage to Jerusalem — left no traces on Bely's soul. He was already absorbed in the turbid abysses of Anthroposophy and moved ever further from Christianity. "Jerusalem," he writes, "remains in my memory as the center of anti-Christian propaganda: propaganda to illustrate the crude morals of the absolutely slovenly Greek clergy."

From Palestine, Bely and his companion returned to Odessa by steamship; from there, they went directly to Bogolyuby, the estate of Asya's stepfather, V. K. Campioni (May, 1911).

* * *

In 1910, in addition to the "silhouette" of Vyacheslav Ivanov, Bely wrote only one article, "The Crisis of Consciousness and Hendrik Ibsen;" in it he summarized his seven years of work on Symbolism.[6] Once again, with new strength, the author points to the crisis experienced by contemporary mankind. He writes:

> Never yet have the fundamental contradictions of human consciousness collided in the soul so sharply; never yet has the duality of consciousness and feeling, contemplation and will, personality and society, science and religion, morality and beauty, been so precisely expressed.

Ibsen's dramas speak of the crisis of consciousness. They are written not to depict tragedy on the stage; they are a signal given by one who experiences tragedy in life itself. Ibsen transforms our goals in life into absurdity. He shows that it is no longer possible to live the way we do. There remains only one path — the path of rebirth. The author continues:

> To put dynamite under history itself in the name of absolute values not yet revealed to consciousness — this is the dreadful conclusion from the lyrics of Nietzsche and the dramas of Ibsen. To break with one's century to aspire to genuine reality is the only way to avoid destruction.

Ibsen proclaims this new reality as the coming kingdom of the Spirit. He teaches us to fight and overcome fate; he calls for the creation of life.

The article concludes with a summons to the religious transformation of the world. Bely writes:

> Three stages must be passed by contemporary individualism: from Baudelaire to Ibsen, from Ibsen to Nietzsche, from Nietzsche to the Apocalypse. The path from Baudelaire to Ibsen is the path from Symbolism as a literary school to Symbolism as an outlook; the path from Ibsen to Nietzsche is the path from Symbolism as an outlook to Symbolism as a disposition. This disposition leads to real symbolics. Finally, the path from Nietzsche to John the Evangelist is the path from individual symbolics to collective symbolics, i.e., to definitive, transforming religion. Symbolics becomes embodiment, Symbolism — theurgy.

The spirit of all of Russian Symbolism is expressed in this last article of Bely's: the end of art, culture, history; the hope for the kingdom of the Spirit; the will to the religious transformation of the world and to the creation of universal brotherhood. The Russian Symbolists loved Ibsen for his proud demand: "all or nothing." Symbolism did not succeed: its plans were limitless.

132

But there was true magnificence in its failure.

In 1910, three books by Bely were published: two collections of his articles from the years 1902-1909: *The Green Meadow* and *Symbolism*, and his first novel, *The Silver Dove*, appearing in chapters in the journal *Scales* for 1909. *The Silver Dove* was written in the winter of 1909 in Bobrovka. In the book *Between Two Revolutions*, Bely tells the history of the creation of this novel. He writes:

> In Bobrovka, I finally, at Gershenzon's insistence, sat down to write my first novel. At once everything became clear: the material for it was collected; the types had lain for a long time in my soul.... I had conversations with the Khlysty; I studied them and their writings (Prugavin, Bonch-Bruevich and others).... I sensed the spirit of Rasputin before Rasputin appeared on the scene.... I fantasized him in the figure of my joiner: he is Rasputin's village past.... The character of my joiner was formed from a number of characters (the joiner I saw plus Merezhkovsky, etc.). The character of Matryona from one peasant woman plus (Lyubov Dmitrievna Blok) plus ... etc. In the novel, a personal note, which tortured me for the entire period of my illness, was reflected: the morbid sensation of "persecution," the feeling of nets and the expectation of destruction: it is in the plot of the *Dove*.

In the spring of that same year, Bely had met Asya Turgeneva. "My perception," he writes, "of the Asya of that time was immediately reflected in the novel, to which I returned when she departed (Katya)."

* * *

Even while he was in Tunis, the poet had sensed his divergence with his old friend, the editor of Medtner, the editor of Musaget.

> A stormy quarrel burst out in letters, at which time I postponed bitterness and sharp annoyance at Medtner, who allowed himself to use sharp words in letters. I remember that even in Tunis I was wandering around the fields with this sharp thought about Musaget and a feeling of growing perplexity toward Medtner.... Upon my arrival in Moscow, it is true, still externally, we came to an agreement; the previous, incomparable relations were at an end; after two years, we quarreled again; and then made it up; in 1915, however, our ways parted forever.

Bely had left Asya in Bogolyuby and had gone himself for a short time to Moscow. Moscow met him with a "quinsied grimace." In Musaget he felt like a foreigner. The group of collaborators at the philosophical journal *The Path*, Rachinsky, E. N. Trubetskoi and M. K. Morozova, were closer to him in spirit.

The two main "Pathniks," Berdyaev and Bulgakov, having become admirers of my art, demonstrated in those days a special attention to me.

A "strange, rainless summer" passed in Bogolyuby. Bely was again on the threshold of a "new life." He decided to go abroad immediately, to write his novel. In his *Memoirs,* he points out the great significance of this summer of 1911.

Gazing from the future, in those days I could have said to myself for the first time that self-knowledge seemed to be churning up my being with burning tongs. Until that fateful summer, someone called Boris Nikolaevich Bugaev, dressed in some sort of transparent cocoon, calling himself Andrei Bely, lived, was, thought; but suddenly this Bely exploded in the process of self-inflamation, the essence of which was incomprehensible to him; nothing of Bely remained. Boris Bugaev, however, proved to be absorbed in catalepsy similar to death — he died: he ate, slept, moved like a mummy. In his own self he heard the remote echoes of some sort of life in which awakening is possible; but how to awaken?

Anxiety, premonitions, worry possessed him. The place where he was living, Lutsk, Bogolyuby, three years later fell into the zone of the Russo-Austrian front. But in the summer of 1911, there was nothing yet that predicted war. And in the meantime, in the fields, on walks, Bely, Asya and her sister Natasha clearly heard the peals of faraway thunder, the rumble of unseen arms. He writes:

Afterwards, the little house of the forester, our little house and the big home built only a year later — all were destroyed by Austrian cannons (here both my books and a collection of knick-knacks from Africa were destroyed); the battles lasted for a year here.... The general impression of the summer was a rumbling quiet.... It rumbled not here, but above the world.... The atmosphere of Russia thundered with the coming misfortunes; and we heard the thunder.

In the autumn, Bely and Asya settled near Moscow, close to the Rastorguevo station. "Here," he remembers, "Asya again fell into torpidity resembling a trance, devouring Blavatsky's book *From the Caves and Jungles of Hindustan.*" The first issue of the journal *Works and Days,* thought up by Blok as a diary for three writers (Blok, Bely and Vyacheslav Ivanov) was published. But the Musaget publishing house placed upon it its ponderous guardianship, and the journal was transformed into the "most boring institution," disappointing both Bely and Blok.

Bely received an official proposal from *Russian Thought* to write twelve galleys of his new novel by January. He writes:

I thought of it as a second part of the novel *The Silver Dove*, under the title of *Wayfarers*; it was about this that we had the conversation with Struve. At the signing of the contract there was no mention of the fact that the manuscript I presented must pass Struve's censorship. Bulgakov and Berdyaev, admirers of *The Silver Dove*, put the worth of the novel before Struve in such a way that there could be no mention of the fact that the continuation could be defective. I was given three months — October, November, December — to write the twelve galleys, for which I was to receive an advance of 1000 rubles. With this money, Asya and I proposed to go to Brussels.... The last negotiations about trifles I conducted with Bryusov, who had become editor of the arts section of *Russian Thought*; he invited Asya and me to his house on Meshchanskaya and gave us a magnificent dinner with expensive wines. While filling our goblets, he cooed gutterally with precious mordancy, twitching with his crooked smile: "*Russian Thought* is a poor journal, and we are obliged to squeeze someone out immediately. Boris Nikolaevich, you are not greedy for money, you're a saint. And, after all, what do you need the money for? So, shall we cut down — on you?"

Bely was experiencing hard times: from Musaget he was receiving 75 rubles a month, and this money was insufficient for life for two. From morning till night he sat bent over the table and wrote about five galleys in a month. There was no time left for other literary earnings.... In order to support him, friends arranged a lecture for him, but even this did not save him. And now, at this difficult moment, Bely received a letter from Blok, in which he wrote that he had heard about Bely's crucial work and financial difficulties; that upon his father's death he had received a small inheritance, and asked him to accept from him 500 rubles as a loan. Bely adds:

This letter was imbued with great delicacy, and I could not refuse A.A.: to the heart-felt, friendly assistance, I responded in all simplicity with the heart-felt acceptance of assistance. Thus Blok's sending 500 rubles was the stimulus to the origin of *Petersburg*. Therefore, I consider Alexander Blok the inspirer of *Petersburg* and the genuine author of its coming to life.

At the end of October, it became so cold at the Rastorguevo country house that Bely and Asya were obliged to return to Moscow. They took shelter in a small room: there was almost no money. Bely worked to the point of nervous over-exhaustion.

At the beginning of December, A. A. Rachinskaya invited them to Bobrovka. Asya was a little afraid of the old house with the portraits of ancestors and creaking floor-boards.

135

I remember how Asya sat at the window (sewing something) in the very, very spacious dining room; I was sitting near the wall, hunched over, crossing out pages written over four times or reading her something just redone, or we would be absorbed in a book on occultism; it was already getting dark, and there was a blizzard at the windows.... Somewhere alongside, people passed with a light.... She and I would darken the lamp and speak about the fact that something very, very big was moving upon us; or we would listen to the tread of events.

In this gloomy house, under the howling of a snowstorm, Bely wrote the "nightmare" scenes of the novel *Petersburg.*

At Christmas, they returned to Moscow. Bely gave *Russian Thought* fourteen galleys of his novel.... But the advance of 1000 rubles was not forthcoming. Bryusov gave evasive replies, saying that the journal was overloaded with Abeldyaev's novel, that editor Struve did not like *Petersburg.* Bely complained to S. N. Bulgakov; he was perplexed, frowned and was angry at Struve's behavior. Finally, Pyotr Berngardovich returned the manuscript to the author with a letter in which it was announced that the novel could not be printed in *Russian Thought,* and that it should not be published at all. Bely created a scandal for Bryusov at a meeting of Free Esthetics, and with his last money, he and Asya went to Petersburg as guests of Vyacheslav Ivanov at the Tower.

* * *

1912

As in the past, literary life was throbbing at the Tower. Asya became friendly with Vyacheslav Ivanov and played chess with him; Kuzmin came out of his room for morning tea. Gumilev, then already married to the poetess Anna Akhmatova, the witty Knyazhin, the good-hearted Yury Verkhovsky, the refined, brilliant N. Nedobrovo, Skaldin, A. N. Chebotarevskaya, Professor Anichkov and others gathered in the evenings. Vyacheslav Ivanov, aroused by the affair with *Petersburg,* organized a series of Bely's readings at his house: his novel was a huge success. On the advice of the owner of the Tower, Bely abandoned the original title, *The Lacquered Carriage,* and replaced it by a new one, weighty and important — *Petersburg.* During the month he was in Petersburg. Bely gave two public lectures in the Society of Zealots for the Artistic Word, on the rhythmics of Russian iambic pentameter, and on the forces in the poetry of Tyutchev, Pushkin and Baratynsky. He wanted very much to see Blok, but because of a quarrel with Lyubov Dmitrievna, he could not decide to go to him. He wrote Blok a letter. Blok made a date with him in a wretched little restaurant near Tavricheskaya Street. Their conversation lasted six hours. Bely spoke about his spiritual quests, about theosophy, about the path of initiation. Blok respected his new faith, but it was foreign and unnecessary to him.

Before his departure abroad in 1912, Bely had finished the novel *Petersburg.*

Chapter Six: *The Silver Dove*

Not one Russian writer has ever performed such intrepid experiments on words as Andrei Bely. There is nothing like his narrative prose in Russian literature. Bely's "stylistic revolution" may be considered a catastrophic failure, but it is impossible to negate its tremendous significance. The author of *The Silver Dove* and *Petersburg* did not leave a stone unturned in the old "literary language." He "reared Russian prose on its hind legs,"[1] turned syntax upside down, flooded the lexicon with new words he invented. Bely's daring attempts, sometimes bordering on madness, placed their imprint on all of the new Soviet literature; he created a school.

The "literary revolution" prepared by the lyrical prose of the *Symphonies* finds its expression in *The Silver Dove*. Bely begins with a student's imitation of Gogol. Stretching them to extreme emotional tension, he makes all the methods of Gogolian stylistics his own... The lyricism, irony, grotesque, hyperbola, conglomerations, contrasts, literary puns, intonations, coloration and rhythm of Gogolian prose are exhibited by Bely through a magnifying glass. In the beginning of *The Silver Dove,* the village of Tselebeevo is described: we at once recognize the Gogolian Mirgorod.

Tselebeevo is a wonderful town, suburban. It lies among knolls and meadows; here and there it is sprinkled with little houses, richly adorned, here with a patterned fretwork exactly like the face of a regular fashionplate in curls, there with a cock made of painted tin, and there with daubed flowers, with cherubs... A wonderful town! Ask the priest's wife: sometimes, as the priest would come from Vorop (his father-in-law has been provost there for ten years), so: he would come from Vorop, take off his cassock, kiss his plump wife, hitch up his underwear and would immediately come out with: "Set up the samovar, my dear."

This is not even an imitation, but a pastiche: the Gogolian mocking narrative style is transmitted with great skill.

The stylistic construction of "A Terrible Vengeance" defines the style of *The Silver Dove*. Describing the meadow in the middle of the town, Bely reproduces the pathetic rhythm of the famous Gogolian tirade "Lovely is the Dnieper in calm weather...."

And how the round dance moves in waves, the rouged maidens, in silks, in beads, how they begin to whoop wildly, and how their legs move in the dance; a wave runs through the grass, the evening breeze hoots — it is strange and merry: you don't know what and how, how it is strange, and what is merry here... and the waves run and run; they will run in fright along the road and break up in a swelling splash: then the brush by the road will sob, and the shaggy dust will leap up....

It is useless to multiply the examples; the entire fabric of Bely's novel is embroidered with complex patterns taken from Gogol. The dark Russia of the folk Bely sees through the romantic folklore of the author of "A Terrible Vengeance."

The Silver Dove is built on the contradiction between the "people" and the "intelligentsia," on the theme of "love-hate" lying at the basis of the Russian historical tragedy.

The hero of the novel, Daryalsky, is a member of the Russian intelligentsia, or, more precisely, a Russian Symbolist poet of the beginning of the 20th century. With lyrical irony worthy of Gogol, Bely depicts the "spiritual storms" of this "eccentric"; in his image, the personal traits of the author are combined with the traits of his Moscow litterateur friends. Daryalsky has written verses "on a lily-white heel, on the myrrh of the mouth, and even on the semi-balm of the nostrils." He has published a book with a fig leaf on the cover. Even as a child, he announced to his father that he didn't believe in God and threw the icon out of his room; he prayed to the red sunrises, wrote verses, read Kant, and bowed down before the red banner. After the death of his parents, he lived a stormy student life: he studied Boehm, Eckhardt, Swedenbourg, and simultaneously was attracted by Marx and Lasalle. He sought the secret of his dawn and found it nowhere.

The author continues:

And now he has already grown wild and no longer attracts anyone; now he is a wanderer, alone among the fields with his strange thoughts which produce no unity, but always with the dawn... and the dawn promises something close to him, some secret approaching him; and he is already in the temple: he is already in the holy places, in Diveev, in Optina, and simultaneously in pagan antiquity with Tibulus and Flaccus... And the feelings are ever warmer, the thoughts ever more subtle, there are more of them, more, and his soul bursts from fullness; it begs for love and tenderness.

Now in his life there appears the "beautiful Katya," living on the estate of Gugolevo with her grandmother, the Baroness Todrabe-Graaben. For two summers, Daryalsky rented a hut in the village of Tselebeevo in order to be close to Katya; on the third summer, the thin, timid girl, with unexpected decisiveness, announces to her grandmother that she is his fiancée. Daryalsky is a stylized self-portrait of Bely and Katya a poetic reflection of Asya Turgeneva.

Look: there over the piano she is engraved in his memory in a snug-waisted, blue, slightly short dress, leaning forward just a bit and slightly hunched over — she seems like, just like, a little girl.... Katya shook her little head and her thick curls were flung over her shoulder; but the lines pushed together between her thin brows, the momentarily compressed little mouth pleading for kisses, the high-held little head, and the waist precisely shaped, slight, austere in its slightness, expressed a sort of strange stubbornness not of childhood.

In this modest little girl is the depth, peace and transparency of a mountain lake. Her silent mystery attracts and excites Daryalsky.

To the right and left of the hero, supplementing his image, stand two other representatives of the "intelligentsia": the theosophist Schmidt and the mystical anarchist Chukholka. Of the first, the author says:

Daryalsky's friend was very unassuming: his last name was not Russian, and he spent his days and nights reading philosophical books. Although he rejected God, however, he often went to the priest; and it was nothing to the government, and in general he was absolutely orthodox, only his last name was Schmidt, and he didn't believe in God. For half the year he lived in the country "in a country house"; he was toothless, bald and gray; he wandered about the neighborhood in a yellow silk coat, leaning on a cane and holding his straw hat in his hand: the village boys and girls surrounded him.

There was a time when Schmidt had controlled Daryalsky's destiny, revealing the path of secret knowledge to him and proposing to go abroad with him to them, the brothers who influenced destiny from afar. But Daryalsky did not follow Schmidt; he remained in wretched "perishing Russia." Not long before his destruction, he goes to Schmidt for the last time; the latter makes him a horoscope and interprets it:

You were born in the year of Mercury, in the day of Mercury, in the hour of the moon, in that place on the starry sky which bears the name "the Tail of the Dragon." The sun, Venus, Mercury are obscured for you by evil aspects: the sun is obscured by quadrature with Mars; Mercury is in opposition to Saturn while Saturn is that part of the starry sky of the soul where the heart breaks, where Cancer defeats the Eagle; and, furthermore, Saturn promises you failure in love, falling in the sixth place of your horoscope; and it is in Pisces. Saturn threatens you with destruction. Come to your senses — it is still not too late to abandon your terrifying path....

The bald head of Schmidt arises from the volumes, tables and sketches; Bely enumerates the books on secret knowledge decorating the bookshelves of the theosophical astrologist. This is a contemporary's important evidence on the occult and mystical strain in the flow of Russian Symbolism. A. Dobrolyubov, Bryusov, Bely, Vyacheslav Ivanov, Ellis, Batyushkov, Ertel, N. Goncharova, A. Minstlova, Asya Turgeneva, and many other people of the Symbolist epoch experienced a passionate attraction to occultism. Schmidt had the following books: the Cabbala in an expensive binding, the Merkabah, volumes of Zohar, manuscript notes from the works of Lucius Fismicus, the astrological commentaries on Ptolemy's *Tetrabiblia*, the *Stromata* of Clement the Alexandrian, the Latin treatises of Hammer, manuscript notes from *The Shepherd of the Peoples.*

On the table were little sheets with signs drawn by a trembling hand: pentagrams, swastikas, circles with a magical Tau inscribed; there was also a table with sacred hieroglyphics.... On one side, on a chair, lay a mystical diagram with ten rays copied out in a certain order — sephiroth: Kether, Canalis Supramundanus... and the eighth sephira, Jod, with the designation "the ancient serpent." There were strange inscriptions on the white wood of the table, like "everything material is calculated by the number four."

Bely speaks of Schmidt with respect, even with apprehension, seemingly. But of the "mystical anarchist" Chukholka he speaks with obvious mockery.

Into the aristocratic estate of the Baroness Todrabe, where Daryalsky is a guest, there bursts "...a stupid being in a gray felt hat, with a small head flattened onto an excessively long and thin body, and introduces himself: Chukholka, Semyon Andreevich, a student at the Imperial Kazan University." With great brilliance, Bely parodies the "gallop of ideas" of this mystical anarchist:

...an incoherent flood, capable at any moment of turning into a veritable ocean of words, in which the names of universal discoveries are mixed with the names of all the universal luminaries; theosophy here would be mixed with jurisprudence, revolution with chemistry; to complete the outrage, chemistry turned into cabbalistics, Lavoisier, Mendeleev and Crookes were explained with the help of Maimonides, and the conclusion was always the same: the Russian people will assert its rights. Chukholka viewed these rights in such a modernistic form, that from certain parts of his speech one might think that he was dealing with such a Decadent as Mallarmé himself had never seen; in fact, Chukholka was a chemistry student, in truth a chemist occupied with occultism which had irrevocably deranged his poor nerves.

Chukholka's presence in Gugolevo ends in a scandal. He brings the Baroness some sort of Spanish onion; the old woman, shaken by this, drives him away. Daryalsky defends his unlucky friend and receives a resounding slap from the enraged Baroness. Thus the break with his fiancee and his departure from the estate into the country takes place — from the world of perishing "civilization" into the mystical darkness of "the people." In the image of Chukholka, Bely collected the traits of his Moscow friends in an expressive *raccourci*, arranging them around the picturesque figure of L. L. Kobylinsky-Ellis. (The surname Chukholka suggests the surname of another "mystical anarchist," Georgy Chulkhov.)

The new generation of Symbolists from the intelligentsia acquires sharp relief on the background of the old world — the nobility becoming extinct. Their western, non-Russian origin is emphasized by the parodized appellation Todrabe-Graaben. The Baroness, a "stocky old woman, all in silk and colored laces and gray, yellowish hair," solemnly passes through the suite of rooms, leaning on a walking stick with a crystal cane-head; haughtily and peevishly, she completes the ritual of the morning cup of coffee, in deep silence, with deathly ceremoniousness. In a lyrical digression, Bely reveals the symbolic meaning of this image, exclaiming:

> Did you not thus, old and dying Russia, proud and frozen in your magnificence, every day, every hour, in thousands of chancellaries, offices, courts and estates, complete these rituals, the rituals of by-gone days? But, oh Exalted, look about you and let your gaze fall: you will realize that beneath your feet an abyss is opening; you will look and collapse into the abyss!...

Bely masterfully depicts the picturesque figure of the son of the Baroness, Senator Pavel Pavlovich Todrabe; thin, long-nosed, with gray hair, clean-shaven and smelling of eau de cologne, he kisses the hand of his mother with careless tenderness and, in a whining, complaining voice, tells about Petersburg, about his travels abroad. Pavel Pavlovich, an eccentric, a fantasist and a man of sense, had lazily created a brilliant career; in Petersburg salons his caustic wit was feared. He educated his children according to the system of Rousseau and was writing a treatise on anthropology. His "philosophy of decadence" is reducible to the following positions:

> All people are divided into parasites and slaves. The parasites are divided in their turn into wizards or magicians, murderers and cads. The magicians are those who invented God and extorted money from this invention. The murderers are the military estate of the whole world. The cads are divided into simply cads, that is, people of means, educated cads, i.e. professors, lawyers, doctors, people of the free professions; and into esthetic cads: to the latter belong the poets, writers, artists and prostitutes.

141

"Cultured" Russia — the nobility, the landowners, the civil servants and the intelligentsia — is doomed to destruction: it stands over the abyss and experiences a sweet giddiness. In passing merciless judgment on it and pronouncing the death sentence, Bely bids farewell to it as his first love.

All the beauty, all the poetic enchantment, all the lyrical sadness of this dying Russia is embodied in Katya. She is the only Beloved, the Bride, the Wife. Daryalsky abandons her, but he knows that to betray her is ruin; he is doomed.

> Katya! There is on earth only one Katya. You can travel the whole world, but you will meet her no more; you will pass over the fields and expanses of our broad native land and go on. In the foreign countries, you will be captivated by black-eyed beauties, but they are not Katyas.... This is what she is like — look at her: she stands alone, lowering her curved blue-black eyelashes as soft as silk; and from under the eyelashes shine the lights of her remote eyes, not quite gray, not quite green....

The lights of "cultured," "European" Russia are burning low, and the darkness of the Russia "of the people," "Asiatic" Russia, is approaching. The mysterious elemental force of the soul of the people Bely finds not in the peasant masses (he does not know the peasantry), but in the world of the petit bourgeoisie and the merchant class. The inhabitants of the village of Tsebeleevo and the out-of-the-way little town Likhov: Luka Silych Eropegin, a millionaire miller, and his wife, the "dumpling," Fekla Matveevna, who joins the secret covenant of "the Dove;" the blacksmith Sukhorukov who exterminates the merchant with a slow poison in order to control his capital for the "covenant;" the poor wanderer Abram, one of the most important members of the sect; and finally, the joiner Mitry Kudeyarov, the secret leader of the covenant — they are all united by a secret pledge, mysterious and sinister. The strangest figure in the novel is Kudeyarov:

> ...not a face, but a gnawed sheep bone; and, moreover, not a face, but half a face; a face, let us suppose, is a face, and it only always seems that it is half a face; one side slyly winks at you; the other is always on the look-out for something, is always afraid of something.

He is gifted with tremendous occult power, a terrible power over souls; this is the wizard with the evil eye, weaving a web of black magic about himself. With him, as a worker, lives the pock-marked woman, Matryona, his submissive and silent "female incarnation." After becoming acquainted with Daryalsky, the joiner decides to lure him into the covenant of the Dove, and bring him together with Matryona so that she might conceive from him a "spiritual offspring." Kudeyarov's sorcery and Matryona's ardor enslave Daryalsky's "free soul." After the break with his fiancee, he goes to work for the joiner and becomes intimate with his "female incarnation."

"The Turgenevian girl" Katya symbolizes "cultured" Russia; the pock-marked woman Matryona — the Russia "of the people." The author devotes a lyrical tirade to her:

If your love is different, if ever she felt the itch of small-pox on her browless face, if her hair is reddish, her breasts withered, her bare feet muddy, and although her stomach protrudes greatly, she is all the same your love; what you sought and found in her is the sacred fatherland of the soul; and you have looked her, the fatherland, here in the eyes, and you no longer see your former love here; your soul converses with you, and your winged guardian angel is indulgent with you.

Daryalsky is absorbed in the terrifying world of fortune-telling, witchcraft, sensual possession, dark mystical ecstasies.

The description of the mystical rites of the "doves" in the bath house of the merchant Eropegin has an almost hypnotic effect. The author attains such force of artistic and mystical inspiration that it is impossible to tear oneself away from the magic circle of his words and incantations. This is no longer "literature," but a genuine and horrifying occult experience, the sweetly disgusting dizziness of mystical rites. We experience the spiritual temptation and spiritual charm of sectism realistically; a new dimension of consciousness is revealed — a ghostly, magic, shining world arises.

In the bath house, there was quiet; in the bath house, there was coolness; the bath house was not filled; but all of it, with shutters closed tightly from within, shone, lit up, floated in light; in the middle of it stood a table, covered, like the sky, with turquoise satin in the middle of which was a red embroidered heart, preyed upon by a beaded dove; in the middle of the table stood an empty goblet, covered with a kerchief; on the goblet a lioness and a lance; fruits, flowers, communion breads adorned this table; and green birch twigs decorated the damp walls; in front of the table pewter lamps were shimmering; above the pewter lamps shone the heavy hanging silver dove.

In white shifts, with candles in their hands, the brothers and sisters slowly circle around, holding hands; they do not dance, but walk, conduct a circle dance, and sing:

Bright, oh bright is the blue air!...
In this air bright the precious spirit be!

Their faces shine like suns, their eyes are lowered; instead of the ceiling, they are seeing the lofty blue sky, studded with stars.

The author continues:

Everyone now seats himself at the table, in a seven-colored rainbow, amidst the heavenly white earth, amidst the green conifer forest and under the skies of Favor; one radiant man, interpreting, passes out the Communion bread, and swallows the red wine of Cana of Galilee from the goblet; and it is as if there is no time and space, but wine, blood, blue air and sweetness. The blessed Assumption and eternal peace are with them. The little silver dove, reviving on the pole, is heard, caressing them, cooing; it has flown from the pole to the table; it scratches the satin with its talons and gives off sparkles....

And Daryalsky, drunk with "spiritual wine," believes that the secret of Russia has been revealed to him. And, rejoicing, he glorifies the Russian land. How much exalted love there is in these lyrical flights:

...The Russian fields know secrets, as the Russian woods know secrets.... You will drink the dawns like precious wines; you will be nourished by the aromas of pine resin; Russian souls are the dawns; firm and resinous are Russian words; if you are Russian, you will have a red secret in your soul.... To live in the fields, to die in the fields, to your own self repeating one soul-flinging word, which no one knows except he who has received that word; and they receive it in silence.... There are many books in the West, many unsaid words in Rus'. Russia is that against which a book explodes, knowledge melts, and life itself is burned to ashes. On that day when the West is grafted onto Russia, a universal fire will engulf it; everything that can be consumed will be consumed, because only from ashen death will the heavenly little soul, the Firebird, fly out.

However, it is not resurrection, but destruction that awaits the dreamer Daryalsky. The "red secret" of Russia is turned about for him in a dark chaos, a sinister mirage. Instead of the religion of the Holy Ghost, he finds in the people the "covenant of the dove," led by the evil wizard Kudeyarov.

Bely portrays the mystical rite in Kudeyarov's hut amazingly, the black magic of the joiner, the materialization of the "spiritual offspring," Matryona's shameless dance to the mumbling of the horrifying old man: "Jesus, Jesus, shorn into brotherhood: bombartsy... God have mercy." Daryalsky's eyes are opened. The author writes:

He had already begun to understand that this was horror, the noose and the pit; not Rus', but some dark abyss of the East preying upon Rus' through these bodies exhausted by mystical rites. "Horror!" he thought.

144

Kudeyarov begins to hate Daryalsky: he lacks the "power"; Matryona did not conceive from him; he must be eliminated. He comes to an agreement with the blacksmith Sukhorukov, lures him into Eropegina's house and there, in an outbuilding, four muzhiks from "the Dove" kill him.

Daryalsky's tragedy is interpreted by the theosophist Schmidt. The author places his most cherished thoughts in his mouth. *The Silver Dove* is a turning point in Bely's personal and literary life. Initially, in his confused consciousness the idea of secret enemies destroying Russia arose, and with it the possibility of fighting them with the help of a "brotherhood of initiates." Bely was suffering from a persecution mania; the fixed idea of "world provocation" gradually took control of his spirit. Simultaneously, he entered upon the path of "secret knowledge" and became a student of the Anthroposophist Steiner. These two tendencies define all his subsequent creative work.

Here is what the "initiated" Schmidt says to Katya about Daryalsky-Bely:

> Pyotr thinks that he left you forever. Yet this is not betrayal, not flight, but a horrifying hypnosis crushing him; he left the circle of help, and the enemies for the present are victorious over him, as the enemy is victorious, mocks at our native land. A thousand innocent victims, while those guilty of everything are still hidden; and none of the simple mortals knows who are truly guilty of all the absurdities which have occurred.... All that is dark is now attacking Pyotr.... Believe me, only great and powerful souls are subject to such temptation; only giants come to an end like Pyotr. He did not accept the hand extended in help; he wanted to achieve everything by himself. His tale is both absurd and ugly: as if it were told by the enemy scoffing at the whole bright future of our native land.

This "enemy" is realized in the delirious images of provocateurs in the novels *Petersburg, Kotik Letaev* and *Moscow.*

The Silver Dove is an astounding work. It contains contradictions, lyrical flights, downfalls, conglomerations, satire, lyricism, philosophy; depiction bordering on hallucination, the magic of words and images. Gogolian grotesque, captivating music, the purest poetry. Bely's art contains flashes of genius and the first symptoms of mental illness: the tragic vision of a great, broken soul.

"Believe me," says Schmidt, "only great and powerful souls are subject to such temptation...."

* * *

The novel was published by the Scorpion publishing house (Moscow, 1910), and was reissued by the Pashukanis publishing house in 1917 and by Epokha (Berlin) in 1922.

145

Bely tells of the genesis of *Petersburg* in his *Memoirs*:

On long autumn nights, I scrutinized the images swarming around me:
from beneath them the central image of Petersburg slowly ripened for
me. It exploded within me so unexpectedly and strangely, that I was
obliged to dwell on it, since then, for the first time, I recognized the
birth of the subject from sound.... I was considering how to continue
the second part of the novel *The Silver Dove.* It was my intention that
it begin this way: after the murder of Daryalsky, the joiner Kudeyarov
disappears, but Daryalsky's letter to Katya, written before the murder,
nevertheless reaches her through very intricate paths. It is the means for
searching for Kudeyarov. Katya's uncle Todrabe-Graaben is chosen for
this search; he goes to Petersburg to take council with his friend Senator
Ableukhov. The second part would open with a Petersburg episode,
with the meeting of the senators. Thus, according to the plan, I came to
rest upon the necessity of giving a characterization of Senator Ableukhov. I gazed at the figure of the senator, which was not clear to me, at
his surrounding environment: but — in vain. Instead of the figure and
the environment, there was something difficult to define: not a color,
not a sound; and I sensed that the image must be ignited from some
sort of dim harmony. Suddenly I heard a sound like "oo." This sound
travels along the entire distance of the novel. "You did not hear this
note of 'oo'?" — "I heard it." *(Petersburg).* The distinct motif of Tschai-
kovsky's opera *The Queen of Spades*, depicting the Winter Canal, was
suddenly united with the note "oo" as well. And immediately there
burst out before me the picture of the Neva with the bend of the Winter Canal: the dim, moonlit, bluish-silver night and the square of the
black carriage with the red lamp. It was as if I were running in thought
behind the carriage, trying to see who was sitting in it. The carriage
stopped before the yellow house of the senator, precisely as it is described in *Petersburg.* The little figure of the senator jumped out of the
carriage, exactly as I portrayed it in the novel: I invented nothing, I
only spied upon the actions of the people appearing before me; and
from these actions, a foreign, unknown life, a room, work, family relations, visitors were painted for me.

Andrei Bely's novel, *Petersburg*, is the most powerful and artistically
expressive of all his works. It is a rendition of delirium unprecedented in literature; by means of subtle and complex literary devices, the author creates a
separate world — unbelievable, fantastic, monstrous, a world of nightmare

147

and horror, a world of distorted perspectives, of disembodied people and living corpses. And this world gazes out at us with the phosphorescent eyes of a dead man, paralyses us with horror, bewitches us with hypnotic suggestion. The most uncanny thing of all is that this world, created by a mad genius, exists in reality. In comparison with it, the fantastic dreams of Hoffman and Edgar Allen Poe, the obsessions of Gogol and Dostoevsky seem harmless and benign. In order to understand the laws of this word, the reader must abandon at the threshold his own logical preconceptions. Here common sense is abolished and causation enfeebled; here human consciousness is torn to shreds and explodes, like the hellish machine "in the shape of a sardine tin." The "topography" of this world is strictly symmetrical: Petersburg with the straight lines of its prospects and the flatness of its squares, is perceived by the author as a system of "pyramids," triangles, parallelipipeds, cubes and trapezoids. This geometric space is peopled by abstract figures. They move mechanically, act like automatons, and seem to read their lines from a script. The novel is laden with events, but they do not destroy its deathly stillness. The only living thing is Petersburg — a ghostly vampire which has materialized from the yellowish fog above the Finnish swamps; the only living thing is the Bronze Horseman, "by whose fateful will"[1] the city was called forth from nothingness.

The hero of the novel is Senator Apollon Apollonovich Ableukhov, who has a mania for regimentation and governs Russia by circulars from the "mathematical point" of his study. Two and a half years before the events described in the novel, his wife, Anna Petrovna, had abandoned him to run off with the Italian singer Mindalini. The senator's son, Nikolai Apollonovich, studies Kant and is interested in "revolutionaries." At one time, he had given the "party" some sort of imprudent promise. He is visited by a terrorist, the student Dudkin, who gives him for safe-keeping the "sardine tin," a bomb with a time mechanism. Nikolai Apollonovich is in love with the wife of Officer Likhutin, Sofya Petrovna, who resembles a Japanese doll. But she does not encourage his attentions. He dons a red domino and frightens her at a ball. A scandal ensues: the red domino is written about in the *Diary of Events*. Likhutin is jealous and suffers; he tries to hang himself but falls to the floor and does not succeed. The provocateur Lippanchenko tosses Ableukhov-son a letter: the party demands that he blow up his father. Likhutin decides to deal directly with his rival, and so he tears off the hem of the latter's jacket. The student Dudkin buys a pair of scissors and stabs Lippanchenko to death. The senator's wife, after an unsuccessful affair with the Italian, returns to her husband. Finally, the bomb explodes in the study of Apollon Apollonovich; he escapes unharmed, goes into retirement, and settles in the country. Nikolai Apollonovich, after traveling in Africa, returns to the country estate and becomes absorbed in reading the philosopher Skovoroda.

In brief narration, the story seems senseless, but narration does not exhaust the intent of the author. By freeing it from the turmoil of detail, he

148

only strengthens the plot's fundamental lines: Bely really saw the world as senseless and with unusual literary skill he demonstrates its monstrous absurdity. In the ghostly city there is a collision between two insane ideas: reaction in the person of Senator Ableukhov, and revolution in the image of the "party-member" Dudkin. Both are equally disliked by the author. Vasilevsky Island, the hotbed of revolution, rises against Petersburg, the bulwark of reacttion. The clamminess of death is given off by the old, perishing world and by the new, which bears its own destruction. For both worlds, there is one symbol — ice. The Tsarist reaction is icy, but the revolution too is an "icy bonfire." The opposites coincide: Petersburg, over which Senator Ableukhov, like a huge bat, has spread out his black wings, is the creation of the "revolutionary will" of Peter. The hellish Flying Dutchman, Peter, "having reared Russia on her hind legs," is the first Russian revolutionary. Ableukhov is of Tatar origin; within him lies the dark Mongolian force, the beginning of Ahriman, immobility, dream, Maya, the ancient, indigenous non-being which threatens to engulf Russia. But socialism is also a "lie of Mongolism" for Bely; the black spirit Shishnarfne, whom the terrorist Dudkin fights and in whose claws he perishes, is the descendant of Xerxes, the force of darkness luring Russia into primordial nothingness.

In the 1922 Berlin edition of *Petersburg,* Dudkin reads a puzzling letter beginning with the words "Your political convictions are clear enough to me." In the rewritten context of this edition, the letter is completely incomprehensible. Its meaning is made clear in the manuscript "journal" edition of 1911. It is worthwhile to quote this incredible document in full:

Your political convictions are clear enough to me; it's all the devil's work, all the triumph of a force, the existence of which I can no longer doubt, for I have seen Him, spoken with Him (not with God). He tried to rip me to pieces, but one holy being tore me from his foul claws. The spiritual incarnation of Christ draws near; a decade remains. The coming of our progenitors and of one special progenitor approaches; who the being was that saved me, progenitor or progenitrix, I do not know. The spiritual incarnation will be especially important for Russia, for in her is the cradle of a new human race, the conception of which Jesus Christ himself has blessed. I see now that Vladimir Soloviev was inspired by the highest disincarnated single spiritual soul (initiation itself), which united in him the path of ecstasy and the cult of Sophia, and unconsciously drove him to Egypt, etc. This ties in with the agonized ravings of the Nizhegorodian sectarian N. P. (you remember her?).... Lev Tolstoi is the reincarnated Socrates: he came to Russia at the proper time for a moral purging. Yasnaya Polyana is the star of Russia. The forces of darkness are mobilizing under the expedient cover of social justice.

In socialism, just as in decadence, ideology passes into eroticism of its own accord. In terrorism there is the same sadism and the same masochism as in the desire to deprave, as in the false quest for the false way of the cross. The longing for the radiant resurrection of humanity turns into a debauched thirst for blood, either another's or one's own (it's all the same). Shake off the sensuous revolutionary tremor, for it is a lie of the approaching Eastern chaos (Panmongolism).

By means of this letter, the ideological conception of *Petersburg* is entirely laid bare. Both old Russia and her new reaction and revolution are in the dark power of Mongolian-Turkish forces. The only salvation is "secret knowledge" — anthroposophy. The "spiritual incarnation" of Christ will save Russia, and in her a new human race will be born.

Having finished his novel, Bely went to Dornach and devoted himself, body and soul, to the "teacher" Rudolph Steiner. The composition of *Petersburg* is conditioned by its anthroposophical foundation.

In preparing the new edition of the novel in 1922, Bely fundamentally altered the text of 1913. Times had changed and with them the mood of the author as well; after the October Revolution of 1917, Bely reversed his attitude toward revolution: sharp attacks against "socialists" and "terrorists" were softened. The chapter "The Meeting" was omitted; the "intellectual party worker," "a conscious proletarian," "an unconscious proletarian," two Jews, a socialist, a Bundist, a mystical anarchist, "Rkhasseia" (the gallicized pronunciation of Rossiya — Russia) and "tva-rryshchy" (co-mmarrads) disappeared. The revolution stopped being "icy" and became fiery. Ivanov-Razumnik, in his article about Bely's *Petersburg,* correctly points out that:

> What in 1913 was the "thesis" five years later had become the "antithesis" — now, instead of seeing in it a hellish mirage, Bely saw in the revolution the truth of the genuine Golgotha. It was not by chance that at the end of 1917 he was the author of the anthology *The Scythians.* For him "Mongolism" was the principle of Ahriman, nihil, stagnation; but "Scythianism" was the principle of Ormazd, reality, "to pan," the category of fire, movement, dynamism, supremacy. Between 1913 and 1922 Bely ceased to equate revolution with Mongolism and equated it instead with Scythianism.[2]

During this period still another idea in the novel changed its appearance: anthroposophy. From a fiery student of Steiner, Bely was converted into his sworn enemy. In the new edition of *Petersburg*, he abridged his discussions and meditations about the "cosmic idea," about the "pulsating primordial force," about the battle of the initiated against the Mongolian forces. The novel took on a different stylistic form and a different ideological illumination; the text was cut by a fourth.

Petersburg is a theater of grotesque masks. Sofya Petrovna Likhutina,

150

"Angel Peri," is surrounded by admirers; here are their names: Count Avon, Ommau Ommergau, Shporishev, Verhefden, Lippanchenko. At times she asks them provocatively, "I'm a doll — am I not?"[3] And then Lippanchenko answers, "You're a darling, a pet, a honey" (49). The terrorist Dudkin complains that he is surrounded not by people, but by a "society of gray wood-lice." At a ball given by the Tsukatovs, the guests merge with the masks, a red domino flashes by, a whirlwind of madness catches up an atomized reality and twirls it about.

> The room became filled with masks. Black capuchin monks formed a chain around their red cohort and began a wild dance; the hems of their cassocks swept the floor, the pointed orbs of their cowls bobbed up and down; their capuchin robes bore the emblem of a skull and crossbones (124).

The provocateur Lippanchenko is also a mask, a faceless monster:

> A deep fold was squeezed out between his back and his neck like a faceless smile: his neck seemed like a face; it was as if a monster with an entirely noseless, eyeless mug had seated itself in the armchair. And the fold in the neck seemed to be a toothless, torn mouth. There, on twisted legs, a clumsy monster had thrown itself.

Dudkin's secret visitor — the Persian Shishnarfne — is a momentarily embodied phantom.

> Here was a man who had entered his room, a three-dimensional creature who pressed against the window becoming a silhouette (that is, two-dimensional), and then just a smear of soot. Now this black soot had decomposed and become shining lunar ash; then this too vanished, leaving no silhouette. The entire substance of the man had assumed a purely vocal nature... (228).

Petersburg is a phantom, and all its inhabitants are phantoms. The world is dematerialized, from three dimensions to one of two dimensions; from objects only silhouettes remain, but even they fly off into a thin smear of soot. These methods of disincarnation are used as preparation for the staggering appearance of the Bronze Horseman. Dudkin hears metallic blows shaking the staircase of his house; with a crash the door to his attic flies from its hinges:

> On the threshold loomed a large luminous body with a bowed head, garlanded and green, and a ponderous greenish arm outstretched.... The Bronze Horseman greeted him, "How do you do, son?" He took three

151

steps that snapped like splitting boards; he lowered his metal body, cast in bronze, into a chair, and let his green gleaming elbow drop with its full weight of bronze clanging onto the table. Slowly the Emperor removed the bronze garland from his brow; the laurel leaves clanged as they fell. He drew out a glowing clinking pipe and, motioning to it with his eyes, said, "Petro Primo Catherina Secunda..." (234).

This appearance is a blinding flash of light in the darkness. Bely here is a worthy heir of Pushkin; for a moment in his hero Dudkin the poor Evgeny of *The Bronze Horseman* comes alive and "the ponderous clangor of galloping hooves" of the mounted tsar fills the novel with its triumphantly majestic rhythm — and it seems that Bely's *Petersburg* is the brilliant continuation of Pushkin's brilliant poem. But only for the moment. In the next chapter, the author has already plunged once more into his delirious twilight world, and the choruses of masks continue their exhausting whirling.

It is difficult to speak of the psychology of Bely's characters. "Dolls," "pets," "wood-lice," faceless and clumsy monsters, mugs and silhouettes flying off into soot do not have a psychology. But in the midst of this succession of phantoms, two characters — Senator Ableukhov and his son Nikolai — preserve traces of some humanity. It is a bloodless and soulless humanity, but it is not conclusively destroyed. Here Bely touches upon reality, upon his personal experience in childhood and youth. The store of these impressions and memories seems inexhaustible for Bely as a writer. In all his novels he continually reworks the real-life material of his early years. There is something frightening, almost maniacal, in the spell of this one theme. Bely's life is not a line of ascent, but rather a closed circle. After complex worldly, ideological and literary wanderings, he always returns to the nursery of the "professorial apartment," to the close world of "family drama."

Bely's narrative prose is defined by three motifs: memories of childhood, the figure of the eccentric father, and the dual family conflict, between father and mother, and between father and son.

In the novel *Petersburg,* the image of Senator Apollon Apollonovich Ableukhov reflects the features of the Procurator of the Holy Synod, K. P. Pobedonostsev, and Aleksei Aleksandrovich Karenin in *Anna Karenina.* But the artificial figure of the sinister old man becomes alive only when it approaches the personality of the author's father — Professor Nikolai Vasilievich Bugaev. Ableukhov is also an "eccentric," a man living by means of abstractions in a world of numbers and geometric lines. He is just as helpless before the "incomprehensibility" of concrete reality as was the mathematician Bugaev; he is just as attached to regimentation, theory, methodology, just as inescapably locked up within his own "skull box."

The motif of "family drama" constitutes the plot of the novel. The conflict between the father and mother is outlined: Ableukhov's wife, having

152

abandoned her husband to run off with the singer Mindalini, returns to him after two and a half years. The conflict between the father and son unfolds as a collision of two worlds, as the symbolic image of the 1905 revolution. The image of the senator's son, Nikolai Apollonovich, the Kantian student, is a stylized portrait of the author himself in the 1905 period. At the center of the novel is an intricate "complex" of relations between the senator and his son. The "problem of the father," which weakened, almost smothered, Bely's consciousness as a child, is laid bare now as love-hate, as an unconscious desire for the death of the father. Bely unsparingly analyzes his dual feeling:

> Nikolai Apollonovich cursed his own mortal self and, insofar as he was the image and likeness of his father, he also cursed his father; his spiritual self hated his father. Nikolai Apollonovich intuitively knew his father, his least sinuosities and his most inarticulate tremors. In his physical perceptions, he was absolutely like his father. He was unsure where he himself ended or where the senator. . . began . . . in him... (80).

* * *

> Whenever father and son came in contact with each other, they resembled two ventilators that had been turned on facing each other; and the result was a most unpleasant draft. Their proximity bore little semblance to love; Nikolai Apollonovich regarded love as a humiliating physical act (81).

The son is a rebel, remotely connected with terrorists, and he despises the reactionary activities of his father. "Nikolai Apollonovich came to the conclusion that his father, Apollon Apollonovich, was a scoundrel" (81).

The son is a potential parricide. Fate rushes along to turn his unconscious desire into reality. He agrees to take "for safekeeping" the bomb which must blow up the senator's house. But at this point, the duality of his consciousness takes over. The thought of killing his father horrifies the son. After all, he loves him.

The relationship of the senator to his son is just as tragically dualized. He fears and hates him. "The senator, in his office, had come to the conclusion that his son was a scoundrel. Thus, the sixty-eight-year-old Father had executed an intellectually comprehensible terroristic act over his own son" (88). Not only is the son a potential parricide, but the father as well is a "comprehensible filicide." But this is only a half-truth; the complete truth is that the filicide is a most loving father. Bely loves the compatibility of incompatibles, truth in untruth, good in evil; he enjoys the tragism of opposites. One of the most powerful scenes in the novel is a conversation between father and son at the dinner table. Nikolai Apollonovich "...in an outburst of nervousness, rushed toward his father and began to knead his fingers.... Apollon Apollonovich impulsively rose before his son — jumped up, one might say"

153

(87). A wretched conversation is wrung out between spaces of tense silence. Finally, the son speaks of Cohen's *Theorie der Erfahrung:* the senator confuses Comte with Kant. "I don't know, my dear boy. In my time it wasn't so considered" (89). And suddenly the old man remembers the time when his Kolenka was a student at the gymnasium and would tell his father all the details about his cohorts. And later, when he had grown up, the father would put his hand on his son's shoulder and say, "If I were you, Kolenka, I would read Mill's *Logic*. A useful book.... In two volumes.... I read it in my time — from cover to cover..." (90). And now there is no more hate. "By the time dessert was served, a semblance of friendship had developed; and sometimes it seemed a pity to interrupt the conversation..." (90). Having eaten, they pace around the suite of rooms. And again the past arises:

> Thus, many years ago, they had paced the empty rooms — he, still a boy, and his father, and patting his fair-haired son on the shoulder, the father had pointed to the stars: "The stars, Kolenka, are far, far away. From the nearest star, it takes the light at least two and a half years to reach the earth.... That's how it is, my dear boy!' " (90).

This entire conversation is an exact rendition of the habitual talks of "Borenka" Bugaev and his father; critics of Bely attest to this. In the novel *Petersburg*, autobiographical material is subordinated to the demands of the invented story; and it is changed, but not distorted. The Ableukhovs — Apollon Apollonovich and Nikolai Apollonovich — at their most essential and profound reflect the author and his father.

In relation to Bely, Freud's doctrine about the Oedipal complex is applicable. The spiritual wound which he had received in early childhood became for him the curse of inheritance. The image of the father and love-hate toward him predetermined his tragic fate. About Ableukhov-son the author writes: "Nikolai Apollonovich became a combination of disgust, fright and lust." This is his "original sin," which he can neither exculpate nor expiate. The "hereditary triad" rules him despotically: lust toward Sofya Petrovna Likhutina, disgust toward his father and toward himself; and everlasting fright: horror before the approaching destruction (the "sardine tin" with the time mechanism must explode). He feebly tries to shift his guilt onto others ("provocateurs"), but knows very well: "the provocation was within his own self." Nikolai Apollonovich suffers from a persecution mania and a feeling of being threatened by everything. On this pathological soil, the splitting of consciousness and the dematerialization of reality takes place. The action of the novel is transformed into a heaping up of "horrors."

Vyacheslav Ivanov devoted a brilliant article, "The Inspiration of Horror," to Bely's *Petersburg*.[4] In it he maintains, "I am convinced that before me is a very unusual work, a work which is unique in its own right." However, he takes Bely to task for his portrayal of Petersburg in 1905 because he omitted, as Ivanov says, ". . . all the real strengths of the Russian earth; because, knowing the Name before which all spirits melt like wax before the flame, he is not satisfied with this Name and tries to tame it to deceptive shadows flitting by." Then Ivanov remembers how the author read him the manuscript of his novel at the Tower:

> I will never forget those evenings in Petersburg when Andrei Bely read from the manuscript his still unfinished work. For my part, I assured him that "Petersburg" was the only title worthy of this work whose main character was the Bronze Horseman himself.... During the time when the poet was reading his *Petersburg* to me, I was delighted by the brilliance and novelty of what I heard, shaken by the strength of its internal meaning and the depth of its many insights.... This book contains the genuine inspiration of Horror. It begins to seem to the reader that the swallowed bomb is the general and comprehensive formula for the condition of personal consciousness to which we are all allotted in the earthly plan. "Know thyself".... Four walls of isolated consciousness — there is the nest of all the furies of horror.

And Vyacheslav Ivanov without hesitation calls *Petersburg* "'Andrei Bely's work of genius."

This evaluation hardly seems exaggerated when Bely's novel is viewed in totality, as a work of literary art. The author himself ascribed to his work a great significance and for ten years worked intensely on its stylistic form.[5] *Petersburg* has come to us in five editions: 1) the typewritten pages of the journal edition of 1911; 2) ten and a half galleys for the "book" edition of 1912; 3) the text printed in the third anthology of Sirin in 1913 and reprinted without alteration in a separate edition in 1916; 4) the text abridged by the author in 1916 for the German translation of 1919; and 5) the fundamentally reworked edition for the two volumes of Epokha (1922).

Bely elaborates on the idea of the birth of the novel from sound in a curious unpublished note of August 31, 1912:

> The external is sometimes more internal than the internal. Thus "clever" people say to me, "Excuse me, but allow me to protest against your interpretation of the dominating alliterations in the third volume of Blok's verses "*tr-dr*;" it's nice that you traced it, but its wrong for you to interpret it as a *tr*agedy of *t*emperance."[6] Meanwhile, when I showed Blok my interpretation in 1918, he was terribly pleased, got up and, jumping up and down (which he did when something touched him deeply), said to me, "Akh, Borya, how glad I am that you noticed this, this 'tragedy of temperance'." That is, he meant not the alliteration, but the content of the volume. It stands to reason that he agreed with my understanding of the tone of the third volume, and, really, the

155

monism of form and content is a postulate for such an interpretation. I, for example, know of the origin of the content of *Petersburg* from "l-k-l-pp-pp-ll" where "k" is a sound of stuffiness, suffocation from "pp-pp" — the pressure of the walls of Ableukhov's yellow house, and "ll" is the gleaming reflection of the "laquers," "glosses," and "lusters" within "pp-pp" — the walls or the covering of the "bomb" (Pepp Peppovich Pepp). And "pl" is the bearer of this glittering prison — A*poll*on A*poll*onovich A*bl*eukhov; and the person experiencing the suffocation "k" in "p" on "l" "lusters" is Ni*k*olai A*poll*onovich, the son of the senator. "No, you are having a fantasy!" — Allow me, for once: did I or did I not write *Petersburg*; there is no *Petersburg*: for I will not allow you to take my offspring from me; I know him to a degree you have never even dreamed of.

Bely was interpreting consonance: from the combination of liquids, labials and gutterals, emotion is born: the sounds are overgrown with images and ideas. Thus the phrase is constructed musically, the chapters are put together in a definite tonality, and the narrative grows up from alliterations and assonances. Bely's prose is instrumentalized. One example:

. . . a desire was born in him that the carriage should speed forward, that prospect after prospect should rush to meet him, that the entire surface of the planet should be embraced, as in the coils of a serpent, by blackish-gray cubes of houses; that the entire earth, prospect bound, should in her linear cosmic rotation intersect infinity on the rectilinear principle; that the network of parallel prospects, intersected by a network of other prospects, should expand and cover the world abysses with square and cubical planes... (12).

The "dominant" of this passage is the prospect; the combinations *pr-sp* color its entire sound fabric; another line of alliteration, *l-k* is joined to them; the vowels accompany the melody in "e" ("prol*e*t*e*la kar*e*ta, prosp*e*kty let*e*li navstrechu... s*e*t' parallelnykh prosp*e*ktov" — the carriage should speed forward... the network of parallel prospects). As in the hero's name — A*poll*on A*poll*onovich, so in the instrumentation of the entire novel, the "glosses" and "lusters" *l* collide with the suffocation *p*. In the second part, the sound *p* grows stronger: "suffocation" is embodied in the consonance "Pepp Peppovich Pepp." A storm of sounds rages, bronze instruments roar, the drums "b" and "p" roll. The orchestra thunders deafeningly "con tutta forza!" The exchange between "k" and "p" becomes the sound-signature of ro*ck*y *P*etersburg.

The massive majesty of the "city of Peter" and the "ponderous clangor of galloping hooves" of the Bronze Horseman are transmitted by the author in the metrical scheme of the anapest. And again, the very names of the major characters, Apollon Apollonovich (uu–/uu–/uu/) and Nikolai Apollonovich (uu–/uu–/uu/), predetermine the structure of the novel. Their anapestic nature becomes rhythmic law for the entire work. In the Sirin edition, this uninterrupted and endless chain of anapests created exhausting monotony. For the Berlin edition, the author decisively altered the rhythmical construction of the novel, mixing "heavy" anapests with "light" amphibrachs. Ivanov-Razumnik calculated that on a page of the Sirin edition (in the scene where the Bronze Horseman appears), there are 58% anapests and 2% amphibrachs, while on the same page of the Berlin edition the number of anapests falls to 38%, and the number of amphibrachs rises to 41%. In varying the rhythm of the narrative, the author achieves more lightness and melodism.

* * *

Bely is the creator of a new literary form, a new musically rhythmic prose. His teachers were Pushkin, the author of *The Bronze Horseman* and "The Queen of Spades," and Dostoevsky, the creator of *Crime and Punishment.* In the image of the lonely "dreamer," the revolutionary Dudkin, Bely combines the features of Evgeny, Herman, Chertkov and Raskolnikov. His *Petersburg* crowns the brilliant tradition of great Russian literature.

Petersburg, rejected by *Russian Thought*, was sold to the publisher Nekrasov, who ceded it to the Sirin publishing house. The novel was printed in Sirin's third anthology in 1916.

* * *

Life Abroad
(1912-1916)

In December 1912, Bely completed the most incredible of his books, *Notes of an Eccentric*. In it, recollections of childhood and youth are interwoven in chaotic disorder with the story of a mystical "three-year-period" spent with Asya Turgeneva abroad. In this "anthroposophic" period of his life, he had a tremendous spiritual experience; he ascended to the summit of "initiation" and was thrown down into the abyss of "nothingness." He saw both the "light of Favor" and demonic darkness; he fell sick with a terrifying emotional illness and by unprecedented will power held himself on the brink of madness. *Notes of an Eccentric* is not an artistic work, but a human document, valuable for the psychologist, the psychiatrist and the mystic.

During the summer of 1912, Bely and Asya arrived in Christiania (Oslo) and settled not far from it in the small town of Lian, on the bank of a fiord; they lived in the boarding house of Frau Nilson in a large, bright room which resembled a boat. Nelli (Asya) drew in an album the "thought-images" which came to her: doves, hexagrams, wings, winged crystals, spiral ornaments, goblete, hippopotami, serpents. Bely recalls an attack of her causeless executioner, when, "tearing herself away from a swarm of papers, on which the most complex schemes, interwoven into images, were sketched, Nelli —cried." But they also had quiet, joyful days, "when Nelli and I, seizing each other gaily by the hand, would prance over hollows, fissures, pits.... And nothing other than a sail, air, airy seaside outlines and water arose before our gaze." Here they read for the first time of the fact that humanity would some day form the tenth hierarchy: love and freedom. In Lian the "rebirth of his consciousness" began. "An incredible amount of work was completed; the cover of the 'biography' was exploded here." "These flying moments were strangely marked. These moments were continued in Dornach; the mountain of experiences became thorny; everything began with Christiania, leading through Bergen (over the mountains) to the crucifixion in Dornach."

After staying in Lian for five weeks, they went to Bergen. In the train between Christiania and Bergen, a meeting took place which defined Bely's entire destiny: for the first time he saw the famous "teacher," the anthroposophist Rudolf Steiner.

The beardless, clean-cut, firm face seems from afar to belong, of course, to a nineteen-year-old boy, and not to a man; and currents of invisible whirlwinds and storms fly off from it, shaking you. And moreover, this face expresses floods of the ecstasies of suffering: the eyes are diamonds. Two tears, addressed not to you, but from you, into their depths.

And Bely understood: the appearance of Steiner was saying to him: "Already the times are — fulfilled." Some nun, having attained the secret of the mysteries, went from the train car in which Steiner traveled to the car of our travelers and began to speak with them. Bely attaches decisive significance to the meeting with this anthroposophian woman.

She spoke of the fact that the aims were raised in the centuries of time (?) and gazed into my heart; her blinding gaze into my broken heart set fire to my sun; and, pressing myself to my own Self, I pressed myself — to a Self not my own.

In Bergen, he experienced a mysterious event inexpressible in words: "We experienced in Bergen days of indescribable importance. I feel them after at least ten years; and — now I am silent; I was seized from my ordinary body."

Bely traveled around Europe with Asya. From Bergen through Newcastle, they went to London, and from there to Paris; from Paris to Switzerland (Basel, Zurich, Montreaux, Lausanne, Lugano, Brunnen, Andermatt, Thun); from Switzerland to Germany (Stuttgart, Nuremberg, Munich, Berlin, Leipzig), and all the paths of travel and wandering led him to Steiner. In Leipzig, he heard a cycle of Steiner's lectures about the Holy Grail; a holy light illuminated him...

The whole room was transformed; appearances and the clear brilliance of unfolded wings grew broader; and a wave of the purest light washed the rows of bowing women under the lecturn. It seemed as if we were in the air: we were borne on extended, shining wings. And Steiner, after putting on his hat, walked among us, throwing an unforgettable glance at me and Nelli. And for a moment, all was torn asunder before my spiritual gaze because of this glance. And there rushed from the future centuries: "You — will be."

Bely was experiencing a mysterion.

These lectures caused the mysterion of the purification of the soul to be completed within me; the concussions of the ethereal body moved into an emotional shock, tearing the soul out of my body, and the purification — the result of the shocks — was prepared by bursts of indescribable, purely spiritual love for all of humanity.

In Leipzig, Bely made the acquaintance of the anthroposophist Morgenstern, with whom, until the very death of the latter, he joined in ardent friendship. Morgenstern became his "older brother"; Bely dedicated several ecstatic poems to him. The experience of spiritual light attained unendurable tension in Leipzig on the day when Bely visited the grave of Nietzsche.

Here I sensed that an incredible sun was being lowered into me; I would say that at that instant I was a light to the entire world. I knew that I in myself was not light, but that the Christ in me was a light for the entire world.

This ecstasy was beyond human endurance: Bely's soul could not bear such great heat, and it exploded. He writes:

The experience at the grave of Nietzsche was reflected within me by the assaults of an incredible illness. Near Basel and in Dornach I bore them uncomplainingly. Dornach became "Dorn" for me.

He understood: "I fell ill because I could not cope with the pressure of the love exploding within me."

Both Bely and Asya sensed that their destiny was inseparably linked with the "teacher" Steiner, that their path was predetermined by his will. On February 1, 1914, they settled in the anthroposophical center, Dornach, and began to work on the construction of "John's Temple." The author gives curious details about the life of the anthroposophical community in Dornach. According to Steiner's plans and drawings, a majestic building of gray-black concrete, crowned with two cupolas, was erected. A gigantic portal led into a

159

huge round hall adorned with twelve fourteen-sided columns, divided into two semicircles: seven colors and seven types of wood. On the columns were architraves with ornaments. "The dance of the columns and the flight of the walls made our heads spin." In the hall was a wooden statue of Christ, and multi-colored glass in the windows. The "brothers" were divided into groups and carved the architraves. They worked from morning to midday, then breakfasted in a canteen and rested until 2:00. They worked again until 6:00, drank coffee and continued to chisel the wood until 7:30. After dinner, a "eurhythmics" session took place. Once every two weeks, each person had night watch duty in the temple. The nights were strange in the not fully constructed fantastic building crammed with lumber and ladders, with yawning gaps, with the antediluvian forms of columns and arches, with the wandering little light of the night guard's lamp. A circle of massive pillars dedicated to the planets supported the gently ascending cupola. Bely, Asya, Asya's sister Kitty and her husband worked on the columns of "Jupiter" and "Mars."

We worked, striking a five-pound hammer against the huge chisel, which, for safety, was firmly tied to the wrist. Doctor Steiner, observing the work, saw all of us almost every day; he outlined the planes with coal.

On weekends, the brothers would meet in the huge workshop and, sitting on stumps, would listen to the lectures of the teacher. And it seemed to Bely that his whole past had vanished without a trace, that the writer "Andrei Bely" had died long ago.

In carving the walls of John's Temple, it was not wooden forms that I was cutting with the chisel, but my life; my life was carved in the cupola; only a sliver was pulled off.... The "I" in me is not "I" but... Christ: it is the Second Coming.

Bely lived with Asya in a small house surrounded by apple trees. The walls of his room he covered with glossy lilac and purple paper, and in there, nights, suffering from insomnia, he wrote the novella *Kotik Letaev*.

During the winter, in the overheated room, I would read passages of the novella *Kotik Letaev* to Nelli; she made corrections. The winds howled at us; grains of snow fell in a covering of ice. From Nelli's breast, growing and clothing me with warmth, like the sun, It arose, my happiness.

With passionate tenderness Bely recalls his strange friend, his guardian angel. He sees her before their parting, on a hill above Dornach:

In a cape flying out in snow-white folds, in her white panama, in a light

160

tunic with a yellow stole, belted with a silver chain, playing with her curls, she pressed her little face to her shoulder.... To me she is a youthful angel: transparent, bright, sun-like. And I admired her from afar. It seemed to me that she was the initiating herald of some forgotten mysterion.

He addresses her with prayerful incantations: "I have recognized Thee!" — — Thou hast descended to me from the air!" — "Thou hast illuminated me!" "Thou art my procession into the mountains." — "The spirit descending into me." He is indebted to her not only for his spiritual rebirth, but for poetic inspiration as well. "From the time I met her, external life became more orderly; my style as a writer defined itself. Nelli passed over it with an efficient stroke."

But when, called into military service, Bely was obliged to abandon Dornach and return to Russia in 1914, Nelli-Asya refused to follow him. And she never did return to him. Their paths diverged forever. Bely never knew why. Did she cease to love him, or had she never loved him? In *Notes of an Eccentric,* he pointed out the total opposition of their natures.

The architechtonics of our cognitive lines is contradictory to the extreme. The terminology of Volkelt, Lask and Kant is familiar to me, and the *Ars Magna* of Raymond is incomprehensible (I got lost in it; Giordano Bruno's commentaries did not help!). Nelli swims like a fish in the refined graphics of the scholastic thought of any Abelard.

Her favorite books were Plutarch, St. Augustine, Leonardo and Steiner. She was silent, intense, terribly quiet, while he was stormy, expansive, made of whirlwinds and "furies." The three-year period with Asya was the period of his mystical shocks and spiritual illness. The break with his "mysterious companion" was prepared already in Dornach.

* * *

In *Notes of an Eccentric*, there is so much confusion, delirium, shouting and madness, so much irritating pretentiousness and tortuous eccentricity, that to make sense of it is not easy. Until now, criticism has avoided this book with uncomfortable silence, as an obviously pathological work. In the meantime, the author wanted to describe in it "a sacred moment, overturning forever his entire previous idea of life," "an event of indescribable importance," the birth in him of a new man, a new mysterious "I." This event is indescribable," "inexpressible," like every mystical experience. It is possible to mumble vaguely about it, or to shout about it in a frenzy; it is impossible to speak about it rationally. However, the imperfection of expression not only does not injure it, but, on the contrary, testifies to the authenticity of the "mystical event." Bely is not lying and not pretending; he really underwent a tremendous spiritual shock and could not find words to describe it. All the literary practices and the stylistic methods of the writer Andrei Bely were powerless before the light blinding him. He writes:

The purpose of this diary is to tear the mask off myself as a writer; and to tell about myself, about the man, once and forever shaken. My whole life was preparation for the shock.... My life gradually became a writer's material for me.... "Tear up your phrase thus; write like... a shoemaker." I write like a shoemaker. About what do I write; I still don't understand.... The print which helped me to read the book of life is dispersed.... I know that the deposit of type sets drove Nietzsche out of his mind. I — will not go out of my mind.... My truth is beyond the sphere of the writer. The novelty of my tale lies in the accumulation of the "most worthless means" and "scaffolding" instead of the building of the tale. I, the stylist-writer, appear before you as the shoemaker of style.

In the light of the new revelation, he understood that his writing was a matter of chance, that his life as a writer was only one of the possibilities; and now, when other possibilities suddenly appeared before him, he wanted "to eliminate Andrei Bely." In him, in the man, was born a man, a mystical infant, his genuine "I." The author addresses the readers:

Love us as we are now unfortunates; not when in the future we erect on the surface of the earth magnificent temples of culture. Love us in the catacombs, in formlessness, perceiving not culture and style, but . . . contemplating without a single word the Vision of the Living God, descending toward us.

Epiphany, theofany, the vision of the light of Favor, the "devouring fire" — in these word-symbols all mystics have spoken — both Simion the New Theologian and St. John of the Cross. All of them, kindled with ecstasy, lived in the light of the Transfiguration. Bely continues:

The Second Coming has begun. With this truth I too was filled, while not apprehending it precisely.... My very being is the most improper cry before the life already doomed to destruction. And what is terrifying is that I am powerful not by means of terror and force, but by means of my complete helplessness.

The "indescribable event" which could have become for Bely the path to salvation and holiness led him to a terrifying catastrophe, almost to destruction. His mystical experience was distorted and twisted into anthroposophical heresy and occult mists. It was not Christ the God-man that appeared to him but His seducing double invented by Dr. Steiner. The ecstasies were transformed into a serious emotional illness. Bely tells about it and attempts to explain it; after the light came darkness, after insight — blindness. "Yes, the appearance of light (to my own eyes) does not surprise me: it was ten years ago. For ten years I have seen nothing like it; and I will not see it. Thus the darkness devoured me." And further: "The light blinded me. Now I have become blind. I don't see anything." In Dornach he fell ill; he lost consciousness and collapsed on the ground. He was taken to bed; he thought he was dying. For five weeks he lay like a corpse. The doctor diagnosed a cardiac illness. The fall and winter months of 1914 passed in anguish. "I was like one consumed by fallen fire; and outside these fiery arrivals I felt like a charred log." It was difficult for him to speak: "I lost every gift for expression."

He explains his "fall into darkness" as spiritual unreadiness, the inability to "cope with the light." It seemed to him that his personal drama was mysteriously connected to the world catastrophe — the beginning of the war in 1914.

> For myself I know: the light of ecstasy, the light of wisdom, in the face of the inability to cope with it, is transformed into blossoming sensual color, just as the light of Christ, falsely perceived, is darkened by the multi-color of Alexandrian syncretism.... I dreamed of the voices of lamenting thunders from the expanse of the soul; conglomerations of monstrous lusts took shape in moments of clarity. It seemed to me in the first autumn of the war that I had summoned it, that it had begun within me. The irreconcilable conscious war with my doubles was surging already in June.... The angel within me, fighting with the devil, was turned into a devil during the battle.... Thus the explosions within me became the explosions of the world; the war raveled out of me — around me....
>
> In the place where a man had lived, a clump of cold ashes remained. The wind blew; the ashes flew off, dispersed in the air, the man was no more.

In the consciousness of his own guilt ("the inability to cope with the light"), there are still glimmers of humility and repentance; but they are soon extinguished in the approaching darkness. The emotional illness appears at first in the form of a "mania grandiosa." Bely is convinced that his internal conflict has given birth to world war. He boldly asserts:

> Hunger, illness, war, the voices of revolution are the results of my strange actions: all that lived within me, tearing me to pieces, flew off around the world.... The catastrophe of Europe and the explosion of my personality are the same event. One might say "I" am the war; and the reverse: the war gave birth to me. I am the prototype. In me, there is something strange: the temple, the brow of the Age.

163

From this to the majestic consciousness of himself as the Tsar of the world is only one step. We are descending ever deeper into the darkness of madness. Bely continues:

> In occult development, there is a shocking moment when "I" recognizes itself as the master of the world. Extending the purest hands, "I" embarks along the red steps, presenting itself to the teeming world. The unification with the cosmos was completed within me. Thoughts of the world congealed up to my shoulders: only up to the shoulders is "I" my own; from the shoulders the heavenly cupola rises. Having removed my own skull from my shoulders, I raise it, like a scepter, with my hand.

Even in madness, Bely remains a poet. There is genuine poetic inspiration in his obsessive ideas.

The mania grandiosa is transformed with fateful inevitability into the persecution mania. He is the culprit of the war; he is a bomb threatening to explode the world, and the "enemies" ruling humanity through the occult must destroy him.

> It is clear to me. They know everything. They know that I am not I, but the bearer of a great "I" filled with the crisis of the world; I am a bomb hurtling to explode into pieces and, in exploding, to explode everything around.

But even if his "enemies" are destroyed — it's all the same — he will blow up the world. "But in the grave, in my native land, on Russian soil, my body, like a bomb, will explode all that is and will rise in a great cloud of smoke over the cities of Russia."

The story of the General Astral Staff of world-wide spies and occultists is among the most incredible inventions of Bely the poet. It is a fantasy of madness.

> Representatives of the state order of all countries and peoples! But the "state" is a screen behind which they have guarded their dreadful secret. By duping the people unconsciously devoted to them, through these people, they blow into the history of international relations the sand storms of world-wide catastrophes — war, "diseases." There, in an astral lamp, apparati like mines are placed: they are placed in such a way that hardly has a soul emerged from its everyday dream and opened like a flower turned toward the light, when . . . — the mine explodes; and the sir informs the proper authorities that an "infant" has been born.

A fantastic invention, worthy of Hoffman and Edgar Allen Poe!

164

* * *

In the summer of 1916, Bely and Pozzo, the husband of Asya's sister, received notice from Russia that they were called up for military service. They set off for Bern to the English Embassy to see about a visa. They were informed that they were required to obtain evidence of loyalty from the Swiss police. Bely was upset: of course, to an English functionary he would seem suspicious. And again incredible invention: the functionary would inform espionage that he was an occultist and had understood at once what was afoot: he would hypnotize Bely, the "human bomb," carry him away while he was sleeping to the General Astral Headquarters, and find out everything he needed. From then on, Bely was convinced that he was under surveillance, a "dark-skinned man in a bowler hat" was attached to him, following in his footsteps. Before obtaining evidence, the travelers had to return to Dornach. Bely ran into John's Temple and found Nelli there; she was carving forms on the smooth wood. They went for the last time to stroll in the mountains.

> Nelli squinted from the sun and covered her face with such a tiny little hand, suggesting the stalk of a flower with five petals. My Nelli, wise, complex, austere, seemed to me on that evening to be a fairy above the water.

Finally, the evidence was obtained; Nelli accompanied them to the station; her gaze was saying: "Love me! Don't forget! Wait for me!" She waved her handkerchief and cried. They left Bern. Bely writes:

> And there is no more firm ground; really, Dornach was for me the clump of earth on which I could stand firmly. Until that time when everything crumbled: the world war began to roar in the expanses of the world, devoured our bodies and our souls with steel teeth. But Nelli still remained in that world which forever, perhaps, had departed from me. Nelli said: "Be silent! I am still with you! I am defending you! A time will come when..."

The French border, police, interrogations, examinations, spies. All Europe was covered with a horrifying "secret war." Bely writes:

> One felt that the irreparable would be completed, right here, right this instant; the world of appearances would crumble; a terrifying secret would come forth. It is the secret of war; it will be revealed: "There is no 'battle;' it is a game played by a gang of scoundrels."

On the train he collided with the "dark-skinned man in the bowler," who identified himself as a doctor from Odessa. But Bely had no doubt: it was the same detective who even in Dornach had stood at the crossroad,

165

watching his house and Steiner's villa. He was frightening to Bely by nature of the fact that he was — nothing.

His appearance near me signified that the world in which you have been living, the world of mysteria, is nothing; your "I," now having issued from your body into the world of the spirit, which is nothing, is nothing.

Arrival in Paris. Heat, dust, confusion; the station without porters. On the steamship from Le Havre to Southampton, a "sir" replaced the "dark-skinned man in the bowler." He was "first-class;" it was the "black arch-angel." However, on the following morning, the "sir" lost his demonic halo and turned out to be a most good-natured Englishman, merry and obliging. London. Searchlights in the sky. Flights of zeppelins. The obliging "sir," the former "black archangel," appeared in the hotel of the Russian travelers and offered to show them the city. He took them to the Curiosity Shop made famous by Dickens and into St. Paul's Cathedral to a requiem Bely thought was for Steiner. Into Bely's mind flitted the terrifying thought that this was a trap and that he was suspected of destroying Steiner. He stared at his own photograph — well, of course, it would give him away: "In it the feverish gaze of villainous, frightened, deep-set eyes would create the impression that the bearer of the affixed card was — the one!" He began running around the offices, forms, delays, insidious questions. They would not give him a pass, they urged him to enter the Canadian army, they considered him a spy! And Bely pathetically exclaimed: "Oh, if only Milyukov, living at the same time in Oxford, knew into what they were transforming his fellow penster!" Finally, he received permission to board the steamship "Hakon VII," going to Bergen. On the North Sea, on a lonely, graying day, he was haunted by memories. He had left Bergen three years before: the straight line of life, running from Bergen to Dornach, had now come full circle: the beginning had become the end. He writes:

There, in the beginning, the Beginning moved toward me with the thousand-degree heat of its fanning wings; here — in the end — to the hulking stones of sharp-sided Norway floated a corpse in a coffin.... In between lay three years: the birth, maturation and demise of the "infant" in me or the "Spirit."

It seemed to him as if he had died — not here, and not in London, but on the train in Bern. Instantaneous death from a heart rupture.... His corpse had already been taken to Dornach, and Steiner and Nelli were burying him. And Bergen was only a dream for him. Around him the figures of lemurs and the sea of the elemental force beyond the grave.... "The soul, having cast off my body, first reads, like a book, its biography in the body...."

166

But Bergen was the same as it had been three years beofre. The same crush and yelling on the trade streets, the same Norwegian women in green, the same signs "Eriksen." In the stores, cheese and fish conserves were sold; from a rotten restaurant, pushing his old-fashioned hat down onto his forehead, "the deceased Henrik Ibsen rushed out headlong."

In Christiana, he sat with his friend in the park and reminisced about Nelli and Kitty.

It was already time for bed: after all, our path extended forward from the morning. We will arise tomorrow to the north, to the Arctic Circle, to Tornio, to Finland; there, after looking the Laplander in the eye, after quietly groaning from the cold, we will descend back to Petersburg.

The journey from Haparanda to Beloostrov was particularly exhausting; three secret services, the English, the French and the Russian, had the suspicious travelers under surveillance. Bely lost his baggage in confusion; he was especially sorry to part with a piece of tile from Dornach. At the Russian border, he was obliged to endure a dreadful moment: he saw in the train how a gendarme felt in his pocket for a revolver in order to shoot him.

Finally, all the horrors were ended, and in Beloostrov he stepped onto Russian soil.

Notes of an Eccentric was finished in Moscow in 1921. In 1922, Bely succeeded in going abroad, and in Berlin, while preparing his book for publication, he added an afterword to it entitled "An Afterword to the manuscript of Leonid Ledyanoi (the Icy), written by someone's hand."

The epilogue to the work of a madman is composed by a man entirely healthy and sober. The author had regained his health; "the anthroposophical period of his life had ended." He judges himself sternly and speaks of his "emotional illness" as an outside observer. He writes:

Notes of an Eccentric is for me a strange book, unique, exclusive; now I almost hate it. In it I see monstrous sins against style, architechtonics, the plot of any artistic work; it is a disgustingly tasteless, boring book, capable of arousing a Homeric chuckle. The hero of the story is psychologically abnormal; the illness, though, from which he suffered, as I can testify, is the illness of the time. "Mania grandiosa" is an illness of very many who do not suspect their illness.... The *Notes* is the only one of my books that is veracious; it tells of a terrifying illness from which I suffered during 1913-1916.... I passed through the illness; Friedrich Nietzsche, the magnificent Schumann and Holderlin fell into madness. And — yes: I remained healthy by removing my skin; and by reviving into health. This is a "satire" on sensations of "self-initiation."

Through my disgust with the "book," I love the *Notes* as the truth of my illness, from which I now am free.

167

* * *

In 1915, in Switzerland, Bely had thought up a grandiose epopee, *My Life*. He mentions it in the foreword to *Notes of an Eccentric*.

> The *Epopee* is a series of volumes I have thought up, which I will write, most probably, in a number of years. *Notes of an Eccentric* — the foreword — is the prologue to the volumes. The theme which can be expressed concretely only in a series of novels, begins here only from afar.

In Dornach, in his room covered with "lilac and purple glossy paper," during sleepless nights, he was writing the *Epopee*. It remained unfinished. Its first part, entitled *Kotik Letaev*, was printed in the anthology *Scythians* (Petrograd, 1917-1918) and came out in a separate edition in 1922 (Epokha, Berlin).

Kotik Letaev is a symphonic story "of childhood," "about the years of infancy." The author writes in the introduction:

> I am — thirty-five: self-consciousness has burst open my brain and hurtled into childhood. The past is extended into my soul; on the brink of my third year I stand before myself... Self-consciousness, as the little child in me, opened its eyes wide, and smashed everything — preceding that first flash of consciousness... meaning is life: my life. Before me is the first consciousness of childhood; and we embrace: "Greetings, you strange one!"[7]

After attempts to compose subjects and invent plots comes the frank admission that "meaning is my life." Bely has found his theme: the realization of the mysterious "I," the strange "being." All of his subsequent works are artistic variations on this single, immense theme.

Kotik Letaev presents an original metaphysics of the consciousness of a child; beneath psychology, both cosmogony and mythology lie hidden. Oceans of delirium rage, snake-legged monsters pursue the child along the labyrinths; like Heraclitus, he experiences "metamorphoses of the universe in the fiery hurricanes of the present." Finally, the melted lava cools; chaos is enclosed by the walls of the nursery. The first images dig into his soul: Nana Aleksandra, Grandmother, Aunt Dotya, Dr. Dorionov. The child fears boundless spaces, the terrifying worlds which move upon his sickly consciousness, threaten him with destruction. Nana defends him; in the corner near her trunk, under the clock, it is not frightening. But there — in the rooms, corridors, "spaces" of the apartment, thunders "fire-breathing papa." The boy sees with terror:

> . . . stinging, ragged, unkempt; he burned from inside; and outside — he sprinkles the ash of his dressing gown; beneath the tucked-in flap of the gown he stings with crimson; and he is like Aetna; lumbering, he embraces us (37).

168

In this first impression of fieriness, the sensation of heat during illness and the later stories about how Papa once set fire to the curtains with a candle merge. "Nana shelters me from Papa, and I — I have premonitions; destruction will come, it will come for Nana and me from Papa" (40).

The child lives in a premonition of catastrophe; the first feeling of fear is connected with the father. Consciousness arises, ill, wounded, from the pain. And the wound is unhealing.

Imagination creates myths. "I subsequently became acquainted with Greek mythology; and clarified my understanding of Papa: he is — Hephaestus; in his study, eyeglasses placed on his nose, there he forges his fires" (44). This cosmic being has been born from unknown "spaces" inimical to the child.

> Now in huge galoshes, in a massive racoon coat, he is running along the corridor right through the entrance door, in order, having opened his coat, to precipitate from there into the cosmos (44).

And now he is already a comet: "Papa dashes through the sky — like an immense comet, in the direction of that distant star they call the 'University,' he is dashing away in space" (44).

Thus the initial chance impressions and emotions create a cosmic myth about the father. The boy reaches the age of four; the world around him loses its fluidity and gaseousness. Constructs grow stronger, forms harden. "I went around — a quiet boy — draped in curls: in a vermillon frock; I was naughty very rarely; but I didn't know how to converse" (69). Nine o'clock in the mormorning: the maid, Raisa Ivanovna, in a red blouse, pours out the tea. Mama is still asleep; she will get up at twelve. Papa, in a uniform jacket, goes to his lectures. After breakfast, the maid takes Kotik to stroll on Prechistenky Boulevard. And in the evenings, Raisa Ivanovna reads to him about kings, swans. They drink tea with his grandmother and the old woman, Serafima Gavrilovna. Mama is at the theater, in her box, at the "Mascott." Papa makes a joke:

> "Serafima Gavrilovna: the Last Judgment won't occur." "What do you mean it won't occur?" "The Judgment trumpet has apparently been stolen by the devil: commotion in heaven.... There've been reports about it in the newspapers." And at this point, Papa, suddenly grown merry, would go off to his club (79).

In a gleam of youth and beauty, clothed in the poetry of rhythmic words, the image of his mother arises.

> My dearest Mommy is — young; and — she is intending to go to her nameday party.... Mama's little cheeks are — a full-blooded, rosy marble;

and her firm hands are — wearing clinking bracelets: she is going with Poliksena Borisovna Bleshchenskaya, in a splendid coach, — to the Marshal's Ball: fans, surah, tulle! In her earlobes hollow-faceted diamond earrings dropped like tears with a shifting flame; Mommy — in a velvet ball dress, in opopanax air, from her delicately cream-colored lace bowed down her wavy head (87-88).

The mother inspires the child with adoration and ecstasy — she is from a different, bright world, where he is borne in sleep "on wafting waltzes in the snow-white sparkle of columns" (89).
The world becomes ever wider:

Moment, room, incident, city are — the four steps taken by me, I have ascended them; and the world has expanded into the countryside; and instead of walls, there are open to me: transparent distances... (114).

The first impressions are of summer life in the village of Demyanovo. Four steps lead from the terrace onto a path, limes, grass, chickens, a lake — and in it is reflected "an itty-bitty boy. . . in a frock with lace" (116). Kotik remembers swimming in the river, the rosy-yellow skimmings, going after mushrooms. And in the autumn — return to Moscow.

Raisa Ivanovna and I are surprised at the cramped feeling of our rooms; the apartment is before me on the palm of my hand; the tightly cramped little corridor and the roach crawling along the wall: the tightly cramped nursery. Is this that Moscow? It wasn't from here that we went away; we went away from a huge world of rooms; it has collapsed (127).

He is five years old; new life experiences take place; he discovers that his development is "premature and abnormal." His mother kisses him and suddenly pushes him away and begins to cry: "He's not like me: he's like — his father..." He is also crying... "Is it really my fault that I — know: — my papa is in correspondence with Darboux; Poincare likes him; but Weierstrasse not particularly; Idealov was in Leipzig with . . . an elliptical function" (130-131).
The discord between the father and mother is experienced by the little boy as a tragedy. The mother complains in tears to the grandmother about her husband:

"With Kot too: he is prematurely developing the baby; raising the baby, — that's my business: I know how to raise children. He buys up all the English booklets — about raising children... A pile of trash... No, just think: about showing a five-year-old the alphabet... A big-foreheaded baby... I don't think much of mathematicians: he will grow up on me with the head of a second mathematician" (155).

And in the morning, before leaving for his lectures, while Mama is still sleeping, Papa embraces him, puts his hand on his own big palms and blows to warm his hands under his cuff. And leaning over him, he whispers: "Kotinka, lad, repeat after me: Our Father Who art in heaven..." (156).

And he no longer fears his father, but loves him, the clear-eyed, kind, "bearded and moustached" giant with the slanting eyes. His consciousness is split.

I love Papa very much; except that: he — teaches; and it is a sin for me to learn (I know that from Mama)... How is it so? Who is right?... With Mama it is easy for me: to chuckle, to turn somersaults; with Papa it is easy for me: to learn "Our Father;" ... I am a sinner: with Mama I sin against Papa; with Papa against Mama. How can I exist and: not sin? (156-157).

In the "prematurely developed" little boy the unity of the soul is sliced in two: from the cleft a little serpent slithers out — the feeling of guilt and sin. Lost is the innocence of childhood: the small sinner is ashamed of his nakedness and hides it under a mask... of pretense. Bely writes:

Because of this, I hid my views... until a very late age; because of this, even in high school I was considered a "dunce;" for the people at home, though, I was "Kotenka," — a good little boy... in a frock, who stood on all fours: to give them all a wag of his tail (163).

Bely's whole destiny — as a man and as a writer — is enclosed, as in a kernel, in this childhood "sin" of his.

Papa came again; he bowed over my forehead with a fattish little volume; and he read: — about Adam, paradise, Eve, the Tree, the ancient serpent, the earth, and good and evil (164).

At night, he suffered from nightmares: he would awaken with a scream. Raisa Ivanovna took him to sleep in her bed. But he didn't sleep: he was silent, hardly breathing; his chest was constricted.

This, thought I — is growth; this, thought I — is the Tree of Knowledge, about which Papa used to read to me; of knowledge — about good and evil, about the snake, the earth, Adam, paradise, the Angel... At night this Tree often arose in me; a snake was wound around it (166).

This is a lofty example of Bely's Symbolist art. Here psychological

171

analysis attains a metaphysical profundity. Spiritual experience is born from emotion, and it is clothed in the Biblical myth of paradise and the Fall. Adam, the serpent, the tree of knowledge of good and evil — these are the secret reality of the human soul.

* * *

On the plane of ordinary existence, exile from paradise is embodied in the parting with Raisa Ivanovna. Grandmother and Aunt Dotya whisper to Mama that the maid is taking her child away. "These coddlings are not natural: this development!" "Outsiders have wormed their way into the house" (183). Mama stares angrily at the "separator." "Raisa Ivanovna is weeping in bed; the mattress under her is having tremors; and I — go to her from my bed; to weep a while, the two of us together" (188). "Our Papa, making the floorboard creak, would steal loudly into the room: to console Raisa Ivanovna and me" (188). But the finale approaches. "I lived in expectation of catastrophe; one day it acually occurred: we — Raisa Ivanovna and I — were driven out: I — from the radiant worlds; but she — into the Arbat" (190).

The first sorrow in life: the boy is seized by "unprecedented sadness"; everywhere he seeks the beloved Raisa Ivanovna. For him, all objects, events, the room are connected with her. Humdrum existence begins. He wanders dejectedly with his grandmother on Prechistenky Boulevard. In the evenings, no one reads to him "about his darling queen."

The child's first love, half conscious, half dream, innocent but erotic, ends with exile from paradise. And the little frock with a lace collar is no more; he is "a boy in a sailor's jacket, in pants." "They had sewn all this for me not long ago; pants... All is ended! The mathematicians are at hand" (194).

Kotik is unhappy and lonely; he pretends to be stupid; he cannot speak. They whisper about him: "He is stupid..." "Always silent." "He doesn't make his own judgments..." "A little monkey of some sort." (209-210).

It's not time for pants yet: he goes about as a sailor with a massive, rose-colored anchor, but without words. He rubs his head against his shoulders in response to caresses. He looks at the world from under pale chestnut locks. "No, I don't like the world: in it all is — difficult and complicated. One can't understand anything there" (121).

With this, the story breaks off. Gazing back on the reality in which he lived in childhood, the author asks himself "What is all tnis? And — where was it?" Neither awake nor dreaming: a special world, about which adult consciousness can speak only in the musical language of symbols and myths.

Chapter Eight: Life in Russia (1916-1921)

In August, 1916, Bely returned to Russia. Sad was his meeting with his native land. He writes in *Notes of an Eccentric*:

My God, it's muddy, gray, bustling, aimless, undisciplined, damp. On the streets — puddles. The streets are covered with brown slush: grayish drizzle, graying wind, and patches on the gray, peeling, unplastered buildings. A gray flood of overcoats; everyone is in overcoats. Soldiers, soldiers, soldiers — without weapons, without bearing; their backs are bent, their chests sunken; their faces dejected and ugly; their eyes wander....
    ... Now my eyes are opened, but — what do I see? That all, all has fallen to pieces; that the old has been destroyed, and a revolution (is this collapse a revolution?) has taken place before the revolution.... I have come to understand that in Russia everything is incorrigible; these sirs have bantered and mocked enough now; the atmosphere of the press is mocked here, and souls are mocked; "I" is mocked, it is fired upon from cannons. "They" need bodies, if only red beef, carcasses; and I was called to Russia to register to become a carcass.

But Bely's life in Moscow did not take shape as tragically as he had expected: he was not accepted into the army; his friends were glad to see him; his lectures were a tremendous success. He recalls the first months of his Moscow life:

I would open a page of the newspaper: in the newspaper I was praised. And I went visiting: to Bulgakov, Gershenzon, Berdyaev and Loseva. They listened to me with genuine attention. I went to "poetic concerts" in the company of the "Jacks of Diamonds"[1] .... My lectures attracted a surprising amount of people. I had a strange influence in my lectures; it seemed to me that I would enter people's subconsious, obliging them to tell me their most cherished thoughts.... The world where I had lived only two months before, "John's Temple," the "I" in it heralding incredible news of Dornach, the Doctor — all this was a dream here in Moscow.

Bely was "in vogue"; he was surrounded by admirers, beseiged by young girls. Vladislav Khodasevich (*Nekropol'*) recalls his meeting with Bely at Berdyaev's house on the evening of the assassination of Rasputin.

Physically coarsened, with toil-hardened hands, he was in a condition of

173

extreme excitement. The balding top of his head with clumps of graying hair seemed to me like a copper sphere which was charged with millions of volts of electricity.

Khodasevich guessed at once that Bely was suffering from a persecution mania and was seeing occult provocateurs everywhere.

Bely responded to the revolution of 1917 with the article "Revolution and Culture" (published by Leman and Sakharov, Moscow, 1917), in which he affirms the revolutionary force of art. The spiritual fire of Prometheus is the hotbed of revolution in the pre-revolutionary period; revolution is the act of the conception of creative forms maturing over the decades. The revolutionary period of the beginning of the century raced across Europe in a wave of Romanticism, while in our time, it passes before us in a wave of Symbolism. The creations of the fathers of Symbolism are already fraught with revolution, world war and much more which has not been completed within our field of vision. He who can penetrate the myths of the recent past will repeat the words of Blok:

> But I recognize you, the beginning
> Of lofty and rebellious days.

The political revolution is only a reflection of the spiritual revolution. In art, this revolution has been taking place for a long time. It is expressed in the rebellion against form.

> It is recognized that creation lies in the creation of new spiritual and emotional forces; its form is not transitory, no, it is not clay, not paint, and not sound. No, it is the soul of man.

And the article concludes with a summons to the "fiery enthusiasm" of genuine revolution. Bely writes:

> The revolution of the spirit is a comet flying toward us from the utmost reality; the overcoming of necessity in the kingdom of freedom; the comprehension of the inner connection of the arts with revolution. It is found in the comprehension of the connection of two images: the comet falling above our heads and the motionless star within us. This is the real intersection of the two Gospel behests: "Feed the hungry," and "Not by bread alone."

The article is written with great, joyful enthusiasm, with faith in the coming of "the kingdom of freedom," and the spiritual rebirth of humanity. Like Blok, Bely also calls for "hearing the music of revolution."

* * *

October 1917 — during the days of the October Revolution — Bely was completing his *Poem about Sound — Glossolalia.*[2]

It is a small treatise on sound as the "gesture of lost content." In the introduction, we read:

> *Glossolalia* is a sound poem. It is the most successful of the poems I have written ("Christ is Risen" and "First Meeting"). And as such I ask that it be accepted. To criticize me scientifically is utterly senseless.

The author attempts to penetrate the secrets of language, its deepest strata where there are neither images nor concepts. The word is earth, lava, flame. Its surface is covered with a cloud of metaphors: this cloud must be dispersed and the threshold crossed: into the night of madness, into the universe of the word where there is neither thought nor image, but only "empty and invisible firmament." But the Holy Spirit moves above it. The author does not hide the fact that his poem is inspired by the "outline of the secret knowledge" of Rudolf Steiner. The dry "science" of anthroposophy Bely adorns with the colors of poetry. In the beginning, there was the sound. "The tongue leaped like a dancer," he writes. "The play of the dancer with a light airy stream, like a gossamer scarf, is now inaudible to us." But the author believes that a time will come when the "mimicry of sounds" will catch fire in us and will be illuminated by consciousness. Now we wander about by touch and are only guessing in the dark. We feel, for example, that the "flying of air into the throat is 'Hah!' and, because of this, 'akh' is surprise, intoxication with air; 'ha' is a salute, an emanation of air, an ember of the soul."

Descending into the "universe of the word," into the "dense and waterless firmament," the poet intends to communicate to us the "wild truth of the word." He writes:

> I am a Scythian. I was born in the world of harmony and have just sensed in this newly discovered world that I am an experiencing sphere, multi-faceted and turned in upon itself. This sphere, this world, is my mouth: sounds rush about in it. The division of the waters has not yet taken place: neither seas, nor lands, nor plants — airy embers play, watery airinesses play. There are no audible sounds.

With the help of anthroposophic secret knowledge, Bely creates a mythology of sounds — one of his most fantastic inventions. In the beginning, there was only a "stream of heat," which rushed to the exit of the throat: the "serpent Ha-hi," full of smothering and cries. But here the tongue enters the battle: it, like Siegfried with the sword "r," beats the serpent with its "R" — the first action, the battle; (ira — anger, fury; ar — furrow, Erde — earth).

175

The sound cosmogony turns about, and we discover many instructive things: thus, for example, it becomes clear that the "crossing of the lines of heat with the line 'r' produces a cross in the circumference: hr = cross, crux, croix; that the stream 'h' falling on the sound 'r' begins to rotate and flies through the teeth to the surface in a luminous whistle: 'z' and 's' — sunny sounds ('swar' — sun, sunrise, zenith; 'zen' — day, light)."

Bely the creator of myths boldly refashions the book of Being. People originated from sound and light:

In ancient, ancient Aeria, in Aeria we also lived at one time — as sound-people. And there we were the sounds of exhaled lights. The sounds of lights live remotely within us; and sometimes we express them with the sound wording, Glossolalia.

After explaining the abstruse, mysterious meaning of all the vowels and consonants of the Russian alphabet, the poet concludes the poem with a pathetic address to the country of Aeria. He writes:

Image and thought are a unity. To overcome the splitting of literature means also to overcome the tragedy of thought without words; and to remember that there is a memory of memory or the formation of speech; the creation of ourselves and everything in which we live, because the sound of speech is the memory of memory, of Aeria, the beloved country, the country of miracle plays, lilies, the winged angel of tears...

Through the fragments of smashed, broken, declining life — to Aeria.

Then there will be brotherhood among peoples; the language of languages will explode languages , and the second coming of the Word will be completed.

The author, of course, is right: to scientifically criticize his anthroposophic linguistics is utterly senseless. *Glossolalia* is a poetic fairy tale about the "beloved country" Aeria, where "airy embers" and "watery airiness" shine like a fantastic rainbow.

* * *

Marina Tsvetaeva recalls Bely in 1917-1918:

Always surrounded, always free... in the eternal accompanying dances of coattails... Old-fashioned, elegant, refined, bird-like — a mixture of the magister and the conjurer, in a double, triple, quadruple dance: of meanings, of words, of swallow coattails, of legs — oh, not of legs! — of the whole body with a separate life to its conductor's back, beyond which in two wings, in two ascending staircases, is an orchestra of dis-

176

embodied spirits... Enticement — that's the word for it. Enticing, and, as everyone says, however, with the tenderest of smiles — a traitor![3]

Marina Tsvetaeva would meet the "enticer" on the staircase of the Theosophical Society and at the Narkompros (People's Committee for Education). Once, on the green lawn of the Palace of the Arts, she was present at one of his lectures. With great skill, she reproduces Bely's improvisation on the Nichevoki.[4]

The Nichevoki, says the lecturer, are fleas in an empty house which the owners have left for the summer... A country house! Not that log cabin in Sokolniki, but a country house — a gift, someone's gift, and here Russian literature was just someone's gift, a country house, but... (finger to his lips, an air of mystery) the own-ers went a-way. And nothing remained... Out of everything, nothing remained, but kkhi-khi... On black legs, little fleas. And how they prickle! Sting! How invulnerable they are! Just like you, gentlemen, are invulnerable in your noth-ingness! Along the edge of a black pit, the sunken pit where Russian literature is buried . . . on matchstick legs little Nichevoki are creeping. And your kids will be dear little Nichevoki.

And Tsvetaeva continues:

This was Bely dancing out the Nichevoki. The smooth lawn, set with little yellow flowers, became a rug beneath his feet — and through it, he circled, arose, leaped, fell down, leaned over, seemed about to fly off the earth: a vision of a girl with a little goat!

In 1920, Bely lived for a while in the Palace of Arts, on Povarskaya Street at Kudrinskaya Square (the home of the Rostovs in Tolstoi's *War and Peace*). Boris Zaitsev recalls his visit to the poet:[5]

Bely was in a little scull-cap with a graying "raggedness" of hair under it, just as elegant, dancing, cloying as ever. The room was covered with books and manuscripts. For some reason, there was a blackboard in it.

They spoke of anthroposophy and revolution. Bely sketched circles, spirals, curls on the blackboard.

Here he was without his habitual nervousness. It was more like a soothing fantasy. "Do you see? The lowest point of the spiral? That is you and I at present. That is the present moment of the revolution. We will not fall further. The spiral goes toward the top, widening. It is already carrying us out of hell into the open air."

177

In the fall of 1921, Bely succeeded in leaving Russia. In Kovno, he was obliged to wait for a German visa. He wrote a letter to Asya in despair: twenty pages of large format, in a small hand, giving a detailed account of his life in Russia during the period of military communism. The letter was not sent, and in 1923, Bely gave it to Vladislav Khodasevich. It was printed in greatly abridged form in the journal *Contemporary Notes.*[6] Bely writes:

Until Christmas of 1918, I gave a course of lectures, conducted seminars for the workers, worked out a program for the Theatrical University, gave lectures in the unheated estate of the Anthroposophical Society, attended meetings of the Society.

As of January 1919, I abandoned everything... I lay under a fur coat and was completely prostrate until the spring, when the thaw warmed my body and soul a little... It is not for us, old men, bearing on our shoulders 1917, 1918, 1919, 1920 and 1921, to tell about Russia. And one wants to say: "Yes, now, when I was lying for two and a half months covered with lice, then for me..." "For two weeks I took a cure for eczema, which was caused by the lice, etc." Or one begins to say: "When next to me, behind a thin partition a typhus victim screamed night and day..." Yes, I lived and went to give lectures, prepared for lectures under this screaming. The temperature in the room was not less than 8° below freezing and not higher than 7° above. Moscow was dark. During the nights, wooden private homes were looted... This is how I lived during that time: in my room a heap of my manuscripts were thrown in a corner, and for five months I used them to light the stove; everywhere heaps of old junk were piled up, and my room resembled the room of a junkman. Amidst the debris and garbage, with the temperature between 6 and 9°, in winter gloves, with a hat on my head, legs numb to the knees, I would sit in the very dim light of a burned-out lamp, either preparing material for the lecture of the next day or working out the project entrusted to me in the Theatrical Society, or writing *Notes of an Eccentric,* throwing myself into bed in exhaustion at four o'clock in the morning: because of which I would wake up at nine o'clock, and no one would have left any hot water for me. Thus, often without tea, shivering from the cold, I would get up and at eleven o'clock would race from Sadovaya to the Kremlin (where the Theatrical Society was), going from meeting to meeting. At three-thirty, in someone else's fur coat, suffocating my chest and throat, I would drag myself from the Kremlin along a disgusting, slippery sidewalk to Devichi Field in order to eat dinner (a dinner better than the "Soviet," for I was fed in a private house, at my friends the Vasilievs). After dinner, I had to go a good distance from Devichi Field to the Smolensk market, in order to provide myself with rotten flat cakes for supper, getting shoved around by a lice-ridden, stinking crowd and sickly dogs. From there, from the Smolensk market, I would drag myself home at five or six o'clock, so that at seven I could already rush back along Povarskaya to Proletcult, where I was teaching young poets to value the poetry of Pushkin, myself becoming excited by their excitement over poetry. And already from there, at eleven o'clock, I would make my way home, in absolute darkness, tripping over the impossible pits and bumps, and almost crying because the tea which they left for me had again grown cold, and ahead would be such cold that one would want to scream from it...

And I found strength all the same: to give lectures which ignited hope among the people (people waited for my lectures as moral support in their darkness); and I overcame the darkness by giving others the strength to bear the darkness, while not having this strength myself and as if I were holding out my own hands for help...

Think how they live in Moscow: for five years I could not sew myself a winter coat; my unmentionables were in such condition, all summer, that I was obliged to wear a Russian shirt all summer in order to hide the impropriety of my pants... My hat was ragged; we all looked like ragamuffins. For three days I walked around in slippers in Petrograd because there were no boots... Think — everywhere lines. From line to line. Think, and I had about six meetings a day. And, returning home, to haul firewood, cut the wood, and get in a line... Those bitter moments of personal desertion I will not forget...

In the beginning of 1920, Bely moved into the apartment of the authoress N., a former Khlystovka and "libertine," a capricious fairweather friend, but a good person.

The room was heated every day or so: the temperature was bearable, from 7 to 9°. Moreover, very often our dinner was cooked in my stove. Potatoes were mixed with manuscripts. At that time, I was giving a course, "Anthroposophy," in the Anthroposophic Society, in an estate where the brain turned to ice from the cold and where everyone sat in fur coats and hats.

Finally, in February 1921, he could not bear it, and fled to Petersburg. Until June, he gave lectures in the Free Philosophical Academy ("Volfila"). "How tens of souls clung to me there as I acquainted them with 'Self Knowledge!' They literally imbibed me, and, imbibed, I rushed back to Moscow, because I could give no more to the people." Bely gave approximately sixty lectures at Volfila.

In September 1920, A. I. Annenkov picked me up and took me to live beyond Moscow with him at a factory. From there, I made runs to lectures (by means of which I lived materially and by means of which many souls lived morally). From September to January, I was writing a book on the philosophy of culture and the draft of *Epopee* (the first volume), working insanely, to the point of nervous exhaustion.

The book on the philosophy of culture (an anthroposophic substantiation of culture) remained unpublished. The author mislaid it. When he was living in Germany in 1922, friends sent him a manuscript from Moscow; its subsequent fate is unknown. The first volume of *Epopee* was not completed; its first chapter appeared in the fourth volume of the journal *Notes of a Dreamer* (1921) under the complex title, *The Crime of Nikolai Letaev. Epopee — Volume One. The Baptized Chinese. Chapter One.* No less grievous is the fate of Bely's third book written in 1920, *Tolstoi and Culture.* The author entrusted it to some "Latvian speculator" who was going abroad and who promised to publish it there. Bely had not succeeded in making a copy — the "speculator" disappeared without a trace — and the book was lost.

In December, 1920, Bely became ill. He writes:

In December, I fell in a bath and for ten days dragged myself into Moscow from under Moscow, until periostitis of the sacrum occurred, and it became evident that I had broken my sacrum. I was dragged to a hospital, where I lay for two and a half months covered with lice...

* * *

During the tragic period of 1918-1920, besides the lost books, *Philosophy of Culture* and *Tolstoi and Culture*, and the incomplete *Crime of Nikolai Letaev*, Bely wrote the poem "Christ is Risen," published three little books, *At the Divide,* and a small collection of verses, *The Princess and Her Knights.*

The poem "Christ is Risen," created in one week in April, 1918, is Bely's response to Blok's poem, *The Twelve,* which appeared in January of the same year.[7]

Blok shows the black night of revolution, a winter storm in the dark streets of Petersburg, in which ominous misshapen phantasms of the perishing world rush past — a bourgeois, a young lady in an astrakhan, a writer, an old woman, prostitutes. Twelve red army soldiers, brigands, walk "with a revolutionary tread." And before them — "Christ in a white halo."

Bely takes up Blok's idea, outlines his fine drawing with coal, emphasizes the contrasts, strengthens the emotional tension. Russia experiences the crucifixion on the cross, but after this will come the resurrection.

In Dostoevsky's *The Idiot*, Holbein's picture "Removal from the Cross" hanging in Rogozhin's gloomy house is described. Prince Myshkin is shaken by the realism of this painting. In the picture, a body is not depicted, but a corpse. "Why, some people might lose their faith by looking at that picture!" he sadly exclaims. With the same unsparing realism, Bely depicts the crucifixion of Christ:

... He extended
His hands
Dying, blue from torture...
The tortured, overwrought Body
Hung
Without thought.

* * *

Some horrible It
With dangling, tangled hair
Expiring,
And spreading torn
Wounded
Hands, —
In the ninth hour
Hoarsely cried from the darkness
At us.
"Eli, . . . sabachthani!"[8]

* * *

Fibers,
Like a yellow cane,
Bandaged
Into rustling shrouds...

And, like Myshkin, the author asks: "God! And this was Christ?"

The resurrection of Christ is depicted by Bely with all the rhetoric of anthroposophic insight. "A universal mystery is completed." "The body flew down to the opened depths, it extended from the earth to the ether, dispersed the ambiance of Lethe." "The body of the Man of the sun became the body of the earth."

The crucifixion of Christ is the crucifixion of Russia; the poet boldly places the equal sign:

My country
Is a grave...
The poor Cross —
Russia.
You are now
The Bride.
Harken to
The news
Of spring...
There ascends
With huge roses
The growing Cross.

Russia is on the cross. Russia is in the grave.

Brigands and ravishers are we.... Over the body of the deceased, we strew his hair with ashes and extinguish the lamps..... We are in our former abyss of disbelief.

There follow, as in Blok's *The Twelve,* ironic sketches of the "old world."

Behind the cannon's roar, the back of a bespectacled, weakened member of the intelligentsia stuck out in a hump... The shaggy head, mouthing angry words about the significance of Constantinople and the straits, is visible.

In Blok:

Betrayers...
Russia has perished...
Perhaps, a writer,
An orator....

In Blok, the Red Army member Vanka kills his rival; in Bely, a railroad worker is killed. "The Browning with a red roar explodes in the air — the body of the bloodied railroad worker falls with a crash. Two atheists lift him."
In Blok:

Close the shutters,
Now there will be looting.

In Bely: "Defending themselves from someone, the whole house committee inundates the gates with firewood."
But crucified Russia will be resurrected. And the poem concludes with a pathetic, apocalyptical address to his native land:

Russia,
My country —
You are yourself
The Woman clothed with the sun...
I see it clearly:
Russia
Mine,
The God-bearer,
Conquering the Dragon...

And something in my throat
Is wrung with tender emotion.

A great shining cloud descends upon Russia, and from the depths resounds: "Beloved sons — Christ is risen!"
The frenzied and hysterical tone of the poem corresponds to its torn, tattered form. The rhythmic prose, broken into pieces and fragments with chance rhymes and unexpected assonances, is tiring in its faltering patter. With the failure of his poem, Bely only emphasized the unity and inimitability of Blok's *The Twelve.*

* * *

Under the general title, *At the Divide,* Bely united three articles written in Switzerland in 1916 and first published in Petersburg in 1918-1920: "The Crisis of Life," published by Alkonost, Petersburg, 1918; "The Crisis of Thought," published by Alkonost, Petersburg, 1918; and "The Crisis of Culture," published by Alkonost, Petersburg, 1920 (in 1923, they were reissued by Grzebin in Berlin).

In the first article, "The Crisis of Life," philosophical meditations are presented in the framework of impressions of the war and life in Dornach. At this point, Bely had already lived for two years in "thundering quiet." And, in Alsace, cannons were thundering day and night.

The tip of the front thunders uninterruptedly. The front beyond it thunders uninterruptedly. All four hundred kilometers thunder uninterruptedly, perhaps. Many fronts thunder. Russia thunders on the east....
I am well aware that all the new hundreds of thousands of people, like rye in a thresher, will be plunged with thunder into a howling zone. Probably I will be plunged into it as well. I will depart from here. While I am here, however, I will assert my humanity in a new way: in an inhuman moment.

Of what are the cannons in Alsace speaking? What does the war signify? The author responds: we have killed the world soul. Our materialistic civilization has destroyed the idea in phenomena, and phenomena have become an object of consumption. The earth has ceased to be the earth and has been transformed into an abstract world of artificial apparati, concepts, aspirations and lusts. The machine has rebelled against man; the lifeless present has disintegrated. Instead of a merging with the world, the devouring and break-up of the world prevails. We are experiencing a crisis of consciousness and, perhaps, a world crisis. Bely's words resound with sincere despair:

I am irrevocably lost; we are all lost, and we will not galvanize our corpses. I have long since abandoned my skin, together with the nature from which I fell.... We are the children of Cain. Our paths lead to destruction.... I am irrevocably lost. This is the only philosophy capable of showing us the way out of the problem....

After the more dreadful war of 1939-1945 which we have lived through, several of Bely's assertions acquire a prophetic meaning. He predicts a new human nature, which he calls the "papooses of the 20th century." They are civilized wild-men, white Negroes, "tango-dancers," "Apaches," Futurists. To them belongs the future.

However, the "philosophy of destruction" leads the author not to despair, but to hope. "The earth shows portents," he writes. "Perhaps there will be portents in the heavens; the firmament of the earth and the heavens — it has trembled within us."

But the world Soul, Sofia, the Divine Wisdom, will return to the unhappay earth: all will be united in Her in a new way, all will enter Her temple.

We are now at the gates. Sofia, Divine Wisdom, kindles starry lamps for us beyond the darkness. In this starry crown, she draws near to us.

And the article concludes with the inspired prophecy of Vladimir Soloviev:

Know that Eternal Femininity now,
In imperishable body, walks the earth.

The second article, "The Crisis of Thought," is filled with the bombastic and confused profundities of the "initiated." Spiritual knowledge, secret knowledge, "the goblet heralding the dove," "the emasculation of the heart in union with Klingsor" — all this anthroposophic declamation is reducible to one simple idea: humanity must strive for the harmonic unification of the head and the heart. Sometimes, vital and original thoughts blaze forth in the thick fog of Steinerism. Feeling is the source of thought. Ancient philosophy was born from ecstasy. The author writes:

In ancient thought, ecstasy was the most necessary condition for thought to be born from the initial chaos of the present. Thought ascends from the body through the soul, and flows from the soul like a spirit.... Ecstasies, the paths of initiation, incredibly difficult life tragedies down through the centuries formed the rationality of thought in the heads of the best, purest, holiest people, thought which runs through a number of brochures, popular treatises, textbooks of logic, the mastering of which is possible for any of us. The paths of ancient initiation are the street.

Bely the anthroposophist considers himself to be a direct heir to the ancient initiating mysteries. And this pretension devaluates his interesting

184

meditations.

Half of the path lies in mysticism, he writes; the other half lies in philosophy. Thought not warmed by the heart is the kingdom of Ahriman and Mephistopheles. Feeling not directed by the mind hides within itself the temptation of Lucifer and attracts us to Khlystovstvo. The author cites his own work as an illustration of his assertion. He announces:

Yes, my novels *Petersburg* and *The Silver Dove* depict two horrors of our life, a life which does not dare enough: liberation in a heartless head, and the insanity of the heart.... Apollon Apollonovich Ableukhov flees from life into his "head"; he wanders, traveling along it. But this "head" is the yellow house of Ahriman, an overgrown skull. And insanity of the heart drives freedom from the brain in Daryalsky. He is consumed in mystical rites; Lucifer gazes at him through the joiner Kudeyarov. He perishes... Our freedom dares to fly above the fire of the heart to the walls of the skull, and to explode the walls of the skull: Nikolai Apollonovich feels the necessity for an explosion within himself: with the motion of the swallowed bomb....

In the third article, "The Crisis of Culture," Bely remembers Basel, his life with Asya in Norway, the building of the temple in Dornach, anthroposophy. "Secret knowledge" he calls the "mathematics of a new soul," "spiritual science." In it, he offers "the culture of the future." Steiner's doctrine was accepted by Bely with all the zeal of the neophyte. Before the philosophy of the "doctor," all his philosophical culture – Kant, Cohen, Lask and Rickert – proved powerless.

The most tragic event in Bely's life abroad before Dornach was the pilgrimage to Nietzsche's grave. He writes:

I brought flowers to the grave of the deceased Friedrich Nietzsche. It was near Leipzig. I remember it, I fell for a moment on the gravestone, touching my forehead to it, and felt clearly that the cone of history suddenly and mysteriously dropped from me. It seemed clear to me that the fact of our traveling to the remains of the deceased Nietzsche was an event of immeasurable cosmic importance, and that I, leaning toward the grave, was standing on the summit of a monstrous historical tower, which toppled, separating from my legs so that I was saying in the emptiness, "Ecce homo." And I – "Ecce homo." So it seemed to me. And it also seemed to me that an incredible Sun descended into me.

* * *

In 1919, the Alkonost publishing house printed a small anthology of Bely's poems, *The Princess and Her Knights*. In it are included ten songs written in 1901-1911.

In the dreadful, icy Moscow of 1919, Bely was living on memories of the past — of the beginning of his love for Asya, and from his old verses he selected the ones dedicated to her. Concerning this period, he writes in *Notes of an Eccentric*:

> The years ran on.... Only Nelli remained alive; and I reached toward her. I loved my Nelli with an elusive, tender love. She, her spirit, dictated the *Notes* to me....

The poems in the cycle, *The Princess and Her Knights,* are united by a fairy-tale theme. An old picture is revived: woods, a cliff, a castle on the cliff. A knight is also revived — on a shaggy steed, he rushes toward the castle: it is too late — all have already died...

> And at times the water
> Spoke dejectedly with the past, with what has been:
> All this was, it was,
> It will be — always, always!

Another scene. The princess languishes in the castle; a voice says to her, "Oh, remember," while a hunchbacked jester drones, "Forget." And now the knight flies in.

> Oh, princess, at hand
> Is your salvation:
> On the iron gates
> A lance is beating.

Still more joyful is the poem "To the Kindred Spirit." The princess cannot sleep; her knight has vanished into the forest distance — and she kindles a light in the tower:

> He has found you, princess!
> He has heard the good news!
> The depths sing melodiously.
> It will be. It was. It is.

The exultant poem, "Prophetic Dream," breathes with faith that there will be joy, that the faithful knight will find his princess. These soaring lines are charming:

> Brooks, converse, converse!
> My soul, be joyful, arise!
> Accept me: do not reject me: I am here,

The friend of fairy tales, half-forgotten, dear!...
How good it is! And — sparkling heights!
And unseen forces above my soul!

After a difficult emotional illness, after the darkness and cold of the grave in which he had been buried alive, Bely returned to life. And hope for resurrection was connected for him with Asya. But this hope deceived him as well: Asya abandoned him. In the same year, 1919, he received news from Dornach to the effect that personal relations between himself and Asya were being discontinued forever. From that day, he lived in the desire to go abroad and have an explanation with his "princess." He succeeded in realizing this desire only in 1921. The meeting with Asya in Berlin tragically concluded the history of his "mystical love."

* * *

In March of 1921, having recovered from his illness, Bely went to Petersburg, settled at a hotel on Gogol Street, gave lectures at "Volfila," and for a long time was a guest of Ivanov-Razumnik at Tsarsky. Khodasevich recalls how he and Bely went "to bow" before the Bronze Horseman. Bely wrote in a letter to Asya of November 11, 1921:

I again attempted to leave and again the council extraordinaire did not allow it (in June). Then I came down with a nervous ailment. I was cured by the neuropathologist Professor Troitsky. At this point, I decided to flee, but the council extraordinaire found out, and the flight collapsed.... Then Blok died, they shot Gumilev, and were ashamed. The youth began to clamor: "Let Bely go abroad or he too will die, like Blok." Friends applied pressure, and they gave permission. How the youth accompanied me to SPB! Yes, Russia loves me well.

After Blok's death, Bely wrote a remarkable letter to Vladislav Khodasevich about his dead friend.[9]

Yes!
What can be said now! It is simply clear to me: such are the times. He expired from the very difficult air of life. Others said aloud: It's suffocating! He was simply silent, yes, and . . . expired. This death for me is the tolling of the fateful hour: I feel that a part of me myself has departed with me. You know, we did not see each other, almost did not speak, while the simple "being" of Blok on a physical plane was like a visual or auditory organ for me: I feel this now. It is also possible for the blind to live. The blind either die or are enlightened from within. This is how his death struck me: either awaken or die; begin or end.... And my soul asks: love or ruin, real human, humane life, or death. The soul cannot live like an orangoutang. And Blok's death was a summons

187

for me: "to perish or love."

In the last month before he went abroad, Bely gave several lectures in Petersburg and Moscow: "The Philosophy of Blok's Poetry," "Reminiscences of Blok," "The Poetry of Blok," and "Dostoevsky and the Crisis of Culture." Marina Tsvetaeva tells in her memoirs of a scandal that occurred at one of Bely's speeches about Blok. The lecturer suddenly lost his self-control and began to scream: "From starvation! From starvation! Gout from starvation, instead of from overeating! Spiritual asthma!" Then, from Blok, he turned to himself.

I have no room! I am a writer of the Russian land, and I don't even have a stone on which to lay my head.... I wrote *Petersburg*! I foresaw the downfall of Tsarist Russia, I had a dream of the end of the tsar in 1905!... I cannot write! It's a disgrace! I must stand in line to get my ration of fish. I want to write! But I also want to eat! I am not a spirit! For you I am not a spirit!... But I am a proletarian — Lumpenproletariat. Because I am all in rags. Because they did away with Blok, and they want to do away with me. I will not permit it! I will scream until I am heard! A-a-a-a!...

After this speech, Professor P. S. Kogan quickly found Bely a room.

The poet went abroad with a dual goal: to have an explanation with Asya and to see Dr. Steiner and tell him of the "difficult spiritual labor pains of Russia." He proudly called himself "Russia's ambassador to anthroposophy." While he was stuck in Kovno, he wrote the letter to Asya already cited: he begged her to see about a visa. If the Doctor had wanted to, he, of course, could have helped Bely, but, he added, "having learned from experience that such a 'great person' is not to be worried by trifles, I will not write anything to the 'great person' — from pride and from mistrust." For the first time, irritation and irony are heard in Bely's tone in relation to the "teacher." His disappointment in Steiner and his abandonment of anthroposophy began. At the end of his letter, he tries to frighten Asya with his return to Russia; he pretends that he no longer wants so much to go to Berlin:

I may be obliged to go back, for in Russia there is at least a meaning to dropping from exhaustion, while there is no sense in sitting here in Kovno.... All that genuinely loves me, all that needs me, is in Russia. Russian emigration is as foreign to me as are the Bolsheviks; in Berlin, I will be alone... Perhaps I will try in the meantime to take a look at Ausland as a sanatorium in which I must strengthen my nerves, write the books I have begun, publish them.... But I have left my mother in Russia and she may be arrested because of me.

Finally, with the help of the Lithuanian ambassador, the poet Yury Baltrushaitis, a German visa was obtained, and Bely went to Berlin.

In 1921, before his departure abroad, Bely published two works: the story "The Baptized Chinese,"[10] and the poem "First Meeting" (Alkonost, 1921).

In the chronicle, *On the Brink of Two Centuries*, Andrei Bely notes: "I will not dwell on the appearance of my father: I described it in 'The Baptized Chinese.' "

The story "The Baptized Chinese" is a continuation of *Kotik Letaev*. It is the first chapter of the unfinished *Epopée*, which received the new title, *The Crime of Nikolai Letaev*. In the forword, Bely announces that his novel is "half biographical, half historical: hence the appearance on the pages of the novel of people who really exist (Usov, Kovalevsky, Anuchin, Veselovsky and others), but the author uses them as historical inventions, with the liberty of the historical novelist."

"The Baptized Chinese" is a new reworking of the old themes of "childhood" and "family drama." But the transition from *Kotik Letaev* to "The Baptized Chinese" is a transition from mythology to history, from cosmic storms to strictly logical consciousness. The figure of the father is placed in the center of the narrative. Earlier, his image had been interpreted in the feverish imagination of a child; the forms were melted, flowed in streams of fiery lava, boiled up in storms, exploded in universal fires. The father — the god of fire — Hephaestus — inspired the child with mystical terror. Now the cosmogony has ended: the father is viewed by a grown-up artist-son, embracing the esthetic value of the unique personality. With the change of the angle of vision, the style changes as well. The musical force — the rhythmic construction of phrases, the sound orchestration, the alternation and repetition of literary images — is muffled. The style becomes simpler, more sober, more logical. We enter the world already known to us of the "professorial apartment," but everything seems different. The Rembrandtian illumination has been replaced by the clear light of day. The "problem of the father" is still not resolved conclusively in this story; in any event, it is cleansed o the "complex" which previously complicated it. In the double unity of "love-hate," the second item is omitted. There remains only tender love and esthetic admiration of the "wise eccentric."

Again and again, his "wild," "Scythian" appearance is depicted. Now he sits alone in his study in a gray robe, and makes calculations. Then he gets up and looks at himself in the mirror:

He could not tear himself away from the preposterously constructed head, full-weight, oppressing and flattening him (he seemed square) and gazing beneath the glass of spectacles with deep-seated, little, very slanting eyes, with a tightly fixed nose. Turning around, he tried to see his own profile (and the profile was Scythian), crooked, curly-haired, beast-like.

He is eccentric in everything; for everything there are "rational means" and "points of view." He loves to give advice, to teach the cook Afrosinia how to clean potatoes. "The cleaning of these potato tubers," he would explain to her, "is, so to speak, an integration of actions, and you are not cleaning them that way." But nothing comes of the "rational advice," and Mama angrily says to him, "Ah, you've muddled everything... You ought to get out of here," and drives him to the club.

Papa puts on a frock-coat, not a frock-coat but a lapserdak[11] (he doesn't dress normally, but in his own way); the lapserdak almost drags on the floor, and it doesn't close over his chest. His handkerchief sticks out from his coat like a tail, and the collar is turned and twisted in the impatience of being put quickly on his shoulders... Papa smells of winter apples, almost snuffed stearin candles and dust.

The striking expressiveness of these external depictions prepare for the perception of the emotional depth of the personality. What is "laughable" in the father is only the guise of the "great" under the mask of the "eccentric" which hides the face of a sage.

He was filled with Confucian wisdom. His favorite phrase was "Everything is a measure of harmony... There is harmony, you know, there is measure! Take water: H_2O: beauty! Simplicity!... The world is a simple and brief ratio: it is the result of polysyllabic processes, yet it is not process, but result." . . . And he sits quietly, in great tenderness – for no reason at all; he smiles brightly, at peace with himself and everything that is, resembling a Chinese sage.

There is a scent of something ancient, eternal, outside of time, about the father. He is both a satyr ("the handkerchief sticks out from behind: just like the tail of a satyr"), and a Scythian ("Papa resembles a Scythian with a lance, defeating the Persians"), and a Samurai ("Papa's face is the face-mask of a Samurai waving his saber"), and a Biblical patriarch. He contains the primordial force of the earth; he gives out the intense heat of the Asiatic ancestral home. And the laughable figure of the Russian mathematician Bugaev is only his latest embodiment. Bely writes:

I know that through the ages he has greatly disguised himself many times. He visited Abraham; bowed farewell – he is no more. But Abraham fulfilled the Behest, because he knew that Papa would appear and call for an account... And later, noticed by no one, he lived in an apartment in Sodom.. He led Lot out of Sodom, then moved on to Greece...

There, after drinking the poison, he appeared in the 16th century as a ragged old man.. and recounted personal impressions of events occurring during the time of August Caesar and Pontius Pilate: there, secreting himself behind rubble, absolutely unseen by Mary, but seen by Him — he received from Him first-hand directions as to how to act and what to do in milleniums of time...

Thus, by accumulating similes, the author attempts to interpret his complex intuition. The father embodies eternal fatherhood. He is the Biblical patriarch, the bearer of the spiritual culture of humanity, the servant of holiness over the ages.

But in his latest emobdiment, the prophet and patriarch is involved with mathematics and, following Leibnitz, he develops his "Monadology." The "eternal and temporal" are intertwined. With great humor, the author demonstrates the "fall of the great into the roar of the funny," in the story of his father's dream.

Papa dreamed a dream: he was sitting at a little table with an unknown man, eating gooseberries and explaining to him his "monadology." The unknown man was in agreement. And suddenly he recognized Christ. "Then I said to Him: 'I am so pleased that You, so to speak, the Universal Monad — the Central One, you know... and of the highest orders in relation to ours, that, so to speak, You understand.' We embraced." Papa proposed that "Our Father" be replaced with "Source of Purest Perfection — or something like, for example: 'Oh, Absolute, so to speak...' And He replied: 'But you, Mikhail Vasilich, should say it without "so to speak." "Oh, Absolute!" and not "So to speak, oh, Absolute!" ' And He,... He, imagine, disappeared!"

* * *

The figure of the mother stands alongside the central figure of the father in the story. In comparison with the vaguely musical image in *Kotik Letaev*, her portrayal in "The Baptized Chinese" seems colorfully picturesque. In the professorial circle, she is not liked: she is a Tintoretto among Flemish *natures mortes*.

Mama is playing the piano. It is poison; it is the sweet poison of the Renaissance, where one loves and perishes without rules — in sounds; not at all moral life — but musical life.

She is a beauty:

I love her face which has grown thin, her face with the proud mole, with a thin, chiseled little nose and rosy cheeks. And her mouth a little insulted: well-formed, like a flower, with pearly, even teeth. Her chin plays with a dimple, barely noticeable.

Mama often tells stories about her childhood. They called her little star then.... She remembers how she lived in Petersburg, near the Moika. A personage from the Tsar's family came to tea!... Then she got married. Papa came for her in a fashionable carriage, in evening dress, with a bouquet of flowers, while Maksim Kovalevsky, in evening dress, with the same kind of bouquet, sat opposite Mama. And at a dinner in Turgenev's honor, "Mama and Saltanova were seated so that Turgenev could see the beauty. And Turgenev, putting on a pince-nez with a very wide black ribbon, gazed at Mama..."

The theme of family discord, only outlined in *Kotik Letaev*, is broadly developed in "The Baptized Chinese." The boy understands that Mama is unhappy, that she married his father "from respect," and that she doesn't love him. He is present, dying of horror, at difficult scenes between his parents. Mama is angry:

> She sits behind a screen near a little dresser, dries little bottles, and nags at Father through the open door of his study: "Some people, who think that they understand science, while in life they are still blockheads with neither a heart, nor feelings, are sitting absorbed in these stupid calculations."

The father, of course, loses his temper:

> He turned his face with very evil, slanting little eyes, with a suddenly very disheveled head. "I will force you to be quiet. I give you five minutes..."

The struggle for the son sometimes takes on crude, ugly forms. The father seats the little boy on his knees, tells him about Russia. But the boy knows that the mother forbids him this and sits "neither alive nor dead."

> I hear how Mama would begin to drag her feet; with an unattractive face, swollen with sleep, having forgotten her housecoat, without her corset, without her bed jacket, without slippers, she would run out to the dining room. "I am your mother? Your mother?"

A quarrel would begin with his father. The mother slaps him across the face and cries. And at night, she comes into the nursery, looks at her son, and whispers: "Big-headed!... Like his father!"

One time, she was about to beat him. His father tore the boy away and took him to his uncle's family. The mother sent the maid for him: she met him at the door, and they cried together. "My dear little one, forgive me, for Christ's sake!"

Around the figures of the father and mother, the secondary characters are placed in receding perspective: relatives, colleagues of the professor, acquaintances and servants. They are depicted in a few sharp strokes, with amazing skill. Here the grandmother "sits in a cretonne armchair, tells fortunes from cards, and complains that carrots have become more expensive." Aunt Dotya, narrow-shouldered, with a small nose, works at the telegraph station and signs, "I want to live." The father's brother, Uncle Vasya (in reality, Vladimir Vasilievich Bugaev) is "without wife or woman and, as they say, not 'brainy,' but he's strong on hindsight." His grandmother, Malinovskaya (her real name is Maria Ivanovna Lyaskovskaya), is the legislatrix of the professorial world: green-nosed, with a green forehead: a gray odor in her black-gray handkerchief!" Everyone is afraid of her and goes to pay their respects to her. On the father's name-day, the whole faculty files into the Bugaevs' living room. The originality of the Moscow learned men is caught in unerringly accurate lines. The style of the "professorial apartment" of the age of Alexander III is reproduced in all its everyday details. And beyond the apartment, the open spaces are revealed in Moscow, on the Arbat and Kislovka: the houses, stores, boulevards, bridge spans, sidewalks, squares, and, above the city, the gay March sun. Andrei Bely is the historiographer and painter of old Moscow.

The poem, "First Meeting," written in May, 1921 and published in the same year by Alkonost, is devoted to recollections of youth: the university years, the hospitable home of Mikhail Sergeevich Soloviev, the friendship with his son, Seryozha, the concerts of Safanov, first verses, first love. Bely's poem is undoubtedly the most enchanting of all his poetic works. One must not, of course, seek simplicity in it: this quality is not in Bely's nature. He is complex, complicated, refined in everything. But in "First Meeting," refinement rarely turns into mannerism; the stylistic subtleties are almost always successful, while the light, "divine" play with images, words and rhythms is striking in its virtuosity. In the "Foreword," the author acknowledges that his goal is the creation of a new poetic form:

> With a miner's pick, the gnome
> Of consonants pulls crackles into volumes.
> I am a stylistic method,
> Lingual idioms!

The first chapter begins with soaring verses:

> Ascend, star of memories;
> The years relived anew;
> A poem — the first meeting,
> A poem — the first love.

Winged imagination flies from the darkness of 1921 to the dawns of 1900.

The year 1900: the dawns, the dawns!
Questions, flung at the dawns.

He sees himself as a student in a green frock-coat, a dandy and melan-
cholic, studying the Upanishads, and reeking with the perfume of Atkinson.
He works in the laboratory on the decomposition of matter; he lives in the
"dense woods of symbols," and listens to lectures on physics by Professor
Umov. Playing with alliterations, consonances on "r," and uncommon rhymes,
the poet jokingly portrays his youth.

> In a wave of music
> The life force splashed me...
> . . . .
> In my strophic days,
> And in symbolic plays
> Purpling, there gazed from the dawns
> (Bagreia, zreli iz zari)
> Dionysian tigers.

His father, Dean Letaev, after listening to his misty verbiage, shakes his
head and says, "Stop, my dear, it makes me sick to hear. You're really talking
nonsense."

The second chapter is devoted to the brilliant characterization of the
Soloviev family. We have already quoted the magnificent verbal portraits of
the brother of Vladimir Soloviev, Mikhail Sergeevich, his wife, the artist Olga
Mikhailovna, and his son, the young theologian and mystic, Seryozha. In the
Soloviev salon, Bely made the acquaintance of Klyuchevsky, Bryusov and
Merezhkovsky. There he saw the philosopher Vladimir Soloviev for the first
time:

> ... A transparent phantom
> Seeming to bend down from stilts,
> Enters, and with an explosive gaze
> Beats at the heart, like a bullet...
> Above the black, disheveled beard,
> Churning the hanging mane
> And acrimoniously blowing with his lips,
> Blowing out macrocosms toward his tea.

Depiction here is obviously sacrificed to "sound repeats" ("chernokos-
my" [disheveled] — "klokocha" [churning] — "kosmy" [mane] — "makro-
kosmy" [macrocosms]). In the third chapter, she appears at last — the object
of the first love of the young Symbolist. At a Safonov concert in the Nobles'
Meeting Hall, amidst the flowerbed of women in laces and diamonds, the eve-

ning dress of Taneev and Scriabin shows black, Morozov's bald spot shines, Trepov's binoculars heave. In the orchestra, the instruments are being tuned up. And now — she enters:

> She passes by — illumined
> By the fires of dawn, unsinged...
> Nadezhda Lvovna Zarina
> Is not her name but "in the name of."

Under the invented name of Zarina is hidden the famous Moscow beauty, the millionairess and patron of the arts, Margarita Kirillovna Morozova. His first — dreamy and platonic — love, Bely crowns with strophes which sparkle and pour forth like precious gems. He remembers Vladimir Soloviev's poem, "Three Meetings," and celebrates Zarina as his "Eternal Friend." The verses resound with Solovievian energy:

> Thus from the gleaming azures
> With eyes filled with fire
> You, in a singing storm,
> Diamondized into me.
> From the heights — revelries of light;
> From the depths — a scent of darkness;
> And I was taken from the lightnings of summer
> To the point of horror. By you! Yourself!
> You descended upon me in dreams
> From soothing silence;
> You caressed the depths
> Of my timid spring.

The finale thunders in triumphant fortissimo:

> And now she comes, with summer lightning fire,
> Illumined by her own self,
> Bearing, like a train, her own "in the name of"
> Nadezhda Lvovna Zarina.
> Her veils — murmuring tears,
> Her bracelets — trembling ecstasy:
> In her eyes — mountainous Swedenbourg,
> Her necklace — diamond frosts.

These verses are an example of "sound orchestration."

In the fourth chapter, the departure after the concert takes place. The poet, in love, is alone in the middle of an empty street in a snowstorm. His soul is shaken by the vision which has visited him. He adjures, prays, pleads:

195

Throw there, into the golden sea,
Into my drowning years —
My sobbing sorrow,
Your shining "Yes."
An inexpressible Hosanna,
An irresistible star,
You, with the Revelation of John,
Have been revealed forever.

The lyrical tension of these stanzas is strengthened by the internal consonances of "moye rydaushchee (my sobbing) — svoyo sverkaushchee (your shining)," "nevyrazimaia (inexpressible) — neotrazimaia (irresistible)," "otkroveniem (Revelation) — priotkryvalas' (have been revealed)."

The poet, initiated into the mystical experience of Vladimir Soloviev, goes at night to the Novodevichy Monastery, to the grave of his teacher, and there he hears:

... And again the summons of familiar words:
"There is the day of meetings, the day of arisings!"
"Who art thou?" "Vladimir Soloviev;
With memory and light
I work at this place."

Bely's "First Meeting" is a poetic response to Vladimir Soloviev's "Three Meetings." Like his teacher, the student attempts "in a humorous poem to describe the most significant thing that has happened to him in his life." Both to him and to Soloviev as well, the "Eternal Friend" had descended. He saw her earthly embodiment in the dazzling and magnificent Zarina; she was for him "an inexpressible hosanna and an irresistible star." And during those same years, the same revelation of Eternal Femininity was experienced by Alexander Blok on the open plains of Shakhmatovo. And the unearthly vision merged for him with the earthly image of the Bride — Lyubov Mendeleeva.

196

Boris Zaitsev met Bely in Berlin. He writes:

Berlin somehow coarsened him. Something gray, Berlinishly dull, covered Bely's entire appearance. His bald spot grew, the fleece of hair at his temples turned gray and became thinner. Toward the end, he also grew a little fat and flabby. He now resembled a drunkard, someone unsuccessful and unrecognized — perhaps an inventor or a professor without a chair.

The picturesque portrait of Bely by Ilya Ehrenburg belongs to the same period:[1]

Huge, wide open eyes, raging bonfires on a pale, emaciated face. A disproportionately high forehead, with a little island of hair standing on end. He reads like a prophetic Sibyl and, while reading, waves his hands, emphasizing the rhythm not of the verse, but of his own secret designs. It is almost laughable, and at times Bely seems like a magnificent clown. But when he is present, everyone is ruled by anxiety and languor, a sensation of some elementally forceful misfortune. A wind in the room.... Andrei Bely is a genius. Only it is strange — why at times do I have before me not a temple, but only a tragic farce?

He is a wandering spirit who has not found a body, a stream without banks.

Bely — in a worker's shirt, building the theosophical temple in Dornach; and Bely with the terrorists, in love with the coming revolution; Bely — the priest, and Bely the esthete, describing the wigs of the marquis. Bely, examining the poems of Venevitinov with students, and Bely in Proletkult, enthusiastically listening to feeble verses about factory whistles.

Such a strange contradiction: the wild, fiery thought, while in his heart, instead of a burning coal, ice... Love and hate can carry people along with them, but not the madness of numbers, not the mathematics of the cosmos. Bely's visions are full of magnificence and coldness.

Bely did not go to Dornach; Asya came with a group to Berlin. An explanation took place between them. The poet briefly mentions it in the last pages of *Notes of an Eccentric*:

I saw Nelli recently. She has changed: she is emaciated and pale. We sat together for a while in a cafe. Twice we spoke of the past, but little: she no longer has time to speak of trifles. "Farewell." To Dornach? "To Dornach." And we said our farewells. For consolation and spiritual edification, she gave me two series of lectures given by Steiner; the series are with me. Nelli is in Dornach. That's all? —Yes... That's all.

In his memoirs, Vladislav Khodasevich portrays Asya's break with Bely more dramatically:

On personal grounds, she not only did not want an explanation with him, but also displayed contempt for him in a public, insufferably insulting form.

Asya not only did not wish to return to her "former husband," but openly appeared everywhere with her new friend, the young poet Kusikov.

Bely's despair was boundless. He chose Marina Tsvetaeva as his confidante and poured forth his misery to her in endless monologues. Tsvetaeva would meet him in the Pragerdiele cafe. Bely would run up to her: "You! I was lonely for you! I was pining for you!... My dove, my dear one, I am a ruined man... With you, at once I am at peace, at rest. I even right this minute, suddenly, wanted to sleep." He would ask her to give him her hand and would bitterly complain about his abandonment: he is doomed to the cafe, he must eternally drink coffee. He would say:

Because the main thing is to be someone's, oh, anyone's! It is absolutely all the same to me — to you also? — whose I am, if only that person would know that I am his, that he would not "forget" me, as I forget my cane in the cafe... But now I would say that three days ago my life was ended.

And here is another conversation about Asya. Bely told Tsvetaeva:

All evening, I went around to cafes, and in one I met her. What do you think about that? Can she love him? It's not true, no? Then what does all this mean? Dramatization? In order to cause me pain? But after all, she doesn't love me, then why does she want to cause me pain? But, you know, this must cause her pain most of all. You know him?... Then he mustn't be a bad person... I tried to read his verses... but I don't feel anything: words. (In an outburst) Oh, you don't know how vicious she is! You think she needs him, that she needs a savage, she, who (throwing his head back) for a millenium... She needs (in a whisper) to wound me in my very heart, she needs to kill the past, to kill herself — the one, — to make it so that that one never existed. It is vengeance. Vengeance which I alone can appreciate. Because for the others, this is simply passion. So natural. After a forty-year-old, balding, stupid man, a twenty-year-old, black-haired, with a dagger, etc. Oh, if only it were so! But you don't know her. She is as cold as a knife. All this is cold calculation. She feels nothing for him. I am even convinced that she hates him... Oh, you don't know how she can keep silent, like this: she sits and is silent, she stands and is silent, she gazes and is silent.

Tsvetaeva asked: why "vengeance?" Bely replied:

For Sicily. "I am no longer your wife." But — will you read my book? Where do I say that she is my wife; She is to me — she. A shimmering vision. A little goat on a cliff's edge. Nelli. What did I say about her? Yes, and the book was already printed... Where did she see "intimacy," "possessiveness," the stamp (not a document) of a husband?... The pride of a demon and the action of a little girl. "I did not expect you so — now I am the wife of another." As if without that I didn't feel it. As if I never knew this... I am so sorry for her...

You have seen her? She is beautiful. During these years of separation, she has grown so, matured so. She was Psyche, she became a Valkyrie. There is strength in her, the strength given her by her loneliness. Oh, if she, like a human being, not on a passage with a group, with a troupe, for a half hour in a cafe, but like a friend, like a human being, like a profound, lofty being — I would have, pouring out my blood, been the first to be present and rejoice... You don't know how I loved her, how I waited for her. How she shone for me...

Bely's mission to Dr. Steiner concluded no less dramatically. He was not admitted to Dornach. Steiner was in Berlin, but assiduously declined a meeting with the "ambassador from Russia to anthroposophy." One time they met by chance at some meeting. The doctor carelessly asked Bely: "Na, wie geht's?" ("Well, how are you?") Bely answered in a fury: "Schwierigkeiten mit dem Wohnungsamt!" ("You have problems with the office that rents apartments!") From that time on, he began to hate the "teacher" with a fierce, bloody hatred. He shouted in the cafe in a frenzied voice: "I will unmask him! I will expose him!"

Tsvetaeva's husband, S. Efron (from whom she had been separated for a long time) returned to her. She waited for Bely. He came, after a delay, in a condition bordering on madness. He explained his delay: he was going to see her, but remembered the arrival of her husband and did not want to cloud their meeting. "You are still in paradise," he said, "while I am burning in hell! I did not want to bring in this sulphurous hell with the doctor conducting in it." That is why he visited the cafe and . . . lost his briefcase with the manuscript of his "poems."

Tsvetaeva and her husband set out with Bely to search for the manuscript. He did not remember which cafe he had visited... In any event, it was

199

not this one, because in it they sell cocaine, and not that one, because in it is sitting a "man with dyed dark hair in glasses with no lenses." At random, they went into a third. Bely shouted to the waiters:

Ich habe hier meine Handschrift vergessen. Manuskript, verstehen Sie? Hier auf diesem Stuhl! Eine schwarze Pappemappe... Ich bin Schriftstel- ler, russischer Schriftsteller! Meine Handschrift ist alles fur mich!
(I have forgotten my manuscript here. Manuscript, understand? Here — on this chair. One black briefcase. I am a writer, a Russian writer. My manuscript is all I have.)

The manuscript was not found. Bely ran out on the street, stopped in the middle of the sidewalk, and, with a terrible smile, said:

And aren't these the tricks of the doctor? Didn't he order that my manuscript disappear from here?... You don't know this man. He is the devil... There is only one devil: Dr. Steiner.

The anthroposophian period of his life — the idyll with Asya in Dornach and the building of John's temple — ended in a grandiose collapse. Bely said to Khodasevich: "I would like to go to Dornach now and shout at Dr. Steiner, the way the street urchins shout: 'Herr Doktor, Sie sind ein alter Affe!' (Doc- tor, you are an old monkey!)."
The teacher of "secret knowledge" proved to be an "old monkey," John's temple — a puppet stage.
Until the fall of 1922, Bely lived in Zossen, a wretched little village near Berlin, not far from a cemetery, in the home of a grave digger. Tsvetaeva visited him there. The poet had a bare room with a white unpainted table in the middle. In the newly built cemetery town, there were neither trees, nor shade, nor birds. All the inhabitants wore black: widowers and widows. Car- riages on their way to the cemetery passed with a rumble, bearing red-faced gentlemen in cylinder hats with bouquets in their hands.
The housekeeper would bring in a big tureen with oatmeal. Bely hated oatmeal and was afraid of the housekeeper. He took Tsvetaeva to dine in Ber- lin, in the Zum Bären restaurant. He ordered three meat dishes.
His amazing face etched itself into her memory. She writes:

Whether it was because it was summer, or because he was always ex- cited, or because he already had his mortal disease of the blood vessels, I never saw him pale, but always rosy, yellow and bright rose, copper. From this rosiness, both the blue of his eyes and the silver of his hair was intensified. Silver, copper, azure — these are the colors in which Bely remains for me... He wore a pelerin cape... On him, it looked like wings. Because he swayed so, the pelerin cape behind him repeated, in- tensified, each of his gestures, like a swollen, blustering shadow.

After the break with Asya, Bely's life entered a dark phase. He began to drink and to visit suspicious "Dielen" (gambling halls). He was possessed by a passion for dancing. His drunken dance in the pot houses was horrifying. Khodasevich calls it a "monstrous pantomine, at times indecent, self-blasphemy, a devilish grimace at his own self." Returning home at night, he completely undressed and again danced. Thus the months stretched out. Marina Tsvetaeva writes about Bely's dancing:

His foxtrot is the purest khlystovstvo: not even a devil's sabbath, but (my word) a Christ's sabbath, i.e., once again the *Silver Dove*, to which he, toward his forties, had physically danced... I know that before me was a persecuted man. Born persecuted.

With the same frenzy with which he devoted himself to the "mystical rites" of the Berlin "hops," he threw himself into writing. He wrote to the point of exhustion, loss of consciousness. It would happen that he wrote almost a printer's galley in one day. In order to forget the present, he became absorbed in the past, in memories of Blok.

Khodasevich notes:

The new pain (Asya) awakened the old one (Lyubov Dmitrievna), and the old proved to be more painful than the new. All that occurred in Bely's love life after 1906 was only his attempt to cure this Petersburg wound.

Bely was possessed by memories of the one who once, "in five minutes, destroyed him." He told Tsvetaeva about Petersburg, the snow storms, the "blue cloak." The noose tightened; Blok, his wife and Bely were in the loop: they could not untie it, could not break it... And suddenly he added: "I met her very badly the last time. Nothing of the past remained in her. Nothing. Emptiness." But Blok continued to love her. "Oh, for his whole life, he worried about her, as one would about a sick person. Her room was always ready, she could always return... to rest, but that was broken. Their lives went separate ways and never more came together."

* * *

In November, 1923, In Prague, Marina Tsvetaeva received a despairing letter from Bely in Berlin. He begged her to find him a room near her: "I am exhausted! I am tormented!" he exclaimed. "If only I could crawl under your wing! My life this year has been a nightmare. You are my only salvation. Perform a miracle! Arrange it! Give me shelter!" Tsvetaeva replied that there was a room, and that M. L. Slonim had promised to arrange a stipend for him. But her letter did not reach Bely. On the very day that he wrote to her for help, he left for Russia. He was carried off by his old friend, the anthroposophist K. N. Vasilieva, whom he later married. According to Khodasevich, during the last days before his departure, Bely was "not in an entirely responsible condition," broke off his relations with the emigrants, sought quarrels with his former friends. After his departure, the housekeeper of the boarding house in which he had lived in Berlin brought to Khodasevich a heap of manuscripts "forgotten" by Bely. He gave them to a person who promised to send them to Moscow. Their fate is unknown.

* * *

The two years in Berlin mark the apogee of Bely's literary activity. During the years 1922-23, sixteen of his works were printed, truly a record number. It includes seven reprints of old works and nine new publications.[2]

Among these publications are included verses of the "anthroposophian period" of 1914-18. "Consciousness," "Self-consciousness," "Spiritual Science" place a heavy imprint on Bely's lyricism. His verses are bloodless; the living flesh of the word is deadened by the icy breath of anthroposophic abstractions. Only "astral bodies" and shimmering "auras" of objects remain. "Spiritual science" decomposes poetry, transforming it into a play of shadows. Amidst the choir of constellations, meteors, crying abysses, the darkness of non-being, abstract forces, and hierarchies of the good, in the interplanetary cold of symbols and correspondences, "Self-consciousness" reigns:

> But — Oh, God!
> Consciousness is
> Ever stricter, ever the same
> Consciousness
> Mine.

Still more profound is the meditation on "I":

> In myself — embraced by myself
> (As by the darkness of non-being) —
> In my very self, taken to pieces
> By bright light, is "I."

And in the same world of phantoms and abstractions, only one image retains a semblance of life: the illuminated image of "love unspoken" — Asya Turgeneva. The verses dedicated to her are full of lofty lyrical excitement. Remembering his faraway friend, Bely ceases to be an "initiate," and becomes a poet. Here, he and Asya are again in Italy:

> ... And again the plane trees blacken in the night for me.
> I crown my suffering with the dream of the past:
> Sicily... And the passionate guitars.
> Palermo, Monreale... Rades... I love...

202

Asya is illuminated in his memory with the "radiance of spring":

> Growing up with warmth from the heart,
> With Thee, as one clothed with the sun,
> With Thee, glistening like the sun,
> In Thee, before Thee is he.

In August of 1916, he says farewell to Asya in Dornach:

> My last, faithful, eternal friend,
> Do not condemn my silence:
> In it is sorrow; there is timid fear in it,
> The knowledge of inexpressible love.

And now he is once again in Russia: Russian pines, fields, roofs, huts, and over it all, with an inextinguishable brilliance, she shines:

> In the remote past — meetings to come,
> In the future — the remoteness of a dream:
> Unspoken words,
> Thou art inexplicable!

Two years pass. Her image is still brighter, her faraway summons still more tender:

> I hear anew thy blue voice,
> Not reaching Thee with my soul:
> How radiant, how beautiful it is with Thee,
> Sweet, precious, good.

And the final verses:

> My eternal light,
> My bright flower,
> I am filled with Thee,
> With Thee as with Destiny.

These sounds and rhythms contain the lightness and transparency of fleshless bodies. They recall the verses of Tyutchev:

> Like a sacred shade, an Elysian shade,
> She died at the proper time...

Like such an "Elysian shade," the image of Asya shone for Bely during the dreadful years of military communism.

Another "living place" in the collection are the verses on Russia. While still in Dornach, before his return to Moscow, Bely was writing inspired verses about the coming resurrection of his native land:

> My country, my native country!
> I am thine, I am thine!
> Accept me, sobbing... and not knowing,
> Cover me with damp grass.
>
> * * *
>
> Let us be in the night! Let it be impassible night...
> Let it be dream upon dream!
> In the peace of sunrises and the tremor preceding dawn,
> After the night comes — He!

These verses echo the famous lines of Blok:

> Let it be night. We will gallop on to the end. We will
>   light up with bonfires
> The distant steppe...

After returning to his native land, the poet blessed the revolution as the eternal Burning Bush:

> *December 1916*
> Shining, whirling, into the frosty confusion melting,
> It throws flames into the sky,
> Pouring out in a thousand-colored light,
> The Holy Bush.
> Arise, rejoice, triumph, Russia!
> Burst forth, like an alarm —
> Free people's force —
> From town to town!

And after two years, after dreadful experiences with cold and darkness, he continued to believe in the mystical meaning of the great Russian revolution. It seemed to him that his youthful presentiments of the descent to the world of the Woman clothed with the sun were close to their embodiment. A magnificent triumphal poem is dedicated to Russia:

> *To the Infant*
> Play, mindless child,
> Shine with flying force:
> With the Freedom-loving light of "I"

Appear, be embodied — Russia.

* * *

We are waiting: the funereal shroud
Falls with gleaming shadows:
Already the Heavenly Bride
More tenderly sprinkles the depths with stars —

* * *

And, becoming full-fledged from spring,
The hierarchies are cast in azure:
From light wings, the face of the Bride
Smiles to joyful Russia.

(March 1918, Moscow)

* * *

Bely's "star of self-consciousness" was drowned in the astral spirits of anthroposophic mist; its rays were decomposed according to the rules of "spiritual science," and were described in the schemes and computations of the mathematics of the beyond. Only rarely does it float out of the theosophian shadow, bursting into pure, crystal, poetic light.

The collection *Verses About Russia* includes poems selected from *Ashes* and *The Star*. Many of them are significantly reworked. The author added to them one of his best addresses to his native land, written in August, 1917. It blazes in glowing, melting metal; it contains the fiery inspiration of the self-immolating Khlysty. From the smoke, sparks and tongues of flame, frenzied invocations burst forth:

Sob, stormy force,
In columns of thundering fire!
Russia, Russia, Russia —
Go mad, immolating me.

* * *

Into your fateful ruins,
Into your remote depths —
Wing-armed spirits pour
Their dawn-lighted dreams.

* * *

Do not weep: bend your knees
There — in hurricanes of fire,
In the thunder of the singing of seraphim,
In the torrent of cosmic days!

* * *

The dry desserts of shame

The seas of unwept tears —
With a ray of his wordless gaze
Are warmed by the descending Christ.

And the finale:

And thou, fiery force,
Go mad, immolating me,
Russia, Russia, Russia —
The Messiah of the coming day!

* * *

The third poetry collection, *After the Parting*, bears the subtitle *A Berlin Songbook*. In it are collected Bely's poetic exercises of 1922. Marina Tsvetaeva tells in her memoirs of the origin of this collection. Bely often complained to her that he had ceased to be a poet; "I never read verses," he said. "And I never write them any more. Three times a year — this is a poet? A person must be doomed to verses, like a wolf to howling. Then — he is a poet." Marina Tsvetaeva sent him her book, *The Parting*. He answered it with a letter.

Dear Marina Ivanovna:
Allow me to express my profound delight with the perfectly winged melody of your book, *The Parting*. I read it all evening, almost aloud, and I almost sang it. It has been a long time since I had such esthetic enjoyment.
And, as concerns the melodics of the verse, so necessary after the slackness of the Muscovites and the deadness of the Acmeists, your book is tops (undoubtedly).

After some time, they met. Bely said to Tsvetaeva:

You know, I am writing verses. You know, after your *Parting*, again I am writing verses... It will be an entire book, *After the Parting* — after the parting with her (Asya), and after your *Parting*.

* * *

In the foreword, the poet outlines the idea of the anthology:

We will seek a melody.
This small notebook is a quest for form. I think that after Symbolism there were no really new shifts toward the future style of poetry; Acmeism was a sensible reaction, temporarily, perhaps a necessary one... All the schools of recent times have omitted one essential aspect of verse: the melody of the whole... Melody in verse is the supremacy of intonational mimicry. Verse is always a distraction from song... Only in the melody, placed in the center of the lyrical work, transforming the

206

poem into a genuine, singing song, are image, sound order, meter and rhythm put in their place. In proclaiming melodism as an absolutely necessary school, in the presented melodic attempts, I am deliberately emphasizing the right of very simple words to be the words of poetry, if only they express the melody precisely.

Theses: 1) A lyrical poem is a song; 2) The poet carries a melody within him; he is a composer; 3) In pure lyricism, the melody is more important than the image; 4) The immoderate usage of the common-place elements of verse (images and sound harmony) as regards melody turns the very wealth of these elements into a sure means of killing verse; 5) There is enough metaphorical oversaturation; less imagism and more song, more simple words, less sound clattering (less horns) — the composers of genius are geniuses not with instruments, but with melo-dies; Beethoven's orchestration is simpler than the orchestration of Strauss.

Before Russian verse lies the wealth of inexhaustible melodic words.

And long live "melodism."

Berlin. Zossen. June 1922.

Bely, the eternal rebel, was contemplating a new "revolution." His inde-fagitable, restless spirit was dreaming of destroying the old poetry and creat-ing in its place a new school of "melodism" He was rebelling against himself primarily: who more than he was guilty of the "immoderate usage of image and sound harmony?" Whose verses were more overloaded with metaphors and "sound clattering?" Who more stubbornly than he had "instrumented" his lines?

But the revolution did not succeed. Bely did not create a school of "melodism," but killed his poetic gift conclusively. *After the Parting* is his last poetry anthology. He wrote no more verses.

The "melodic attempts" of the author are striking in their poverty. For the transmission of "intonational mimicry," he resorted to one method alone: he broke the poetic phrase into small pieces (most often into separate words) and wrote them out in a column, one under the other. This was supposed to depict sometimes a "mandolin," sometimes a "violincello," sometimes a "gui-tar," sometimes a "balalaika:"

We are drowning
In the night,
Drowning are
We —
In corroding
Eyes,
In attacking

207

Multitudes!
Drowning are
We —
We are drowning
In multitudes!

And in terms of content, *After the Parting* is a cry of pain and despair. Asya has abandoned him, Asya has departed forever: she is cold, caustic, vicious... He remembers the year 1921; he is sick, he lies in a hospital, alone...

The Hospital

I see you again
You are caustic...
But — not caustic, merely cold: you have forgotten.
. . . .
Suffocated, I gaze fixedly at you, faraway.
Your appearance is unfriendly.
Oh, this long dream!
Beyond the windows is the sunrise.
Ward No. Six, a pile of gray junk.

* * *

The dreamless groan of the sick, my hospital robe,
And the gnawing pain, and the nimble rustle of a mouse.
. . . .
Disappearance, cover my eyes
With a stern hand, with an icy hand.

* * *

Forgotten are the "quests for form" and "melodism;" here are living, human words of genuine misery. Feeble complaints, powerless tears, a sinking whisper, and entreaties and reproaches.

He asks her:

Do not speak dead words
Do not repeat, —
Dear!

She replies:

To you, one thing is precious, to me —
Another.

And her ghost disappears; she is a deception. He calls her the "shade of shades":

You are the shade of shades...
I will not name you.
Your face is
Cold and evil.

. . . .

Lost poet,
Find her, lost somewhere;
You, myself I embrace, trembling,
In the tremblings of the lost night.

* * *

The tragic explanations with Asya in the Berlin cafes, the intimate "elu-
cidations of relations" are set forth in detail in the original form of a "lyrical
monologue," sarcastically entitled:

> *A Small Puppet Show on the Small Planet "Earth"*
> (Screamed into a Casement Window)
> Boom, boom —
> It has begun! —
> The heart — has cried itself out; to cry —
> There is no / Strength! —
> Heart of mine —
> Be silent: and stand still...

And there begin passionate, despairing, embittered, hysterical accusations of
Asya:

> ... Why / — Are you slandering / The spirit?
> Why / — This / Monstrous / Distortion / Of life —
> — The cold / Obsequious / Face —
> — S — / "It means / It is so destined!" —
> — S — / "Were / We, / Or — / Not?"
> — S — / "We loved — / We forgot!" —
> So what / , If it is so destined, —
> Destroy!

* * *

> Yes, — / You / With bombastic / Lies / Drew
> An evil / Circle / Around / Yourself,
> — And — / You / With a genuine / Shudder / Depart
> Evil / Friend / From / Me —
> — Without / An answer
> And — / I — / Never will see / You —
> And — I hate / Myself / For / It!

But Asya is not to blame for the "parting": the "devil," Doctor Steiner, who separated them forever, is to blame. Bely never tires of damning him:

Oh, — / Accursed / Accursed / Accursed / —
— That devil — / Accursed / — Who —
In the broken / Fatherland / From the firmament / Destroyed
Our lives — / In the spray of death, / — Who
Forever — / Separated me / — From you...

And again the "screams of the heart" and "wild cries" and "quiet sorrow" and "years of forgetfulness" and the "sprays of the exploding firmament" and even the "screech of death." The finale:

Boom,
Boom, —
— It is ended!
(The casement window slams. The room is filled with the sounds of a merry shimmy.)

* * *

The verses in *After the Parting* are not songs, but wails, a dreadful lacerating howl of a mortally wounded beast. Bely had said to Tsvetaeva: "A man must be doomed to verses, like a wolf to howling. Then he is a poet." He could not help writing his *Berlin Songbook*: he was doomed to it.

During the period of 1922-23, Bely wrote three volumes of memoirs, *The Turn of the Century* (approximately seventy-five galleys) for the Epokha publishing house. The first volume was prepared in Berlin in 1922, but the publishing house went out of existence, and Bely left for Russia in 1923. Neither the manuscript nor the proofs of the first volume were preserved. Half of the second volume was lost as well. From this edition, the following appeared in print: 1) "From My Reminiscences. 1. Belgium. 2. "A Transitional Period," in the journal *Conversation*, No. 2, Berlin, 1923; 2) "Echoes of the Former Moscow," in *Contemporary Notes*, book XVI, 1923; 3) "The Arbat — An Essay," in *Contemporary Notes*, book XVII, 1923.

These passages contain interesting material illuminating the literary life of Moscow at the turn of the century. The surviving half of the manuscript the author fundamentally reworked in 1930. The chronicle *The Turn of the Century* was issued by the Gikhl publishing house in 1933.

* * *

The fate of Bely's other memoir work was more fortunate: he succeeded, in four issues of the journal *Epopee* (Gelikon, Berlin, 1922-23), in publishing his remarkable "Reminiscences of Blok." And, to the present day, this work remains the best monument of the Symbolist era. The author has a striking gift for literary depiction: Blok, his age, his environment and his contemporaries are brought to life before us in blinding poetic brilliance. Of course, Bely is not an historian, but a poet. He creates an enchanting myth from his life and that of his friend. But we are all bewitched by this myth, and long ago it became for us the only reality. The knight of the "Lady Beautiful" lives even now in a fairy-tale aura, created for him by Bely.

* * *

In addition to the *Travel Notes* and *Notes of an Eccentric* already mentioned, Bely published a small book in 1922.[3] It is a polemical response to Vyacheslav Ivanov's book, *The Native and Universal.* Bely attacks Ivanov's articles, seeing in them reaction and betrayal of the revolution. The political lining of his criticism gives it an unpleasantly tendentious character. It is disgraceful to read that Vyacheslav Ivanov "creates a spurious ideology of pious, orthodox, honeyed Dionysianism in his latest 'peace-bearing' articles, social-kadetishly—anarchistically—mystically—emotionally nodding tenderly to all sides," and that "in the light of the coming era, Ivanov seems to us like a Tantalus thrown into hell, supporting the edge of the dark, extinguished sphere of his ideologies." This pompously perfidious article remains a black mark on the memory of Andrei Bely.

* * *

Of the books reprinted by Bely in Berlin, a very special place belongs to a large volume of five hundred pages, *Poems*, published by Z. I. Grzhebin in 1923. Marina Tsvetaeva tells in her memoirs of how the poet reworked his old books. The publisher complained to her:

My dear Marina Ivanovna, persuade Boris Nikolaevich. Convince him that before it was also good. You know, he has not left a stone unturned in the original text. There was conversation about a reprint, but this is a new book, unknown. You know, each of his corrections is a whole new book! The book grows newer uncontrollably and unceasingly: the type-setter is wringing his hands!

In the foreword to this "collection of selected poems," the author expounds his "methods:"

Each poet's lyrical creation is reflected not in the group of separate and self-contained works, but in the modulations of a few basic themes of lyrical excitement, the imprinted gradations of the written verses expressed at various times. Each lyricist has an unwritten lyrical poem beyond all the lyrical passages... Just as the lyrical poem often originates in the poet's soul, from the middle, from the end, so in the general aspect of all his creative works, chronology does not play a role. Cycles of verses, their mutual interconnections, must be discovered in the sum of the verses. In approaching the selection of those of my poems which

211

went into this book, I was ruled not by the voice of self-criticism, but by the memory of the leit-motifs which I heard over a number of years and which dictated certain passages... Some of them (often less perfect) meant more to me than others (technically perfect); and I made this biographical significance of the individual poems to me the criterion of selection... Everything I have written is a novel in verse; the contents of the novel, moreover, is my quest for truth, with its achievements and failures.

Thus Bely eliminates chronological sequence and esthetic evaluation. He uses his anthologies of verse as raw material, performing decisive operations on it, breaking down old cycles and creating new ones, changing, abridging, modifying and shredding his verses. The results obtained are most lamentable: thus, for example, the poet ruins his best poem, "First Meeting," by tearing it to shreds and distributing it in various sections. A "new book, unrecognizable" is obtained in reality. Having set himself a fantastic task — to write the "unwritten lyrical poem" which hides behind all the individual poems, Bely leaves no stone unturned in his poetic past. He sacrifices artistry for the sake of "ideology" and arranges the lines of his lyrics like the stages of a single, initiated path.

Each new section is preceded by a foreword explaining its "esoteric" meaning. A treatise on "secret knowledge" with lyrical illustrations is the result.

In 1922, Bely reviewed his poetic creative work of twenty years, reinterpreting it as his spiritual biography. This biography is a myth, but a myth artistically constructed, internally unified and ideologically convincing.

Bely's life tragedy grows from the material of the forewords.

The author divides the section *Gold in Azure* into three cycles: in the first ("In the Fields"), verses of the earliest period are "overflowing with bright and joyful expectation." In the second cycle ("In the Mountains"), the leit-motif of religious expectation is replaced by fairy-tale ecstasy and the Luciferian theme is aroused. The ruling leit-motif of the third cycle ("Not He") is disappointment in the feeling of his own chosenness; the sensation of mountain illumination is dispersed; the author feels himself to be in "sober reality," like a prison.

The following section, *Ashes*, is divided into two cycles: "Remote Russia" and "Before and Now." He writes in the foreword:

Strictly speaking, all the poems in *Ashes*, in the period of 1904-08, are one poem speaking of the remote, unawakened expanses of the Russian land: in this poem, themes of the reaction of 1907 and 1908 are equally interwoven with themes of the author's disappointment in the achievements of the former, bright paths.

212

The second cycle, "Before and Now," reveals the poet's view of reality as a stylized picture:

The past and present seem equally remote for a soul that has lost itself: everyone is only masks. The appearance in the midst of the masks of deceased reality, the "domino," is the appearance of fate shaking off the ashes of the past. The lyrical subject of this section is the corpse gradually becoming conscious of itself.

The foreword to the third section, *The Urn*, reads:

The general idea of this section is that the poet collects in an urn the ashes of his consumed ecstasy which had once burst forth for him in "gold" and "azure." Concentrated sorrow, now condensed into despair, now enlightened by philosophical reflection, is dominant in this section.

The section falls into four subsections:

In the first, "The Snow Maiden," are collected verses depicting disappointment in love; this love, replaced by passion, is dispersed by a snowstorm... The leit-motif accompanying it in mood is the leit-motif of the snowstorm: if "she" is only a cold snow maiden, then all of life as well is only a snowy transparent maelstrom.

In the second subsection, "Years of Forgetfulness," "the note of philosphical reflection is dominant." In the third, "The Tempter," are verses united around one theme — philosophy. The fourth subsection is entitled "The Corpse." The author explains:

The "I," disappointed in religious and esthetic aspirations ("Gold in Azure"), oppressed by the stagnant expanses of political and moral reaction ("Ashes"), disappointed in personal love ("The Urn"), and in the philosophical, supra-personal path ("The Tempter"), becomes a living corpse, buried alive: and these experiences of death in life lead to blasphemous cries of pain: the theme of "blasphemy" from pain is the theme of the poem.

Bely produces an interesting foreword to the poem "Christ is Risen:"

The poem was written near the time of the writing of Blok's *The Twelve*; together with *The Twelve*, it was subjected to misinterpretation. The author was accused of almost joining with the Communist party. To this "nonsense," the author could not even respond in print (under the conditions of the time), but to him it was clear that if the Sermon

213

on the Mount had appeared in 1918, then it too would have been examined from the point of view of "Bolshevism" or "anti-Bolshevism." That a representative of spiritual consciousness and an anthroposophist cannot so simply associate himself with political slogans occurred to no one. In the meantime, the theme of the poem is the most intimate of individual experiences, independent of country, of parties, of astronomical time. That about which I was writing Meister Eckhart had already known; the Apostle Paul wrote about it. Contemporaneity is only the external covering of the poem. Its inner core does not know time.

The anthology *The Princess and Her Knights* is included as a whole in the collection of poems. This cycle seems to the author to be a transition from the gloomy despair of "The Urn" to the consciousness of "The Star."

To one who has awakened from the unconsciousness of the grave to living life, this life sounds like a fairy tale. And hence the essence of the cycle is the essence of a fairy tale of the past.

The following foreword is preaffixed by the poet to the cycle "The Star:"

The poems of the cycle, "The Star," embrace the period of 1914-18. This period is adorned for the author by the encounter with spiritual science, illuminating for him his former ideological wanderings. Thus, here is the synthesis of the poetic ideology of the author. The themes of *Gold in Azure* here encounter the themes of *The Urn*, which were reembodied anew by anthroposophy. And again there comes the theme of Russia torturously seeking its spiritual self-definition. The author thinks that this section is the most conscious. "The Star" is "the star of self-consciousness."

The last section of the collection of poems is entitled "After the Star"; in it, in reworked form, is included the anthology of verses of 1922, *After the Parting*. The author speaks briefly of it:

The poems of this period conclude the book. They were written recently, and I can say nothing about them. I know only that they are not a "star" and that they are after "The Star"...
I am now attracted to different themes: the music of the "paths of initiation" has been replaced for me by the music of the foxtrot, the boston and the shimmy: I prefer a good jazz band to the bells of Parsival; I would like in the future to write verses corresponding to the foxtrot...

Thus Bely's life tragedy is revealed before us. The bright religious hopes of youth, the ecstasies of the mystic sensing the approach of Sofia, Divine Wisdom, and faith in his lofty calling conclude with a dreadful downfall into Luciferianism. The unwreathed prophet recognizes himself as a corpse, and reality appears to him as the "remote, unawakened expanses of Russia," under the yoke of reaction. She, with whom the period of mystical illumination was connected for him (Lyubov Dmitrievna Blok), has abandoned him. She is not the beloved, but the cold Snow Maiden... The poet seeks salvation in philosophy, but it leads him to "callous sensuality." After the "mystical" catastrophe follows the "philosophical" catastrophe. And again the face of Lucifer lies in wait for him here.

The third period is "living death," the blasphemous cries of one buried alive. But now the meeting with the second beloved, Asya Turgeneva, takes place. The corpse comes to life. Asya reveals to him a new path — the path of initiation. The fourth period (1912-1921) is a new mystical wave, a new illumination by the light of Favor and a new dreadful downfall: Asya departs from him, "spiritual science" leads him into total darkness, Doctor Steiner throws off his mask. Again, for the third time, the face of Lucifer smiles before him.

The music of mystical sunrises and anthroposophical initiations is deadened by the rumble of the foxtrot and the shimmy, the bells of Parsival by the jazz band. The ruin of a great soul is accompanied by the sounds of a Negro orchestra.

Chapter Ten: The Final Years (1924-1933)

We know almost nothing of how Bely lived the last ten years of his life in Russia. He married his old friend, the anthroposophist K. B. Vasilieva, in the summer of 1923, while visiting M. Voloshin in the Crimea, and made his peace with Bryusov. In 1924, he revised *Petersburg* into a drama, *The Downfall of a Senator*. In connection with this, the author conducted negotiations with Mikhail Chekhov, Meyerhold, Zavadsky and Tairov. The first performance of the drama in the Moscow Art Theater took place on November 14, 1925. Mikhail Chekhov played the part of the Senator. The drama concluded with the explosion of a real bomb, killing Apollon Apollonovich. His son Nikolai goes mad.

In 1924, Bely began to write the novel *Moscow*. It was published in two volumes by the Krug publishing house. The first volume is entitled *A Moscow Eccentric*, the second, *Moscow under Assault*. In July-August of 1927, he reworked it into a play, but this revision was never performed.

In his new novel, the author returns to the irresistible attraction of the "themes of the father."

In the chronicle *On the Brink of Two Centuries*, he warns the reader: "Korobkin (the hero of the novel *Moscow*) is not a father: any trait in him is taken only in the reflection of an uncanny caricature."

The idea of the novel is the "decomposition of the bases of the pre-revolutionary way of life and of individual consciousness in a a bourgeois, petit bourgeois and intelligentsia circle." A battle takes place between the German spy, Mandro, who belongs to a secret society, "The Oppressors of Humanity," and Professor Korobkin, a scholar of international importance, who has made a great discovery. It was the author's intention that this battle symbolize the "skirmish of essentially free science with the capitalist system." The old, perishing world is depicted in "uncanny caricature." The structure and style of the novel are defined by this goal.

The familiar features of the writer's father are distorted in a monstrous grotesque: his "eccentricity" is exaggerated into a mania. His ideas, his science, his discovery which must overturn the world are shown on a plane of quiet madness. The style of the novel is the mad fantasies of Bruegel, the sinister deviltry of Bosch. The author adopts the motif of the father's gazing at himself in the mirror from "The Baptized Chinese," but his face is melted into a beastly grimace:

In the mirror he encountered slanted eyes the color of snuff. His face went into prominent cheek bones from there. His cheeks puffed out; his nose was stuck on any old way. And the crowning column of the rubbish of his hair stood straight up; and it was very brown!

216

But a realistic description of the past Korobkin-Bugaev erupts into the caricatures. His father was a military doctor, sent to the Caucasus. The son was born in a fortress, left home, studied in the best Moscow gymnasium, was a first-rate student. In the fifth grade, he received news of the death of his father. He rented a corner in the kitchen of a cook, gave lessons, went hungry...

A cheerless life took shape; and it is understandable that Vanya came to the conclusion that the disorder of his life prevailed with the clarity only of proven theses. Thus, Russian science was enriched by a scholar.

The philosophy of Korobkin is a precise repetition of the philosophy of the mathematician Bugaev. The author writes:

The table of his world-view was based on two points. The first point: the universe is rolling toward clarity, toward measure, toward quantity. The second point: mathematics has already reached this stage: the world is the best.

After these openings into reality, the action is again submerged in "disorder" (Bely's favorite word). Korobkin's lecture in the University is described in a tone of crude caricature. Going out on the street, the absent-minded professor writes his calculations in chalk on the black square of a stopped carriage and falls under the horses. He is carried home, and he lies for a long time with his arm in a cast. Stupid and incredible things happen to him. Thus, leaving Mandro, instead of his hat, he puts on his head . . . a cat. The celebration in honor of Korobkin as the founder of a "Mathematical Collection" ends with a scene of buffoonery. The students toss the hero of the day in the air, tear his clothing, crush him; he jumps down the stairs on one leg, torn to pieces, disheveled, beast-like. We read:

Korobkin's jumping, in accompaniment to the kicks and even pinches of the yelling and sweating people causing him pain, resembled delirium in the style of Bruegel, who sooner depicted castigation than glorification.

The summer before the war arrives (1914); Korobkin is living in a summer house near Moscow, reading the "Mathematique Amusable," and observing the life of ants. And suddenly he understands: in the world in which he lives, his discovery will bring only ruin — it must be destroyed. "If the kingdom of science had come," he says, "our servants would act for us. But it is not of this world... A cruel time will come when the murderer will shout that he is serving the truth; remember — I said this." He goes to Moscow in order to burn his papers; the spy Mandro penetrates the house and demands that he be given the "document." Korobkin refuses. Then the provocateur subjects him to monstrous torture, the description of which is almost unendurable to read. Blinded, bleeding and insane with pain, Korobkin is taken to a lunatic asylum. Boys are running along the streets with papers: "Mobilization!"

The world conflagration had begun; somewhere, lightning struck.

* * *

The "theme of the father" is deformed in the distorting mirror of caricature. And together with it, the accompanying theme of "family drama" is distorted into parody. Korobkin's wife, Vasilisa Sergeevna, betrays her husband with Professor Zadopyatov, in whose features Professor N. I. Storozhenko is spitefully caricatured. The meeting of Zadopyatov with his "Sylfochka" is rendered in the tones of an indecent farce. Zadopyatov has "whitening curls of hair," "a meaty overhang of a nose," and a "puckered little brow." "Zadopyatov would be seated — he was taller than anyone: a giant. He would rise — of medium height, somehow short-legged." He has a jealous wife, Anna Pavlovna, "a round-headed, corpulent lady," strict, firm and honest. She prefers I. I. and P. I. Petrunkevich to all the other kadets and attends "Courses in dress-cutting." The housekeeper of the furnished room in which the meetings of the horse-complexioned professor with Korobkin's wife, Vasilisa Sergeevna, take place, eavesdrops on a conversation of the lovers:

"Yes..."
"It is said at Kareev's — oof, oof, oof..." and the divan creaked, "that the ideas of progress shine like a guiding star, as I express it, to the ages and the peoples..."
"You expressed this same thing in 'Ideals of Humanity,' " a feminine voice said dejectedly.
"But I maintain..."
"Apropos," interrupted the feminine voice, "when Milyukov wrote to you from Bulgaria..."

The son of Professor Korobkin, the high school student Mitenka, is the author's self-portrait. His features are shown in a crooked mirror, transforming his face into an ugly mug. Bely jeers at his own self, at his uncomely appearance and worthless, flaccid little soul:

A slouching youth stepped across the alley, in a rough cap and pants of the same sort. The growth on his cheeks roughened unpleasantly; and the forehead, overdeveloped, gave to the expression of the face something stupid. The eyes barely gazed out from the browless bottom of his forehead. The whole face was unhealthy, gray, yellowing, with red pimples.

Mitya steals books from his father's library and sells them at the Smolensk market. In one of the books a little paper with computations is found by chance: Korobkin has made the discovery which must overturn the world. The paper falls into the hands of the agents of the German spy, Mandro; thus the son unwittingly becomes the guilty party in his father's destruction.

Mandro, a "dark-skinned man, striking one with his sideburns, succulent portliness and the rotundity of his stance," enchants Mitya with his amiability and patronizes him in courting his daughter, Lizanka. Korobkin discovers the loss of his books and accuses his son of stealing them. The mother defends him; the father ceases to speak to him. The discord in Bely's family is interpreted this way in the novel. There are also other sins on Mitya's conscience: he skips lessons in the gymnasium, forges his father's signature in the excuse book. He is called in by the director, Vedenyapin, in whose image the features of the pedagogue L. I. Polivanov are brought to life.

Lev Petrovich Vedenyapin inspired horror in him: stooped, tall, thin, with a gray, stiff, combed mane, with a clipped beard, in gold eyeglasses, in a blue jacket too short and tight, the director seemed like Attila; under the gray bristle, he pressed his lips into a ring, lips capable of bursting open to his ears in elephantine roars, of showing a black tongue...

Mitya admits everything to the director and cries; in his soul a feeling of honor and responsibility is aroused. He is morally reborn.

Mitenka began to clean his teeth. But formerly, he went around bedraggled. Now he put his jacket into shape. He somehow fixed up his face: the pimples went away, and his cheeks were not purpled from scratching.

In this episode, the author freely orders the material of his own biography. The fantastic story of Mandro, the Jesuit, Mason, and Satanist, becoming the tool of Doctor Donner (to be read Steiner) and an international provocateur, recalls the most delirious pages of *Notes of an Eccentric*. Mandro is only a mask; behind it is hidden the ancient serpent-devil. Speaking of Mandro's home in Moscow, the author announces: "It would be possible to equip a museum, hang up a sign, 'Here lived a most interesting reptile, a very rare and ancient reptile — Mandro.' " Around the major "reptile," smaller reptiles hiss more gently from beast-like mugs, the offspring of a sick and depraved fantasy. Complex, vile intrigues are woven, disgusting scenes of sadism and masochism are portrayed. Ugly shadows with broken mouths, with crushed-in noses, flit about in a devil's sabbath. Bely's novel is a sinister piece of buffonery, literary hysteria, a nightmare stretched over two volumes. His pathological instincts, at last finding free expression in this book, Bely tries to justify ideologically: he is exposing the decomposing capitalist world. All these "international villains," spies, blackmailers, provocateurs, perpetrators of incest,

219

murderers are representatives of the "old world." Professor Korobkin says to Mandro:

I erred in thinking that clarity of thought, in which alone we sense freedom, had arrived. It is at present an illusion. It is even an illusion that there is some kind of history. We are in a prehistoric abyss, my dear sir, in the ice age, where we still dream dreams of culture.

Possessed by a thirst for destruction, Bely mocks at the past, and primarily at his own past. The beginning of the century for him is now a "prehistoric abyss," in which not people, but reptiles and orangoutangs were living. Until 1917, there was no Russian history: it was the "ice age." The literary life of Moscow is portrayed in the outlines of crude caricature: either a puppet show or a lunatic asylum. The Satanist, Mandro, is a refined dandy attending the Society of Free Esthetics and loving in his spare time to read the verses of Bryusov.

Mandro was lying on a couch. Opening a book bound in blue leather, he read through the *Assyrian Flowers*, the drama *Earth*. From Valery Bryusov he knew by heart:
> After raising the collar of my overcoat,
> And pushing the cap over my eyes,
> I run into unliving woods
> And behind me no one pursues...
In the verses of Valery Bryusov, "they pursued" often, and Mandro liked this. He really loved Bryusov's *Earth*: it had an excellent description of how the order of stranglers enact pursuit through the rooms, throwing a loop around the neck.

After the caricature of Bryusov follows slander of Blok. At a meeting of "Esthetics," the following conversation takes place:

It was great at Vibustina's... Balk (Blok), instead of "petit jeu," proposed a mysterion to everyone...
Well?
You are prosaic there with your "well." Well, they stuck Isai Isaakovich Rozmarin with a pin and drank his blood, mixing it with Bordeaux. Well, they circled around him holding hands!
Did they disinfect it?
What?
The pin.
Of course... Pfui!

That is all that Bely the communist remembered of his mystical sunrises at the beginning of the century.

* * *

In 1924, a book of Bely's, *One of the Inhabitants of the Kingdom of Shades* was published by Gosizdat; in 1928, *Wind from the Caucasus. Impressions* was published by Federatsia. In 1929, he published his research "Rhythm as Dialectics and *The Bronze Horseman*" (put out by Federatsia).

In the last years of his life, Bely returned to his work on the rhythn of Russian verse. Since his remarkable articles on the morphology of the Russian iambic tetrameter (the collection *Symbolism*) had appeared, a whole school for the study of verse had arisen. Originating from Bely's "discoveries," it subjected his "statistical method" to stiff criticism. At the end of the 1920s, the former Symbolist felt isolated, unrecognized, surrounded by enemies. His work "Rhythm as Dialectics" is filled with bitter complaints and polemical attacks. He writes:

> Until the arrival of the verse-studying professors, the rooms of Bryusov and Vyacheslav Ivanov were the first-rate verse-studying studios... My method of statistics, of the morphological study of the backbone of verse, flowered against me; for seventeen years, I have been attacked... One might say that one half of me was used to attack the other... A surprising fact was obtained: Andrei Bely already in 1910 had begun that which others developed. And − he lapsed into silence. These others, for eighteen years, in the form of "criticism" of Bely's stupidities, took from him his point of origin, and the not too bright fellow, Bely somewhere in silence thanked them and bowed to them.

And the research concludes in "self justification." The author writes:

> In fighting with the theories of Andrei Bely and exposing Andrei Bely's mistakes, Professor Zhirmunsky attacks not the Bely of 1910-1927, but the Bely of 1906-09, the Bely who allowed himself to sail on the sea of questions of systematics, statistics, and the resolution of all the disputed cases of interpretation, about which in those years they did not write and did not "stew." For a man with one finger writing articles on gnoseology, with another polemicizing with "mystical anarchism," with a third writing the novel *The Silver Dove,* with a fourth − verses, and with a fifth resolving cases in versification unresolved before him, it is not a sin to make a few mistakes.

Bely's new research on the rhythm of *The Bronze Horseman* in its fancifulness and arbitrariness stands beyond the limits of the "science of verse." By complex means, into which we cannot delve here, he calculates the "curve of the rhythm" of Pushkin's poem... Using scissors to cut out passages standing at the middle level of the curve, and sticking them together, he obtains the major theme of *The Bronze Horseman*: magnificence, austerity, regularity, supreme power — an image in the Empire style. But into this imperial construction something romantic intrudes, upsetting the order: some Evgeny, after sitting on the imperial guard lion, did not return home. The passages standing on the lower levels of the curve strengthen this contrast:

> Within the granite and the sternly harmonious iron, some sort of disorder begins. On the one hand, the "fateful will" of the Horseman, destroying destinies; on the other, the horror of human suffering and rebellion. The skillful interweaving of these two rhythmic themes defines the composition of the poem.

But Bely is not content with these modest conclusions. He wants to prove that the hero of the poem is not Peter, but Nikolai I, "who stabilized the personality of Peter by pouring into him his own Nikolaian personality of autocracy." And then, he asks:

> Is not Evgeny one of many, one of the thousands of rebels? Is it not November-December? The misfortune on the banks of the Neva is not the flood, but the crushing of the Decembrist uprising, the reprisals for the Decembrists.

Bely strengthens his unexpected guess with the following unconvincing conjectures:

> "And illuminated by a pale moon..." The Bronze Horseman, it is clear, is Nikolai, and not Peter; he rushes after the rebelling Evgeny. The arena of pursuit is the Senate Square.
>
> The primary theme of the rhythm, the imperial theme, is the stratagem of the cipher; the outward theme, since it concerns some sort of eccentric, does not require a cipher...
>
> "There was a dreadful time"... The dreadful time is the Nikolaian regime.

The author foresees the argument: "Pushkin loved 'Peter's creation' and with his poem glorified the 'miracle-working builder.' How, from 'praise' for Peter is it possible to deduce an 'accusation' of Nikolai?"

Bely is not disturbed by this: he asserts the monstrous idea that the creative work of the artist is unconscious; he himself does not understand what he is writing, for it is not he who is creating, but the collective that creates through him. The author announces:

> That by which Pushkin lives in us has no relation to Alexander Sergeevich reflecting upon the meaning of *The Bronze Horseman*. This latter,

for example, might suppose that he wrote "to the glory" of the regime of Nikolai, while the living being of the images in the dialectics of their flow, in the musical counterpoint of levels shouts at this regime: "May you rest in peace..."

The work is created previous to the act of its conception in the soul of the artist — by the collective; from collective to collective — this is the path of creation. And this path goes not through abstract consciousness, but through the will: the consciousness of the creator in the artist of the collective gives will to the body. And the will to rhythm responds to this will... The rhythmic curve is in fact a sign of authentic meaning replacing the non-authentic meaning...

The paradox of the conclusion is a death sentence to method. If the language of rhythm speaks to the researcher in direct opposition to the language of images and words, then either the work is not artistic or the researcher is mistaken. *The Bronze Horseman* is not a stratagem of secret ciphers, but a unified work living in the undecomposing unity of form and content.

Bely concludes his investigation with a quotation from Rozanov. He writes:

The demonstration is unsuccessful, perhaps. Perhaps I am not gifted in it. But I know that my theme is gifted. And with this repetition of Rozanov's aphorism I conclude my essay.

The study of "rhythm as dialectics" is in reality a "gifted" theme; and in spite of Bely's "unsuccessful demonstration," the future belongs to it.

* * *

During the last years of his life, Bely was occupied with writing his memoirs. In the spring of 1929, he worked on the chronicle, *On the Brink of Two Centuries*, which was published by the Earth and Factory publishing house in 1930; in the second half of 1930, he began to revise the text of *The Turn of the Century* of 1923. This second half of the chronicle appeared in a Gikhl publishing house edition in 1933; finally, in 1933, the author finished the third volume of reminiscences, *Between Two Revolutions*. This book, published by the Writers publishing house in Leningrad, was dated 1934; in reality, it appeared only in 1935, already after Bely's death. In September, 1933, mortally ill, he began to dictate the continuation of his memoirs, but soon became so weak that he was obliged to discontinue the dictation.

Bely's three-volume chronicle, embracing thirty years (1880-1910), includes a tremendous amount of valuable material on the history of the age of Russian Symbolism. Unfortunately, this material is not absolutely reliable. The author stylizes his past, portraying it as a rebellion against the old order, a "permanent revolution" not only spiritual, but political as well. However, Bely's works until 1917 obviously contradict such a concept; socialism was totally foreign to the young mystic, the metaphysician and theoretician of Symbolism. But under the conditions of Soviet reality in the 1930s, he attempts to rehabilitate himself. He does this unconvincingly, ambiguously, with shameful cowardice. In "reinterpreting" his past, he portrays it in tones of malicious satire. He jeers at former friends. He does not stop even at sharp "devaluations" of Blok's personality. In Bely's chronicle, there are many inaccuracies, exaggerations and distortions, but there are great merits in it as well: the literary portraiture, observation, the sharpness of the sketching; cartoons, parodies, caricatures, grotesques. Bely is not an historian, but a poet and visionary. He creates a "myth of Russian Symbolism" full of light and sound.

* * *

Bely's last book, *The Art of Gogol,* was published by the Ogiz-Gikhl publishing house in 1934, after the author's death.

There is something profoundly symbolic in the fact that during the last year of his life, Bely turned to Gogol, his faithful guide, teacher and inspiration. The author as the writer of *The Silver Dove* and *Petersburg* is indebted to Gogol for everything. And his last book before his death is the gift of reverent and grateful love.

The Art of Gogol is one of Bely's most brilliant critical works: in it, he lays out new methods for the study of Russian literary prose, this terra incognita still awaiting its conquerors. In the science of prose, as in the science of verse, Bely is the "discoverer of new worlds."

His book is divided into five chapters: 1. Gogol's Creative Process; 2. Gogol's Subject; 3. Gogol's Portraiture; 4. Gogol's Prose Style; and 5. Gogol in the 19th and 20th Centuries.

In the first chapter, the author gives a general characterization of Gogol's prose. He writes:

All the sweep of lyricism provided by rhythms, from which Pushkin disassociates himself in prose, Gogol places in prose.... Gogol is the very epopée of prose. His consciousness suggests a quiescent volcano. Instead of Pushkin's Doric phraseology, and Karamzin's Gothic phraseology — assymetrical baroque. Gogol's phraseology begins a period, the fruits of which we are still plucking.

The author divides Gogol's creative work into three periods: the first — before Petersburg, until 1831; the second — the Petersburg (1833-1836); and the third — the period of *Dead Souls.*

The first period is characterized by the spirit of music: the wealth of sounds, the melody reared on the style of the Ukrainian epos. In the second period, the "thunder of the Ukrainian nightingale" falls silent, the melody runs dry; the hyperbole of glorification is transformed into the hyperbole of derision: the panegric becomes irony. A complete collapse of gesture, speech and melody takes place. Mechanical atomism is contrasted to organism. In the third period, Gogol's style grows rigid, and all Russian reality appears to him as a kingdom of corpses.

In the second chapter, "Gogol's Subject," Bely explains the origin of the Ukrainian tales from Gogol's fidelity to "ancient custom." The author of the *Evenings* glorifies the patriarchal way of life already doomed to destruction. Therefore, the crime against kin is connected for him with sin and the "evil spirit." The "renegades" and the "alienated" are dangerous people, villains or wizards. The author notes:

> The theme of being without kith or kin is the theme of Gogol's creative work. Piskarev, Bashmachkin and Popryshchin are renegades, and Gogol is a renegade as well. The theme of kinship for Gogol is the theme of the earth. For one alienated from his kin, the earth is a "bewitched place." The wizard in "A Terrible Vengeance" is "not a Cossack, not a Pole, not a Hungarian, not a Turk"; and in the eyes of the collective, he is a wizard.

The subject of *Dead Souls* is connected with the age of the decomposition in Russia of the natural economy. Bely calls Chichikov the "future Shchukin,"[1] prepared to cover Persia with chintz, and considers the history of Chichikov the "history of capitalism in Russia."

In the third chapter, "Gogol's Portraiture," many interesting observations are collected on the literary art of the writer. Bely writes:

> Gogol's painting is born from motion, the displacement of the body, a backwards look at objects. The origin of both lines and relief, and colors, is from music. If one sits motionlessly before an easel, there is one perspective; if he runs and turns his head to the side, obliquely, upwards, there is a different perspective: the kind which the Japanese depict.

The quality of the Japanese, the mixture of perspectives and the glassy landscape are characteristic of the first period. The mechanical naturalism of the second and third periods is the same sort of stylization as the "Japanese" of the first.

> Hyperbola there, hyperbola here; dithyramb there, mockery here; Hokusai there, Watteau here, the island of Crete, vases, even Mexico.

The analogy is paradoxical, disputable, but undoubtedly revealing of some new aspects, previously unnoticed in Gogol's art. No less brilliant are Bely's remarks on Gogol's "nature:"

> The estate house, the garden, yard, field and woods are rendered by the mature Gogol in the genre of the itinerants and in the spirit of the land-

225

scapes shown by Polenov and Shishkin. Where, however, the landowner and the way of life in his home appear, there is an entirely different school of painting: Bakst, Benois, Somov.

In the fourth chapter, "Gogol's Prose Style," the author studies the dynamics of Gogolian verbs, the hyperbolism of the epithets, the language of nouns, sound-writing and the figures of the repeat.

In the last, fifth, chapter ("Gogol in the 19th and 20th Centuries), Bely quotes the words of Chernyshevsky: the reform produced by Gogol is the reform of the language itself. From this reform came all the new Russian literature. The author gives a detailed discussion of the "Gogolism" of the Symbolist school and explains the influence of the creator of *Dead Souls* on Sologub, Blok, Bely and Mayakovsky. In conclusion, he writes:

Pre-classical style spilled into us through Gogol. Gogol is the most characteristic representative in Russia, not only of the peculiarities of the Asiatic style: in him, Homer, Arabism, Baroque and Gothic are originally interpreted.

On July 17, 1933, in Koktebel, Bely suffered a sun stroke; he died in Moscow on January 8, 1934. He had predicted his death in a poem of 1907:

I trusted the gold brilliance,
But died from the sun's arrows.
I measured the centuries in thought,
But could not live my own life well.

Many manuscripts remained. The major ones are "The Poetry of the Word. Calls of the Times," "On Poetic Meaning," "Four Crises," "Concerning the Rhythmic Gesture," "A Dictionary of Rhymes," and huge correspondence.

NOTES

Chapter One

1. Grades of Excellent (*Translator's note*).
2. Peredonov: The hero of Sologub's *Petty Demon*, a teacher embodying calculating desire (*Translator's note*).
3. "The Man in a Case:" title of a story by Chekhov about a servile, withdrawn teacher (*Translator's note*).
4. The Russian word, *nozhnitsy*, means both scissors and discrepancies (*Translator's note*).

Chapter Two

1. Vlas: the hero and title of a poem by Nikolai Nekrasov. Vlas was an embodiment of humility, piousness and submission (*Translator's note*).
2. B. K. Zaitsev, "Andrei Belyi (Vospominaniia, vstrechi)." June, 1938.
3. Blok's first signed article: "A. Belyi. *Simfoniia (Vtoraia dramaticheskaia)*. Moskva, 1902." It appeared in the fourth volume of the *New Path* for 1903.
4. Bely's article on Tolstoi and Dostoevsky was published in No. 1 of *Novyi Put'* for 1903.
5. It appeared in No. 11 of *Mir Iskusstva* for 1902.
6. It was published in No. 12 of *Mir Iskusstva* for 1902.
7. *Nachalo veka*, Moscow, 1933.
8. A. Belyi, "Vospominaniia o Bloke," *Epopeia*, Berlin, 1922.
9. In *Nachalo veka*, Bely, without any hesitation, announces that "Sokolov stole Ellis' slogan and gave it to Ryabushinsky as the title for the journal *Golden Fleece*."
10. V. F. Khodasevich, "Konets Renaty" in the book *Nekropol'*, Petropolis, Bruxelles, 1939.
11. A. Belyi, "Vospominaniia o Bloke."
12. A. Belyi, *Zoloto v lazuri*, Scorpion, Moscow, 1904. In the edition of Z. I. Grzhebin: A. Belyi. *Stikhotvoreniia, Berlin 1923 — Zoloto v lazuri*. It was not published in its entirety.

Chapter Three

1. Khlystovstvo: Belief in self-flagellation as practiced by a Russian religious sect calling themselves "God's people," but commonly known as Khlysty (flagellants). In their rites, they performed a "circle procession," moving faster and faster and accompanying their mutual- and self-flagellation by the incantation, "Khlyshchu, khlyschu, Khrista ishchu" (I flagellate, flagellate, seeking Christ) (*Translator's note*).
2. It appeared in *Novyi Put'*. Later it was included in the book *Arabeski*, Moscow, 1911.
3. The lecture "Psikhologiia i teoriia znaniia," reworked into an article entitled "O granitsakh psikhologii," was included by the author in his book *Simvolizm*, Moscow, 1910.

The article "O nauchnom dogmatizme" was also included in *Simvolizm*. The article "Apokalipsis v russkoi poezii" was included in the anthology *Lug zelenyi*, Moscow, 1910.

4. The article of 1904, "Krititsizm i sir[blacked out] included in the anthology *Simvolizm*, Moscow, 1910.

5. Subsequently a professor on the facult[blacked out] ance philology at St. Petersburg University.

6. Georgi Chulkov, *Gody stranstvii*, Federatsiia, Moscow, 1930.

Chapter Four

1. It was published in 1909.

2. The articles "Smysl iskusstva" and "Budushchee iskusstvo," were included in Bely's book of essays *Simvolizm*, Moscow, 1910.

3. Mitrofanushka: The hero of *The Minor*, a play by Fonvizin. He is an embodiment of crudeness and vulgar, brutal selfishness (*Translator's note*).

4. *chik*: a Russian suffix which adds the meaning of "dear, little" to a word (*Translator's note*).

5. Manilov: a character in Gogol's *Dead Souls* representing cloying sweetness, smug complacency, inactivity, futile daydreaming (*Translator's note*).

6. *Sanin*: a vulgarly erotic novel by Artsybashev.

Translator's note: The novel was very popular because it openly espoused a "new" philosophy of life to Russian readers: men need only be true to their sensual desires because life is meaningless and only death is real.

7. Kriks Varaks: one of Remizov's many invented names (*Translator's note*).

8. Of Bely's critical articles of 1908 we will mention the articles on Balmont, Z. Gippius ("Literaturnyi Dnevnik") and V. Ivanov ("Realiora").

9. Narodnik: an adherent of "Narodnichestvo," a form of radical populism, urging peasant uprising (*Translator's note*).

10. Raskolniki: "Old Believers" who refused to accept reforms in Russian Orthodoxy adopted in 1667. In protest, some employed self-immolation (*Translator's note*).

11. Sorrow-Misfortune: a folk embodiment of man's ill-luck, a kind of guardian devil staying with one from cradle to grave (*Translator's note*).

12. According to tradition, a maiden wore a scarf on her head; this is what the merchant offers. The youth, however, gives her a thicker, carpet scarf, such as married women would wear (*Translator's note*).

13. Trykalka: that which makes the sound "try," i.e., the balalaika (*Translator's note*).

14. Red Jacket: from Gogol's story, "The Sorochintsy Fair." The red jacket is said to belong to the Devil. It was cut up, and he searches for the pieces at the fair (*Translator's note*).

15. These words proved to be prophetic: Bely died in the Crimia from sunstroke.

Chapter Five

1. B. Zaitsev, "Andrei Belyi (Vospominaniia, vstrechi)," *Russkie zapiski*, July, 1938.

2. Of Bely's other articles of 1909 we will mention "Charles Baudelaire," "Weininger o pole i kharaktere," and "Anatema L. Andreeva." They all were included in the anthology *Arabesques*.

3. Under the influence of the conversations with Vyacheslav Ivanov at the Tower, Bely wrote the article "Vyacheslav Ivanov, Silhouettes." It was included in the anthology *Arabesques*.

4. M. Tsvetaeva, "Plennyi dukh (O Belom)," *Sovremennye zapiski*, No. 55, 1934.

228

5. Bely's monumental was never completed. It broke off in the first part of the third volume, wł :d in 1934 under the title *Mezhdu dvukh revolutsii* (until 1910). Of the second part only two chapters were written. They appeared in print in the 27th-28th issues of *Literaturnoe nasledstvo* in 1937.

6. This article was included by the author in his *Arabesques*.

Chapter Six

1. Reference to Pushkin's poem, *The Bronze Horseman,* the horseman (Peter the Great) "rearing Russia on its hind legs" (*Translator's note*).

Chapter Seven

1. From Pushkin's poem, *The Bronze Horseman (Translator's note).*

2. Ivanov-Razumnik, *Vershiny. Aleksandr Blok. Andrei Belyi,* Kolos Publishing House, Petrograd, 1923.

3. Andrei Belyi, *St. Petersburg,* John Cournos, trans., Grove Press, New York, 1959, p. 49. Henceforth, page numbers will be given in the text in parentheses when the quotation corresponds to the translated text (*Translator's note*).

4. V. Ivanov, *Rodnoe i vselenskoe. Stat'i 1914-1916 i 1917 g. g.,* published by Leman and Sakharov, 1918.

5. See Ivanov-Razumnik, *Vershiny,* Petrograd, 1923.

6. In Russian: "*t*ragediia *t*rezvosti" (*Translator's note*).

7. Andrei Bely, *Kotik Letaev,* Gerald Janecek, trans., Ardis, 1971, pp. 3-6. Henceforth, references to the book's pages will be given in parentheses (*Translator's note*).

Chapter Eight

1. Jacks of Diamonds: a group of "Formalist" painters opposed to realism in painting (*Translator's note*).

2. It appeared in print only after five years. *Glossaloliia. Poema o zvuke*, Epokha, Berlin, 1922.

3. M. Tsvetaeva, "Plennyi dukh (Moia vstrecha s Andreem Belym)," *Sovremennye zapiski,* No. 55, 1934.

4. Nichevoki: a small, post-revolutionary group of nihilist writers who sought to distinguish themselves by writing nothing at all (*Translator's note*).

5. B. Zaitsev, "Andrei Belyi," *Russkie zapiski,* July, 1938.

6. V. Khodasevich, "Tri pis'ma Andreia Belogo," *Sovremennye zapiski,* 1934.

7. It came out in a separate booklet from the Alkonost publishing house (1918) and was included in the collection of poems published by Grzhebin, Berlin, 1923.

8. "Eli, . . . sabachthani:" "My God, why hast thou forsaken me?" (Mat. 27:46) (*Translator's note*).

9. V. Khodasevich published it in the 55th issue of *Sovremennye zapiski,* 1934.

10. It was first printed in the journal *Zapiski mechtatelei,* No. 4, 1921. It was reprinted in *Sovremennye zapiski,* 1922.

11. Lapserdak: A long dark coat, such as that worn by the Hassidism (*Translator's note*).

Chapter Nine

1. Ilia Ehrenburg, *Portrety russkikh poetov*, Argonaut Publishing House, Berlin, 1922.

2. Reprints: 1. *Tret'ia simfoniia. Vozvrat.*, Ogonki, Berlin, 1922. 2. *Serebrianyi golub'*, Epokha, Berlin, 1922. 3. *Petersburg,* Epokha, Berlin, 1922. 4. *Kotik Letaev*, Epokha, Berlin, 1922. 5. *Na perevale*, published by Grzhebin, Berlin, 1923. 6. "Kreshchenyi Kitaets," *Sovremennye zapiski*, Paris, 1922. 7. *Stikhotvoreniia*, published by Grzhebin, Berlin, 1923.

Published for the first time: 1. *Putevye zapiski*, published by Gelikon, Berlin, 1922. 2. *Zvezda*, Gosizdat, Moscow, 1922. 3. *Stikhi o Rossii*, published by Epokha, Berlin, 1922. 4. *Posle razluki,* Epokha, Berlin, 1922. 5. "Return to My Native Land," Moscow, 1922. 6. "Sirin uchenogo varvarstva," *Scythians,* Berlin, 1922. 7. *Zapiski chudaka,* Gelikon, Berlin, 1922. 8. *Glossolaliia,* Epokha, Berlin, 1922. 9. "Vospominaniia o Bloke," *Epopeia,* Berlin, 1923.

3. Andrei Belyi, "Sirin uchenogo varvastva (po povodu knigi I. Ivanova *Rodnoe i vselenskoe)*."

Chapter Ten

1. Shchukin: a wealthy merchant and art collector in Moscow (*Translator's note).*